The Co
Therap of Desire

Most of the best contemporary theology is being done under the rubric of 'historical theology,' and so all theologians must read Dr. Boone's book. He presents the basic options – as true today as in Augustine's time: Epicurean materialism with its attempt to repress hope and moderate desire in the face of everlasting death; Stoic fatalism or determinism for which desire must be rendered docile to whatever happens; and desire for God according to which humans are created irrepressibly to desire union with the immaterial God who comes to us in Christ Jesus and his Church. Boone makes a superb contribution to the ongoing discussion of Augustine's early writings. Above all, he makes crystal clear how much we could gain by being taught anew by Augustine, how much each of us – and our communities – need him today!

Matthew Levering,
James N. and Mary D. Perry, Jr., Professor of Theology,
Mundelein Seminary, and author of *The Theology of Augustine*

The Cassiciacum dialogues are Augustine's earliest writings on theology and philosophy, but have been overshadowed by his later works. Boone shows the importance of the Cassiciacum texts in their own right – as developing a uniquely Christian account of desire and its satisfaction – and as setting the stage for his later works. No future discussion of the Cassicacum texts will be able to avoid reckoning with this book.

Brian Harding,
Associate Professor of Philosophy,
Department of Psychology and Philosophy, Texas Woman's University
and author of *Augustine and Roman Virtue*

In this lucid, accessible, and well-informed study, Mark Boone uses desire as a kind of lens to bring Augustine's early writings into focus. Fully aware of Augustine's philosophical as well as religious background, Boone helps us see young Augustine's fundamental project and the way it opens out into his mature thought.

Phillip Cary,
Author of *Augustine's Invention of the Inner Self*

The Conversion and Therapy of Desire

Augustine's Theology of Desire in the Cassiciacum Dialogues

Mark J. Boone

Foreword by Michael P. Foley

James Clarke & Co

James Clarke & Co
P.O. Box 60
Cambridge
CB1 2NT
United Kingdom

www.jamesclarke.co
publishing@jamesclarke.co

ISBN: 978 0 227 17666 5

British Library Cataloguing in Publication Data
A record is available from the British Library

First published by James Clarke & Co, 2017

Published by arrangement
with Pickwick Publications

Portions of chapter 1 appeared previously in Mark Boone,
"The Role of Platonism in Augustine's 386 Conversion to Christianity."
Religion Compass 9.5 (May 2015) 151-61. © 2015 John Wiley & Sons Ltd.
Available at onlinelibrary.wiley.com/doi/10.1111/rec3.12149/abstract.
Reused with permission.

Contents

Foreword

DESPITE AUGUSTINE'S ENORMOUS IMPACT on Western thought and his abiding popularity (or notoriety) in both Catholic and Protestant circles, modern scholarship has by and large paid scant attention or the wrong kind of attention to Augustine's earliest writings as a Christian: *Against the Academics*, *On the Happy Life*, *On Order*, and *Soliloquies*. Known collectively as the Cassiciacum dialogues because of their setting at a friend's villa somewhere north of Milan, these early writings abound in literary charm and philosophical maturity. Nonetheless, for the bulk of the late nineteenth and twentieth centuries, professional readers of Cassiciacum focused on a dry and narrow set of questions concerning Augustine's neo-Platonic (as opposed to authentically Christian) beliefs at the time of his conversion to Christianity in AD 386. Although the protracted debate that ensued from this topic was not without its merit, it came at a cost. To use a rough analogy, the Augustinian studies from this period more or less strip-mined the texts for evidence of Augustine's alleged neo-Platonism instead of respecting the delicate ecology of Augustine's compositional art by attending to his dexterous use of the dialogue genre, his pedagogical intent, and his often subtle engagement of the great authors of classical antiquity beyond that of neo-Platonists like Plotinus or Porphyry.

Fortunately, a new generation of scholars arose in the late twentieth and early twenty-first century with a more environmentally-sensitive set of questions, so to speak, and a greater respect for Augustine's own goals in writing the Cassiciacum works. Yet the new wave of secondary resources is not without its defects either. Whereas much of the earlier scholarship in the twentieth century tended to read the Cassiciacum corpus through the flattening lens of Enlightenment presuppositions or modern historical criticism, the more recent scholarship has tended to read it through the blurry lens of post-modern indeterminacy. Neither pair of goggles, at the end of day, quite captures the spirit of Cassiciacum.

It is in part because of this current state of affairs that Mark Boone's *The Conversion and Therapy of Desire* is such a valuable work. Boone clearly profits from the strengths of contemporary advances in Cassiciacum research but he is careful to avoid its infelicities. *Conversion and Therapy* returns us to the mind of a young Augustine who has spent over a decade wrestling with an astonishing array of philosophical, literary, and religious claims and is now ready to talk. It follows Augustine whither he goes through the distinct subjects of each work, and it catches one of the central threads tying not only the dialogues to each other but also to the great Western conversation from which it draws and to which it contributes: desire.

In the fourth century AD, a keen interest in the nature, value, and direction of human desire was hardly novel. As Boone aptly explains in the first chapter, it was divergent analyses of desire that, as much as anything else, distinguished the great philosophical schools of antiquity and the Middle Ages from each other. But Augustine's exploration of human desire places the Bishop of Hippo in a category all his own. Augustine's anthropology is so driven by the subject that it would not be much of an exaggeration to assert that for Augustine, man is the desiring animal, a unique creature consisting of an erotic intellect attached to animal appetites.

Augustine's analysis of human eros arguably reaches its apex in the *Confessions* and *On Christian Doctrine*, where Augustine pursues an understanding of human longing both in its turn away from its Ultimate Good and in its return. But one of the contributions of *Conversion and Therapy* is to demonstrate how the theme of desire was operative in Augustine's thinking from the very beginning. As Boone notes, each dialogue explores, or drives the reader to explore, what we ought to desire, what has gone wrong with our desires, and what we need to do to desire the right things.

Boone is also to be commended for drawing our attention to two aspects of Augustine's erotic anthropology: conversion and therapy. An important theme in each of the Cassiciacum dialogues is a conversion, or turning, of the subject. Augustine's goal for his pupils and his readers is to convert their minds to the true and their hearts to the good; indeed, as Joseph Pucci has pointed out in his recent book *Augustine's Virgilian Retreat*, he even endeavors to "convert" the words of classical *auctores*. This conversion process, which involves a reorienting or reordering of one's intellect and will, is essentially therapeutic in nature, and hence Boone rightly yokes his focus on conversion with a focus on therapy. The *Soliloquies* alone maintains a conspicuous therapeutic dimension of great psychological depth, but for the other three dialogues as well, a "healing" of wounds is never far from the surface.

For these reasons and more, Mark Boone's *The Conversion and Therapy of Desire* is required reading for anyone interested in the mind of Augustine at Cassiciacum.

Michael P. Foley
Associate Professor of Patristics
Baylor University
March 19, 2015

Acknowledgments

I WISH TO THANK Michael P. Foley, Thomas S. Hibbs, Robert C. Roberts, Robert B. Kruschwitz, and David Lyle Jeffrey for their help with earlier versions of this text. I am also grateful to Phillip Cary for the insightful e-mail conversations about Augustine at Cassiciacum. I am also grateful to Augustine J. Curley for the edifying work on Augustine and the Church Fathers on which we have collaborated.

I am grateful to John Wiley & Sons for allowing me to reuse some material that was published in *Religion Compass* under the title "The Role of Platonism in Augustine's 386 A. D. Conversion to Christianity."

Most of all, I am grateful to my wife for all of her support, and to God for everything.

Abbreviations

Conf.	Augustine's *The Confessions*
Ord.	Augustine's *On Order*
b. Vita	Augustine's *On the Happy Life*
c. Acad.	Augustine's *Against the Academics*
Sol.	Augustine's *Soliloquia*

1

Augustine at Cassiciacum

Augustine's commitment to the Christian faith in AD 386 is a pivotal event not only in his own life, but also in the history of Christianity and the history of the world, for the writings and teachings of Augustine set the course of theological and cultural development in western Christendom. But to what exactly was Augustine converted?[1] Scholars have long debated several questions pertaining to Augustine's conversion: whether he really converted to Christianity in 386, whether he was a neo-Platonist, and, if he adhered to both neo-Platonism and Christianity, which of the two was dominant in his thought. These are important questions, and I hope that this book will help to answer them. But these are not the questions that Augustine himself was asking when he abandoned his worldly pursuits of money, fame, and physical pleasures in 386. At this time he retreated with a few friends and relations to Cassiciacum, to the country home of his friend Verecundus. Here he wrote his first post-conversion writings, the Cassiciacum dialogues: *Contra Academicos*, or *Against the Academics*; *De beata vita*, or *On the Happy Life*; *De ordine*, or *On Order*; and *Soliloquia*, or *Soliloqies*. Ernest L. Fortin remarks that scholars often approach these earliest writings with their own questions rather than Augustine's own questions.[2] Augustine himself was more interested in questions such as "What is

1. Some scholars object to the word "conversion" to describe Augustine's change of life in 386. I am sympathetic to their concerns, although I continue to use the word in the broad sense of a life transformation whereby one abandons a morally and spiritually inferior way of life and adopts a morally and spiritually superior one. See below, chapter 2, under the subheading "Christ: Towards a Christian Theology of Desire."

"2. Fortin, "Foreword," x. There are excellent studies that do allow Augustine to speak for himself. To name a few: Foley, "Cicero, Augustine"; Foley, "The Other Happy

the nature of the soul?"; "What is the nature of happiness?"; and "How does one become happy?" In this volume I investigate three questions important to Augustine during his retreat at Cassiciacum: "What ought we to desire?"; "What has gone wrong with our desires?"; and "How do we come to desire the right things?"

Yet if we are attentive to the questions that motivated Augustine, we are more likely to find the answers to the questions that have motivated so many scholars. In letting the dialogues speak for themselves—in allowing Augustine's own questions and answers to emerge from the dialogues—it will be easier to discover to what degree Augustine is a Christian, to what degree he is a neo-Platonist, and how the Christian and neo-Platonic elements of his thinking interact. In this book I shall defend the thesis that Augustine's philosophy of desire in the Cassiciacum dialogues is a distinctively Christian one. In order to show this I shall investigate Augustine's own questions and answers pertaining to desire; what emerges will prove to be a distinctively Christian philosophy of desire. Indeed, it would not be amiss to call it a *theology* of desire.

There are two components to my thesis. The first is that Augustine's theology of desire at Cassiciacum is a distinctively Christian one incorporating some neo-Platonic elements—not a merely neo-Platonic one. The second component is that the Christian elements help to determine the shape of the whole; they help to determine the significance and application of the neo-Platonic elements.

Now this theology of desire is not exactly an anti-Platonic one; it has neo-Platonic elements. Nor will I argue that it is *thoroughly* Christian—only that it is *distinctively* so. Non-Christian regions may remain in the thinking of this newly converted Christian, so honest about his theological questions, so committed to *seeking* truths he has not yet found—and to *understanding* truths he has found but not yet fully comprehended.

In short, Augustine at Cassiciacum is developing a theology of desire that borrows heavily from neo-Platonism; yet its Christian characteristics determine the shape of its overall structure: trinitarianism, Christology, sin, grace, and the quest to understand God and the soul.

Before explaining the major distinctives of Augustine's theology of desire, it would be helpful to review the major alternative interpretations of Augustine's conversion and early writings. To this I now turn, after which I shall explain why a look at the Cassiciacum dialogues' analysis of desire is so useful for understanding Augustine—and for some other reasons.

Life"; Cary, "What Licentius Learned"; Silk, "Boethius's Consolatio"; Kevane, "Christian Philosophy"; Kolbet, *Augustine and the Cure of Souls*; and Topping, *Happiness and Wisdom*.

Following that, I shall review the major philosophical schools with which Augustine interacts at Cassiciacum; finally, I shall summarize what his own views on desire at Cassiciacum actually are.

WAYS OF UNDERSTANDING AUGUSTINE'S CONVERSION AND EARLY WRITINGS

The nature of Augustine's conversion and the character of the early writings have been subjects of significant debate for about one and a quarter centuries. Perspectives on Augustine in 386 and the years following generally fall into one of four categories. After discussing the nature of this dispute, I shall outline these four major perspectives on young Augustine, and endorse one of them.[3]

Augustine's worldview at Cassiciacum has been the subject of a great dispute concerning the nature of his commitment to Christianity. Intertwined with this debate are questions concerning the notion of Christian neo-Platonism and the extent to which the two were reconcilable in Augustine's world. There is also the question concerning, to whatever extent they were not, which one figures more prominently in his thought at Cassiciacum. This debate more or less began in 1888 with two scholarly works on Augustine, which inspired the first of the four perspectives on young Augustine's thought.

The first of these was Gaston Boissier's comparably modest article on the alleged change of views between Augustine's early and later writings. The second was Adolph von Harnack's work, which explicitly reads the *Confessions* as a misrepresentation of his mind in 386 and the years after.[4] Later Prosper Alfaric championed this interpretation of Augustine.[5] One crucial aspect of this rather uncharitable reading is the idea that Augustine was insincere, a convert to neo-Platonism but not to Christianity, which he allegedly saw as an inferior substitute for Platonism, fit only for the less

3. Much of this material has appeared previously in Boone, "The Role of Platonism in Augustine's Conversion." My characterization of the four perspectives is the same here, but the text has been modified for clarity and expanded in places. The reader interested in a direct look at views on the early Augustine's relationship to neo-Platonism should consult that article, available at http://onlinelibrary.wiley.com/doi/10.1111/rec3.12149/abstract.

4. Boissier, "La Conversion;" von Harnack, "Augustins Konfessionen." Among the English sources discussing Boissier and von Harnack is a succinct paragraph in O'Meara, *Studies in Augustine and Eriguena*, 146.

5. Alfaric, *L'évolution intellectuelle*. O'Meara provides a helpful summary of Alfaric's book in *Studies in Augustine and Eriguena*, 121–22.

intelligent masses. Only much later, so the story goes, did he finally commit to Christianity. This interpretation approaches Augustine as being at different times two very different thinkers, in the early dialogues a neo-Platonist and in later works such as the *Confessions* a genuine Christian. A genuine Christian, but deceptive about his past, for such a reading tends to suspect Augustine of dissembling and deception.

Charles Boyer was a formidable adversary of Alfaric.[6] Thanks largely to his efforts, this reading is now widely considered discredited. Yet its effects have not ceased to linger in Augustinian scholarship. Two more recent scholars associated with this reading of Augustine are Paula Fredrekson and Leo C. Ferrari.[7] Brian Dobell's reading[8] is also similar to Alfaric's, though Dobell is explicit that the *Confessions* is not deceptive.[9]

This interpretation has also influenced a rather common tendency to view Augustine's intellectual development as a dramatic shift from a philosophical optimism present in his early writings to a theological pessimism in the later writings. Supposedly in his early days, influenced by Stoicism and neo-Platonism, he trusted reason to gain knowledge of God and had ambitious plans for *thinking* his way into the happy life. In his later days, chastened by failure to do just this and more knowledgeable of the writings of the Apostle Paul, he abandoned this approach and began to rely on God's grace. Carol Harrison's *Rethinking Augustine's Early Theology* is aimed primarily at combating this view of Augustine's intellectual development, which corresponds to the old "two Augustines" theory of Alfaric: "the young Augustine is seen as an optimistic devotee of a Christian philosophy which promises the attainment of perfection, moral purity and tranquility, and the contemplation of wisdom."[10] Harrison cites Peter Brown's influential biography *Augustine of Hippo*[11] as a leading purveyor of this perspective, noting, however, that Brown retracts it in the new edition of his book.[12]

Before going on to the next general strategy for interpreting the early Augustine, I must pause to note that one of the major disagreements in the scholarly literature is his alleged belief in the possibility of perfect happiness in this life. Harrison is against this reading.[13] Among those saying that

6. Boyer, *Christianisme et* Néo-Platonisme; discussed in O'Meara, *Studies in Augustine and Eriguena*, 148–49.

7. Fredrekson, "Paul and Augustine," 3–34; Ferrari, *The Conversions*; Ferrari, "Truth and Augustine's Conversion," 9–19.

8. Dobell, *Augustine's Intellectual Conversion.*

9. Ibid., 25–26.

10. Harrison, *Rethinking Augustine's Early Theology*, 16.

11. Brown, *Augustine.*

12. Harrison, *Rethinking*, 14–17.

13. Ibid., 63–67.

Augustine did indeed hold to the possibility of perfect happiness pre-mortem are Brown in his biography, Frederick Van Fleteren,[14] Eugene TeSelle,[15] Phillip Cary,[16] Leo Ferrari,[17] Ryan Topping,[18] and Paul Kolbet.[19] I lean—cautiously—towards Harrison's view. I think Augustine's eventual considered view that happiness in this life is neither complete nor perpetual has roots in his early writings, even at Cassiciacum. At Cassiciacum he thinks that happiness, though it may be *complete* whenever one has a fleeting vision of God, cannot in this life *last*. I will present for this view evidence, such as I have it, from the Cassiciacum dialogues. I have no delusions that what I say here will be the final word on the subject. I only hope to present some evidence that young Augustine did not believe in a perfect and perpetual pre-mortem happiness—or at any rate that, if he did, his views on the subject were not entirely clear and consistent. The subject is interesting, and my understanding of it would lend a modicum of support to my overall thesis in this book, but my thesis can stand without it.

In *The Irrational Augustine*[20] Catherine Conybeare articulates a view which is more or less the opposite of Alfaric's. Instead of reading the early Augustine as a neo-Platonist and *not* a Christian, Conybeare argues that he is a Christian and *not* a neo-Platonist. Instead of discovering *later in life* that the neo-Platonic, rationalistic quest for the happy life is doomed to failure and needs to be rethought, Conybeare thinks Augustine was developing this critique immediately after his conversion and wrote about it at Cassiciacum. He was indeed to reject the neo-Platonic understanding of the universe, of man's place in it, and of salvation, but this rejection took place much earlier. Conybeare reads Augustine at Cassiciacum as an earthy fellow, resistant to neo-Platonism and the other-worldly.

Conybeare's thesis is best understood in terms of Augustine's developing response to pagan philosophy. The Cassiciacum dialogues interact a great deal with various pagan philosophers—especially the Stoics, Plotinus, and Cicero. These ancient philosophers promised that one could attain a stable happiness by means of reasoning and philosophical practices—reasoning

14. Van Fleteren says that *b. Vita* implies "that man has the ability to reach this knowledge or vision [of happiness] in this life." See "The Cassiciacum Dialogues and Augustine's Ascent," 61.

15. TeSelle, *Augustine the Theologian*, 61, 73.

16. Cary, "What Licentius Learned."

17. Ferrari, *The Conversions*, 72–73.

18. Topping, *Happiness and Wisdom*, 157–66.

19. Although Kolbet's reading of Augustine is more or less that of Harrison, he departs from Harrison in this particular, siding with Van Fleteren and others; see *Augustine and the Cure of Souls*, 104 and 189.

20. Conybeare, *The Irrational Augustine*.

that would identify the correct stable object of desire, and practices that would help us come to desire it and so attain the satisfaction in which happiness consists. It is easy to read these passages and conclude that Augustine is endorsing this philosophical project aimed at producing a rational and stable happy life. However, according to Conybeare, Augustine is *interacting* with this project not to endorse it so much as to *reconsider* it. And, in reconsidering, he ultimately *rejects* it. Thus Augustine abandons the rationalism of the Stoics and the neo-Platonists, along with the otherworldliness of the neo-Platonists. In its place he adopts a more nuanced understanding of the good life: as an embodied activity, not a quest for disembodied intellectualism; a communal and inclusive affair, rather than the privilege of a few learned men; and a moral, rather than an intellectual, process. This new conception of the good life is inspired by Christianity, not by philosophy.

Conybeare's view is the mirror image of Alfaric's. According to the one, young Augustine is a neo-Platonist, not yet a Christian; he has experienced a mental conversion to neo-Platonic immaterialism. According to the other, he is already a Christian, not a neo-Platonist; having experienced a *moral* conversion to the Christian faith, he has already left neo-Platonism behind.

A third way of understanding Augustine in the fall of 386 and the years following is to see him as committed to Christianity *and* to neo-Platonism. Championed by such scholars as Pierre Courcelle and Robert J. O'Connell, this particular reading has it that Augustine in 386 has converted to Christianity *and* to neo-Platonism, which he sees as essentially compatible, the former the completion of the latter. The dual influences of neo-Platonism and Christianity are easy enough to find in Augustine's early writings. From the Christian side there are strong emphases on God, immortality, sin, and Jesus Christ. From the neo-Platonist side there are emphases on the immaterial nature of God and the soul, the superiority of the immaterial over the physical, and intellectual ascent to knowledge of immaterial reality. It is easy to assume that Augustine considers himself fully a Christian and a neo-Platonist, integrating the two. In this integration sin would be understood as an attachment to carnal reality, salvation as liberation from this attachment.

Pierre Courcelle exemplifies this way of reading Augustine. Courcelle has shown that there was a Christian neo-Platonic community at Milan at the time of Augustine's conversion.[21] For Courcelle, this is evidence supporting Augustine's own neo-Platonism. Courcelle is the father of the modern

21. Courcelle's major works are *Recherches sur les Confessions* and *Les Confessions de Saint Augustin*. One of the many English sources discussing Courcelle is a brief but rewarding discussion in O'Donnell's commentary on the conversion scene in *The Confessions of Augustine: An Electronic Edition*, commentary on 8.12.28–29. O'Donnell mentions as "The sternest rejoinder to Courcelle" Bolgiani, *La conversion*; referenced in O'Donnell, commentary on 8.12.29.

view that young Augustine was both neo-Platonic and Christian, but in one important respect his reading resembles Alfaric's. Recall that Alfaric treats Augustine's autobiographical account of his state of mind in 386 as a misrepresentation. Courcelle, while he views Augustine as being a Christian neo-Platonist in his early and his later writings, views the famous conversion scene in book VIII, chapter 12, of *Confessions* as a fictional narrative.[22]

The legacy of Courcelle continues in more recent scholars including Van Fleteren, Jon Beane, and Roland Teske.[23] John O'Meara, a keen commenter on Augustine's "synthesis" of neo-Platonism and Christianity, also falls into this camp.[24] There is also Phillip Cary, who argues that Augustine is influenced by the neo-Platonic idea of the soul's divinity, an idea he accepts in the early writings.[25] Henry Chadwick offers a nice summary of this interpretive tradition, saying of post-conversion Augustine that "Ambrose has convinced him of the incorporeality of God, and preached so profound a fusion of Christianity with Platonic mysticism that Augustine thinks of Christ and Plato as different teachers converging in the same truths, complementary to each other."[26]

In recent decades O'Connell has been particularly influential in promoting this understanding of Augustine's conversion.[27] In addition to his studies of the relationship of Augustine's early writings to Plotinus,[28] O'Connell has distinguished himself by his idea that Augustine had adopted Plotinus's view of the fall of the soul.[29] Plato had suggested in *Meno* that the soul existed before it came to be in the body. Plotinus elaborates in the *En-*

22. O'Donnell disagrees with Courcelle: "There is no convincing reason to doubt the facts of the narrative of this garden scene as A. presents them, and so we should depart from Courcelle;" commentary on 8.12.29.

23. Van Fleteren, "The Cassiciacum Dialogues and Augustine's Ascent." Beane, "Augustine's Silence." Teske, *To Know God and the Soul.*

24. O'Meara, *Studies in Augustine and Eriguena*, 130–31, 136–38, 155–56.

25. Cary, *Augustine's Invention*, *Inner Grace*, and *Outward Signs*. For example, in *Augustine's Invention*, Cary explains that Augustine was in 386 converted to Platonist philosophy *and* to Catholic Christianity, and "to the latter by means of the former;" afterwards, his "Platonism grew in tandem with his Christian orthodoxy" (35). In an earlier article Cary argues that Augustine's idea of the soul's divinity is, at Cassiciacum, transforming from a Manichean idea to a Platonic; Cary, "God in the Soul," 69–79.

26. Chadwick, *Augustine of Hippo*, 29–30.

27. Rombs provides a valuable summary of O'Connell's work and its place in Augustine scholarship in the Introduction to his *Saint Augustine and the Fall.*

28. O'Connell, "Enneads VI."

29. O'Connell, *Saint Augustine's Early Theory*. Elsewhere O'Connell says that the "Incarnation, about which Plotinus himself may never have dreamt, Augustine fits neatly into the scheme of the Plotinian universe;" O'Connell, "The Enneads," 160. O'Connell also provides a very helpful refutation of the Alfaric reading of young Augustine in O'Connell, "The Visage of Philosophy."

neads: The human soul "fell" into an embodied state as the result of sin committed in a former, disembodied state. If indeed this is young Augustine's view, he has adopted a view on the origins of the soul although the Christian church had not decided the question. Moreover, he views embodiment as a bad state; the body is not the soul's true home, and embodiment is a punishment. The soul's purpose is to return to its original, disembodied state. Salvation is an escape from the body, not just an escape from sin; indeed, the two escapes are one.

Courcelle, O'Connell, and others in this tradition differ from Conybeare in taking Augustine to be a committed neo-Platonist; they differ from Alfaric in taking Augustine to be a committed Christian from the time of his conversion. This strategy for interpreting Augustine leaves room for development in his thought, a development which is, perhaps, necessary for a maturing Christian neo-Platonist. Yet this view eschews the notion of a radical division between an early and a late Augustine; the division is avoided largely by making both the early and the late Augustine into a Christian neo-Platonist—the late perhaps somewhat less Platonic than the early.

O'Connell's reading of Augustine is somewhat problematic. The early writings display a Christian metaphysics which is not entirely consistent with neo-Platonism. Rombs rightly remarks that part of O'Connell's legacy has been a "neglect of the context of Augustine's assimilation of that Plotinian thought. Such Plotinian elements are found in Augustine's early texts alongside competing or incompatible metaphysical principles."[30] As a theist Augustine knows that the Principle governing the universe is a personal God who hears our prayers. Moreover, Augustine emphasizes the Son's equality with the Father in *De ordine* 1.10.29; this Nicene orthodoxy excludes any "Platonizing notions of a hierarchy of divine beings."[31] Scholars also point to the metaphysical distinction between creator and creation.[32] Etienne Gilson summarizes: "The single fact that Augustine held from the very beginning of his conversion the doctrines of creation and of the equality of the divine Persons would suffice by itself to establish that he was Catholic *and not Plotinian* from the outset."[33]

30. Rombs. *Saint Augustine*, xxiv.

31. Rist, "Plotinus and Christian Philosophy," 394–96. Clark emphasizes the significance of this distinction between Christianity and Platonism, which she says even O'Connell acknowledges. See Clark, Review of *St. Augustine's Early Theory*, 435.

32. An article by Kevane and a recent book by Harrison are particularly helpful in elaborating this metaphysical difference. Kevane, "Christian Philosophy" and Harrison, *Rethinking*. Writing in the Courcelle-O'Connell tradition, Cary, in an earlier book, also mentions this; Cary, *Augustine's Invention*, 59.

33. Gilson, *Revue Philosophique*, 503; quoted in Kevane, "Christian Philosophy," 80,

Moreover, in the early writings even the elements in common with neo-Platonism are set in a Christian context and oriented towards Christian purposes. Could Augustine at Cassiciacum really have believed in such dynamic ideas as the Trinity and the Incarnation—yet maintained certain large regions of his worldview that were identical to regions of a neo-Platonic worldview?[34] I think not. On the contrary, he hopes to use neo-Platonic insights to understand the doctrines he received by faith from the church (*Contra Academicos* 3.20.43). Above all, he directs neo-Platonic insights to the goal of understanding two realities with which Christian theology is closely concerned, which Ambrose taught him not to conceive in carnal terms (*De beata vita* 1.4). He summarizes his intent thus: *Deum et animam scire cupio*: "I yearn to know God and the soul" (*Soliloquia* 1.2.7).

While we need not decide what, if any, view of the soul's origin Augustine held at Cassiciacum,[35] my concerns with O'Connell's reading have implications for my understanding of Augustine's diagnosis of desire and prescription for its healing. For example, the soul's desperate need for grace to convert its desires will emerge as an effect of Augustine's Christianity on his theology of desire—not (or not only) of neo-Platonic influences.[36]

In later chapters I shall from time to time revisit these first three interpretations and their major proponents.

A fourth interpretation is exemplified by Carol Harrison in her book *Rethinking Augustine's Early Theology*. Harrison argues that there is only one Augustine and that he takes neo-Platonist insights very seriously while always giving preeminence to Christianity over Platonism. Platonism provides conceptual resources for answering objections to Christianity, especially the problem of evil (*Confessions* VII), and for explaining Christian doctrines.

---

n. 99; emphasis added. Kevane's article is a helpful source on the significance of the distinction Augustine recognizes between creation and creator; Kevane also recommends Anderson, *St. Augustine and Being*, 61; quoted in Kevane, "Christian Philosophy," 80–81 n. 101.

34. Fortin is helpful on this theme; see "Reflections," 99.

35. And I confess that I lean against O'Connell on this point. I agree with O'Daly's analysis of Augustine's use of language suggesting the soul's return to God: It is a metaphorical way of expressing a truth about the divine origin of *knowledge*, not about the soul's preexistence; O'Daly, *Augustine's Philosophy of Mind*, 199–201.

36. While suggesting that Augustine realized slowly that Christianity and Plotinus depart on the distinction between creation and creator and the treatment of human beings as both body and soul, Rist notes that Augustine knew "at the outset" that we need God's gracious help to return to him. See "Plotinus and Christian Philosophy," 407–8. Cary, in the Courcelle-O'Connell tradition, recognizes this also, treating the idea of grace as a Platonic idea rooted in the divinity of the Good, from which all goodness derives, and which draws us to it by its own goodness; see his *Inner Grace*. I will not argue against this particular view of Cary, but I do argue that Augustine at Cassiciacum has a noticeably Christian notion of grace.

But Platonism is not itself Christianity, and it does not on its own authority establish the truth of Christian doctrine.[37] According to Harrison, the later Augustine's emphases on sin and grace and on Christian faith and practice rather than philosophy as the way to the happy life are already present in the early writings. His thought as it develops undergoes "less a revolution" than a "natural evolution."[38] Even in the early days, he is a *distinctively* Christian thinker—if a less *thoroughly* Christian thinker than he would be after a few decades of writing, thinking, serving, and maturing.

How then, on this reading, is Augustine's relationship to neo-Platonism to be understood? Very simply: He is a Christian, but he appreciates the insights of the neo-Platonists. He finds them insightful and helpful, yet he subordinates them to the revealed truths of the Christian faith, which they are helpful for understanding. He is a "Platonist" in a very broad sense, for he believes in the existence of immaterial reality and in its superiority over physical reality. But he does not accept all the trappings of ancient neo-Platonism. His thought is controlled by Christianity, and not by Plotinus or Porphyry.

Other scholars have a similar interpretation to Harrison. Harrison herself acknowledges her indebtedness to Goulven Madec.[39] John Mourant's article in the inaugural issue of *Augustinian Studies* helpfully collects myriad details from the Cassiciacum and other early dialogues, presenting them as evidence for "the extensive presence in virtually all of the dialogues of the Christian spirit and the Christian faith."[40] Eugene Kevane remarks that in the early dialogues "Something immensely illuminating was emerging, a new kind of philosophy, linked somehow with the new religion which had emerged powerfully out of Palestine into the Graeco-Roman world," a kind of philosophy that would "reorient all the arts and disciplines" and see them "placed at the service of God Incarnate."[41] Or, as Curley quotes Maurice Testard: "One must not forget, the Augustine of Cassiciacum is a Christian!"[42] Carl J. Vaught aptly summarizes this way of understanding Augustine in 386: "Augustine is a Christian who subordinates Neoplatonism to his own purposes rather than a Neoplatonist who disguises himself as a Christian theologian."[43] Paul Kolbet's recent book on Augustine's ethics and use of rhetoric supports the

37. Harrison, *Rethinking*, chapters 3 and 4.

38. Ibid., 151.

39. Most of Madec's studies are in French. To my knowledge only one of Madec's writings is in English: "The Notion."

40. Mourant, "The Emergence," 70.

41. Kevane, "Christian Philosophy," 52.

42. Testard, *Saint Augustin et Cicéron*, 174; quoted in Curley, *Augustine's Critique of Skepticism*, 73.

43. Vaught, *Encounters with God*, 9–10.

idea that his early thought has some neo-Platonic elements but is controlled by Christianity.[44] Ryan Topping's recent book on Augustine's early pedagogy also seems to lend some (admittedly ambiguous) support to the idea that his early thought has neo-Platonic elements, but is controlled by Christianity.[45] Other scholars who understand Augustine's early thought in much the same way include Etienne Gilson,[46] Mary Clark,[47] John Rist,[48] G. R. Evans,[49] Joanne McWilliam,[50] Laura Holt,[51] Brian Harding,[52] Ernest Fortin,[53] Michael Foley,[54] and William Mallard.[55]

When we are considering the relationship of Augustine's thought to neo-Platonism we are dealing with a complex set of issues, and it is easy to get confused about them. One issue in particular deserves special note: Both Harrison's reading and that of O'Connell and others emphasize the continuity of Augustine's thought. The disagreement concerns the nature of that continuity. Is Augustine's thought—both early and late—simply a Platonically informed Christianity (Harrison et al), or is it a more thoroughgoing

44. Kolbet explicitly links himself to the Madec-Harrison interpretive tradition; Kolbet, *Augustine and the Cure of Souls*, 14–16, 220 n. 68.

45. Topping explains how Augustine's goal in the early years was to understand immaterial reality (3), but also had "a distinctive Christian moral theory" (17). However, he endorses the same perspective on Augustine's early views as the O'Connell tradition: that Augustine considers Christianity and Platonism to be fully consistent (66). Yet he does not explicitly stake out a position on Augustine's early relation to neo-Platonism, a question he seems (understandably) to prefer to bracket in a study focused on other matters (66–7). Addressing Harrison in detail, Topping agrees with her on some points but objects on one, saying Augustine did at first hold to the possibility of moral perfection and happiness pre-mortem, with the help of grace (157–166). Topping sounds quite a bit like Harrison when he explains how reason in Augustine's thought follows on faith; its job is to explore that "which Christ through his Church" teaches it (169–70). His final word is that Harrison was wrong on pre-mortem happiness and right on grace, and "that past discussions have often failed to acknowledge how Catholic the young Augustine was" (230).

46. Gilson, *The Christian Philosophy*.

47. Clark, Review of *Augustine's Early Theory of Man* and *Odyssey of Soul*.

48. Rist, "Plotinus and Christian Philosophy."

49. Evans, *Augustine on Evil*. Evans takes Augustine's reference in *c. Acad.* to true philosophy to refer to Christianity (30) and says that "he wove" neo-Platonic ideas "into his Christian philosophy" (29). Evans also explains how Augustine's ethics in *b. Vita* are Christian and not merely Stoical (151–53).

50. McWilliam, "The Cassiciacum Autobiography."

51. Holt, "Wisdom's Teacher."

52. Harding, "Skepticism, Illumination."

53. Fortin, Review of *St. Augustine's Early Theory*, 309–11.

54. Foley, "Cicero, Augustine" and "The Other Happy Life."

55. Mallard argues that Augustine's early Christology is orthodox, though pre-Chalcedonian; "The Incarnation in Augustine's Conversion."

Christian neo-Platonism (Courcelle, O'Connell, et al)? Cary, for example, representing the latter tradition, points out that he sides with Madec as well as O'Connell on the question of continuity, although he departs from Madec on "the sources and character of Augustine's Platonism."[56]

One other, and particularly important, lesson we can learn from studying Harrison's approach is that how we interpret Augustine's early writings is not merely a matter of examining his theology vis-à-vis Neo-Platonism's. There is a methodological difference between Harrison and other scholars arising from the approach they take to Augustine's biography. If we interpret the early Augustine in one manner commonly employed by scholars, then we will assume that he is a neo-Platonist except where we can demonstrate a difference between him and the relevant neo-Platonic philosopher—usually taken to be Plotinus. If we read Augustine in Harrison's way, then we will assume that he was always as much of a Christian as he could be given his developing understanding of Christian doctrine, and we accept no commonality with neo-Platonic thought save where we can demonstrate one.

This particular interpretation of the Christian character of Augustine's early writings is also my own. The book you are reading could aptly be said to be an application of this interpretation to an important but underappreciated region of young Augustine's thought, his early theology of desire. It is also a limited defense of this way of reading young Augustine, a defense based on the Christian characteristics of his analysis of desire and on the relationship they bear to the neo-Platonic elements—facts which fit Harrison's interpretation somewhat better than the others. (To be fair, although my way of reading Augustine comes from a different interpretive tradition, my findings may in fact be consistent with the analyses of some writers in the Courcelle-O'Connell tradition.)

The facts, if my view is correct, are these: At Cassiciacum there are, first, truths Augustine has gleaned from neo-Platonism and to which he will cling for the rest of his life, finding them always to be salutary and consistent with Christianity. Second, there may be some ideas which Augustine has gleaned from neo-Platonism which he will give up as he grows and reflects more deeply on the mysteries of his own faith. These are both coupled with a third category, truths received from the Christian Scriptures and the testimony of the church. The joining of neo-Platonist insights to Christian calls for a rethinking and correction of the former. This rethinking is far from complete, but the point is that it has already begun.

Determining with precision into which categories various ideas fit is no easy task, but we can say with confidence that into the first category fall

56. Cary, *Inner Grace*, 149 n. 110.

the immateriality of God and the soul and the need for intellectual training to contemplate them. Into the second category may well fall the allegedly disembodied state of the afterlife (on which see chapter 3, below), or the Plotinian view of the fall of the soul. The third category includes the doctrines of the Trinity, the Incarnation, the existence of a personal God (as distinct from the impersonal Principle or One of neo-Platonism), and the radical distinction between creator and creation. These truths impart a new significance to the insights in the first category, placing them within a new worldview.[57] O'Connell and his ilk fail to understand, or at least to properly emphasize, this fact. Meanwhile, Alfaric and his ilk miss the third category altogether, and undermine the significance of the first category.

The three interpretations I reject lend themselves to mutual correction and themselves suggest the contours of my own reading of Augustine. The Courcelle-O'Connell interpretation, itself the closest to my own, corrects the Alfaric reading by calling attention to the Christian aspects of the dialogues.[58] In return the Alfaric reading correctly emphasizes the differences between neo-Platonism and Christianity. Each of these is right in seeing that the dialogues have neo-Platonic aspects, yet either reduces their theology to neo-Platonism or at least fails to appreciate the differences. Conybeare prevents the identification of Augustine's thought with neo-Platonism, but loses sight of Augustine's commitment to neo-Platonic insights.

In short, the perspective on Augustine which I am developing in this book is nothing original; it contains elements from Alfaric, Courcelle, O'Connell, Cary, Conybeare, and others. In understanding these elements the way I do, I stand on the shoulders of other Augustine scholars, including Etienne Gilson, Ernest L. Fortin, Eugene Kevane, Augustine J. Curley, Michael Foley, Goulven Madec, and Carol Harrison. But it must be admitted that so much ink has been spilt in the disagreements over how to read Augustine rightly that rarely have we done the actual reading.

I shall now explain why this particular exercise in reading is so important.

57. If O'Connell is right about the preexistence and pre-natal fall of the soul, this would not detract from the significance of the third category and its effects on the things in the second. I do not endorse O'Connell's reading, and the literature provides ample cause for suspicion. See criticisms of O'Connell's view in Clark and in O'Daly, "Did St. Augustine Ever?"

58. A particularly helpful refutation of the Alfaric reading from O'Connell's perspective appears in O'Connell, "The Visage of Philosophy."

WHY EXAMINE THE DIALOGUES' THEOLOGY OF DESIRE?

The analysis of desire is an important part of the work of ancient and medieval philosophers and is vitally important for understanding the figure who looms largest in the transition from the ancient to the medieval world. But there are other reasons we might benefit from understanding Augustine's early theology of desire.

One reason is simply that the theme of desire's maladies and their healing is central to the Cassiciacum dialogues. Unfortunately, it has generally been neglected. Many studies on Augustine's early writings focus on uncovering his sources or on the nature of his conversion. Some opportunities to exegete the early writings, to let him speak for himself, have been lost. The excellent studies that do let Augustine speak for himself[59] rarely if ever focus directly on desire, making it a lacuna even in the best scholarship. Yet desire is an important theme in the dialogues, replete as they are with the language of desire, words such as: *amare*, *appetere*, *quaerere*, *velle*, *cupere*, *sitire*, *diligere*, *libido*, *cupiditas*, and *voluntas*. The disordered state of our affections and their need for renewal is a ubiquitous theme, intertwined with the other central themes of the Cassiciacum dialogues.

The literature itself points to the need to fill this lacuna. Various scholars[60] have observed that the arguments and claims advanced in the dialogues have an ethical purpose, the restoration of happiness in men. For example, Topping: "From Cassiciacum onward Augustine considered the end of philosophy (or what we might term his 'moral theology') to be beatitude, the satisfaction of human aspiration for union with God."[61] Since happiness requires the satisfaction of desire, an understanding of desire in the dialogues is necessary if we are to understand how the dialogues are meant to help us reach happiness.

Several books focusing on Augustine's classical education and his turning it towards more pious ends go some way towards filling this gap.

59. See above, footnote 2.

60. As Kevane says, Augustine's philosophy "was a way of life" based in Christian doctrine and practice; "Christian Philosophy," 48. Gilson commends this aspect of Augustine to our study in chapter 1 of *The Christian Philosophy*. Foley, Silk, and Curley also read the dialogues with close attention to their ethical dimension. Others studies are Heil, "Augustine's Attack on Skepticism;" Harding, "Epistemology and Eudaimonism;" Harding, "Skepticism, Illumination;" Neiman, "Augustine's Philosophizing Person;" and Cary, "What Licentius Learned."

61. Topping, *Happiness and Wisdom*, 8. Another memorable remark on ethics at Cassiciacum: "while Augustine adopted the eudaimonism he found in Cicero's *Hortensius*, already by 386 he had learned how to adapt this to Christian ends" (ibid., 227).

Joseph Pucci's *Augustine's Virgilian Retreat* examines Augustine's reuse of pagan authors in service of Christian truth.[62] Topping's *Happiness and Wisdom* is an admirable study in Augustine's early pedagogy. It is, however, limited in this regard in that it focuses on pedagogy rather than on desire and in that it looks at various other early writings and does not thoroughly cover Cassiciacum. Much the same can be said of Eugene Kevane's magisterial *Augustine the Educator*, which covers, from Cassiciacum onward, Augustine's pedagogy—a topic intersecting with desire. Kevane's is a fine book which, in my view, deserves much more attention from Augustine scholars. But it does not cover in sufficient depth Augustine's teaching on desire at Cassiciacum. In addition, Kolbet's *Augustine and the Cure of Souls* is a fine study of Augustine's psychagogy—his use of rhetoric and philosophy to heal the soul—but it is not sufficiently attentive to the formative period at Cassiciacum. Of the literature I have mentioned, only Conybeare presents a systematic reading of the Cassiciacum dialogues, a reading problematic in some respects and in any case not focused directly on the crucial topic of desire. The lacuna remains.

There are at least three other reasons for such an investigation.

One is that an understanding of Augustine's early thinking on the status of desire and the means of its renovation will inform his later thought on the same subjects. A typical entry point into the *Confessions*, for example, is the notion that sin involves disordered loves—and redemption rightly ordered loves. Indeed, it is difficult to imagine a quality study of the *Confessions* that does *not* discuss this theme at some length. Why, then, would we neglect the same topic in the early writings of the same author? Augustine's views on the disorder of desire in sinful man and the reordering of desire in redeemed man did not emerge fully developed as he was writing the *Confessions*. The doctrine grew with him into maturity. If we are to appreciate fully this topic in the later works, therefore, we must examine it in the earlier ones.

Also, the theology of desire in the early writings of Augustine has the potential to inform contemporary debates on the nature of desire. The current philosophical discussion is thoroughly analytical. It seeks to determine what desire is, typically characterizing it as a requirement for action; coupled with beliefs about the way the world is and the way it could be, a desire that it be a certain way results in action.[63] Although I do not object

62. Pucci, *Augustine's Virgilian Retreat*.

63. A good summary of this view appears in Pettit, "Desire." In trying to determine what desire is Schroeder takes a different approach, analyzing the biological substrata of desire. Although his approach presupposes materialism and treats *all* desires as rooted in or identical to bodily states, I find his theory a plausible account of as many

to the accuracy of this analysis of what desire is,[64] I do not believe it can be a complete analysis of desire. Desire is more than that which together with belief equals action. It is as much a condition for satisfaction as a condition for action. The ancient-medieval perspective on desire suggests an ethical definition: Desire is that which together with an attainment of the object of desire equals satisfaction.[65] Moreover, as a component of the happy life desire calls for more than an analytic treatment; it calls for an active, even a spiritual, treatment that brings us to happiness by renovating our desires. We must understand the value of desire and the nature of healthy desire. From the ancient-medieval perspective, the recent books of David Naugle and James Smith[66] on reaching happiness by reordering our loves are just as important, if not more so, than the analytical approach which is currently the standard in philosophy.

Scholars of the ancient philosophers know well how they treated desire. This ethical and spiritual treatment of desire by the ancients has been called "therapy," and rightly so, for this is therapy as it was practiced millennia before the emergence of modern psychology. These ancient philosophers write with a view toward bringing people to happiness, which they understand as the satisfaction of desire. They diagnose the absence of happiness as a malfunction of desire, and prescribe for its restoration the healing of desire. The nature of the diagnosis and the cure prescribed vary according to the worldview of the philosopher—be it Epicurean, Stoic, Skeptical, or neo-Platonic.

And this is a final reason to understand Augustine's theology of desire in the early dialogues: It is a fitting extension to our understanding of ancient philosophical therapies of desire.

Since this philosophical approach is also the background to Augustine's own analysis, it would behoove us to review some of the views of the philosophical schools of the ancient world, particularly their understanding of desire. After this I shall turn to a summary of Augustine's early theology of desire.

---

of our desires as are rooted in the body; not being a materialist, I doubt it is true of *all* desires. See Schroeder, "Desire." Milliken critiques the standard analysis of desire in "In a Fitter Direction."

64. Indeed, Burt says something similar when he remarks that acts of love require knowledge of an object as well as delight in the same object. *"Let Me Know You,"* 69–70. Moreover, this definition of "desire" is close to the Stoic notion of *horme* as well as to Augustine's use of *voluntas*; see Byers, "The Meaning of *Voluntas*."

65. ". . . happiness depends on the fulfillment of our basic desires . . ." Burt, *"Let Me Know You,"* 10.

66. Naugle, *Reordered Loves*. Smith, *Desiring the Kingdom*.

ANCIENT PHILOSOPHERS AND THEIR THERAPIES FOR DESIRE

The philosophical schools of late antiquity were intensely interested in the problem of desire—in the ubiquity of dissatisfaction and the strategies or therapies one can apply to desire to make satisfaction possible. One can tell the story of late antique philosophy in terms of the philosophies of desire of its various schools. After describing some common elements of ancient philosophical therapy, I shall trace these elements through some of the chapters in this story which are particularly relevant at Cassiciacum: the Epicurean, Stoic, and neo-Platonist schools of thought.[67]

Ancient philosophical therapy is commonly developed according to a medical analogy. Philosophy is, so to speak, spiritual medicine. It observes the evidence of pathology in a person's life, as a doctor would observe *symptoms*; it provides an explanation of the underlying pathology, as a doctor would make a *diagnosis*; it provides a *therapy* for a person's life; finally, it describes the ideal of spiritual *health* to which therapy should bring one. Martha Nussbaum's *The Therapy of Desire* and Pierre Hadot's *What Is Ancient Philosophy?* are very helpful studies of these themes in the ancients.[68] Kolbet and Topping review the same material, focusing on the therapeutic uses of, respectively, rhetoric and education, in their books before going on to explore Augustine's use of the same types of therapy throughout his career.[69]

Epicureanism

Epicureanism sees symptoms of spiritual pathology in the obsessions, fears, and disappointments with which our lives are rife. Nussbaum describes the Epicurean criticism of many people's lives: "We see people rushing frenetically about after money, after fame, after gastronomic luxuries, after passionate love . . . ."[70] Lucretius, the Roman Epicurean, also describes sexual

67. This is not a complete survey, for there are other chapters in the story; for example, Kolbet reviews the therapeutic use of rhetoric in Cicero, Manicheanism, Ambrose, and neo-Platonism in chapter 3 of *Augustine and the Cure of Souls*.

68. Nussbaum, *The Therapy of Desire*; Hadot, *What Is Ancient Philosophy?*. Topping summarizes Hadot nicely: "the ancient school primarily offered an education in virtue" (41).

69. Kolbet, *Augustine and the Cure of Souls*; Topping, *Happiness and Wisdom*. Referring to the work of Diognon, Topping says that "the Cassiciacum dialogues present a pedagogy in action" (71).

70. Nussbaum, *Therapy of Desire*, 103.

obsession.[71] The Epicurean philosopher, above all, sees as symptomatic of spiritual pathology the fact that nearly everyone is "poisoned by the fear of death," desperately trying to secure for themselves a happy position in the afterlife.[72]

Epicureanism analyzes these disorders as rooted in desires that exceed what can naturally be achieved: "The flesh took the limits of pleasure to be unlimited."[73] These desires are rooted in false beliefs about what is good for us, beliefs strengthened by a society that has lost sight of the natural human good.[74] The fear of death is especially significant. We have been trained to believe in an afterlife in which we may be rewarded or punished; we have been trained to believe in gods who punish us when we vex them. Accordingly we live our lives fearing death and the wrath of the gods. We have been led to believe by "conversations all around us glorifying wealth and power" that these are good things.[75] Lucretius goes deeper still, analyzing the accumulation of wealth and power as frantic attempts to achieve invulnerability and rooted in the fear of death.[76]

As therapy, Epicureanism prescribes that we rid ourselves of these false beliefs and learn the truth of the universe and of our existence in it. The Epicurean therapy is rooted in a materialist conception of reality. The universe is composed of atoms in a void; human beings are material creatures, composed of atoms. In a telling piece, Epicurus describes to Herodotus the physical makeup of the universe and explains how the truths of materialism remove anxiety.[77] When we die our atoms simply dissipate, so there is no afterlife to fear. By ceasing to believe in the afterlife we can accept the fact of death and live contentedly in its expectation. The gods are happy, invulnerable creatures who do not need anything from us; accordingly, they do nothing to harm us and we need not fear them. Epicurus explains in a letter to Pythocles that meteorological events are the result of the movements of atoms, not the portents of the gods; by ceasing to believe in gods looming wrathfully over us we cease to fear them.[78] Epicureanism recommends constant meditation on these truths in order to "become intensely aware of,

71. Nussbaum has an excellent discussion of this theme in Lucretius; ibid., chapter 5.

72. Ibid.

73. Epicurus, *Epicurus Reader*, xx.

74. Nussbaum, *Therapy of Desire*, 105, 113.

75. Ibid., 107.

76. Ibid., 198.

77. Epicurus, "Letter to Herodotus," in *Epicurus Reader*.

78. Epicurus, "Letter to Pythocles," in *Epicurus Reader*. The exact Epicurean account of the gods is not entirely clear; for an account Augustine almost certainly read, see Cicero in Book I of *The Nature of the Gods*.

and assimilate within ourselves," the truth about the universe.[79] Epicureans also learned to be content with simple and natural pleasures and cultivated friendships to help one another live by these truths.[80]

Finally, happiness is achieved when we live within our natural limits. The Epicurean ideal is a life free from the psychological torment of unachievable expectations and content with bodily existence. Not seeking to live forever or to placate the gods, the happy person is content to live as a body for a time and then die. Not seeking to accumulate wealth or rise precipitously to political power, the happy person is satisfied with being relatively free from pain and experiencing a modicum of physical pleasure. This achieves the happy life, a state of *ataraxia*, or tranquility.[81] In short, Epicureanism counsels that we limit our desires to the very modest goal we are able to achieve; desire for what we cannot attain and retain results in disappointment, so we should understand what is attainable and trim our desires to accept it.

Stoicism

Like the Epicurean, the Stoic school of thought addresses spiritual pathology, seeing as evidence of pathology the emotions that disturb our lives: the likes of fear, anxiety, grief, disappointment, envy, anger, hatred, and regret. For example, Seneca opens his *On Anger* with an account of the misery associated with anger: bloodlust, a loss of self-control, outbursts of violent speech, wars, etc.[82] In *On the Tranquility of the Soul* he describes the boredom and laziness of some lives, a condition which digresses into envy: "they desire the ruin of everyone, as they have not been able to succeed themselves; then . . . the mind of these men becomes angry at Fortune and complains about the times, withdrawing into corners and brooding over its sorry fate until it becomes irritated with itself."[83] The great sadness we often experience at the death of a loved one is also taken as an example of spiritual ill health.

The Stoic diagnoses these disorderly emotions in terms of mistaken judgments; according to Stoic psychology, emotions are a kind of false judgment.[84] The devastating emotions which disturb our lives are judgments that the universe does not measure up to how it should be; for example,

79. Hadot, *What Is Ancient Philosophy?*, 122.

80. Ibid., 123.

81. See Nussbaum, *Therapy of Desire*, 109.

82. Seneca, *On Anger*, 1.1–2.3.

83. Seneca, *Tranquility of the Mind*, 116–17.

84. Nussbaum, *Therapy of Desire*, 366–69.

grief is the judgment that I have lost something of great value.[85] As the Stoic sees it, these judgments show that we are failing to see the universe for what it is and failing to see our place in it.

To cure us of these emotions, Stoic therapy aims to help us learn the truth about the universe. Philosophy of desire is again linked to metaphysics: Nothing happens without divine permission; our fate is acceptable to God and is indeed God's very decree.[86] The universe is determined, and the way things are is the way they ought to be. Marcus Aurelius in his *Meditations* reflects on the order of the universe: a systematic whole which is law-like, beautiful, and good. We must learn to accept the universe as it is and to consider it from the perspective of the whole.[87] We experience disturbing emotions because our desires are based on our own perspective: a selfish, individual view which does not take into account the good of the whole. What seems a misfortune is actually good; by reflecting on the universe as a whole we will come to see this and accept our place in the universe.[88] By changing our perception of things, we change our desires; by changing our desires, we are no longer hurt by shifting fortune. Since emotions are a false judgment, removing the judgment removes the emotion. The key to happiness is to cut desire down to size, or even to extirpate it completely—to proportion desire to the way things are. Arguments help to cultivate the soul's understanding of the truth and thus are central in its therapy.[89] Stoic therapy also includes constantly paying attention to oneself and reminding oneself of one's place in the universe.[90]

Finally, the Stoic explains spiritual health. The person who lives properly understands that the soul's true good is its own virtue: "virtue all by itself suffices for a completely good human life . . . ."[91] Thus the Stoic ideal is the state of *apatheia*, the utterly stable contentment of one whose desires line up with the way things are. The heart of this prescription for happiness is the principle that we should desire only that which is under our direct control, namely our own virtue; nothing else is consistently attainable.

85. Ibid., 375–86.

86. Aurelius, *Meditations*, 4.40.

87. Ibid., 4.7.

88. On this theme see Seneca's *On Providence*.

89. For example, see chapter 11 of Nussbaum's *Therapy of Desire* on how Seneca's *On Anger* uses arguments as therapy to heal the reader's soul.

90. Hadot, *What Is Ancient Philosophy?*, 138.

91. Nussbaum, *Therapy of Desire*, 359; also see Hadot, *What Is Ancient Philosophy?*, 127: "The good person believes that the only evil is moral evil and that there is no good but moral good—namely, what we call duty or virtue."

Everything else can go by the wayside; we do not need it, and should not want it, to be happy.

Neo-Platonism

In a revealing passage Plotinus explains what things do *not* affect the happy man, thus showing the sort of things the neo-Platonist sees as evidence of poor spiritual health.[92] These are the fears and disappointments common to men, such as: distress at the death of a child or the loss of possessions; despair when political winds bring change; and the fear of an ignoble death, of not being buried, or of not having an imposing tombstone to stand as monument. By fearing the possibility of such things and despairing at their realization men show that they are not spiritually healthy.

Neo-Platonism diagnoses not the *strength* but the *direction* of desire as what has gone wrong. Desire for physical things is the root of spiritual pathology. Although Epicurus and the Stoics are correct that our desires exceed anything attainable in this world, we should not be desiring *this* world in the first place.[93] Lust for sensory things pulls us off the pursuit of what would make us happy; the right object of desire is immaterial and accessible only to the intellect.[94] Plotinus says, "the mortal . . . is not the authentic object of our love nor the good we really seek. Only in the world beyond does the real object of our love exist . . . ."[95]

The soul's therapy consists in being trained to know immaterial reality. At the heart of neo-Platonism are the insights that there is such a thing as an immaterial world; that it is better than the physical world; that it lends to the physical world such continuity, organization, and rationality as it admits of; that our souls are immaterial realities themselves; that it is the soul and not the body that knows immateriality; and that we must be trained in order to know it. Neo-Platonic therapy helps us know the immaterial world by living "in accordance with the highest part of ourselves, namely the intellect," in order to be healed.[96] We must also contemplate immateriality and practice

92. From the treatise on *Happiness* in Plotinus, *The Essential Plotinus*, 1.4.7.

93. Stoics such as Marcus, who desire the good of the universe, bear a resemblance to the Platonists in that they recommend *redirecting* our desire towards something higher than money, power, fame, and physical pleasure. From the Platonic perspective, the problem is that they still fail to redirect desire towards an immaterial world.

94. Plato's *Symposium* is the paradigmatic mediation on love for the divine.

95. From Plotinus, the treatise on *The Good or the One* in *Enneads*, 6.9.9.

96. Hadot, *What Is Ancient Philosophy?*, 158.

asceticism in order to learn to live for the immaterial world.[97] Finally, in Plato's Academy it was taught that the fear of death was to be avoided.[98]

The happy life is the life lived in accordance with reason and in contemplation of immateriality, and it culminates in union with the divine.[99] Happiness depends on the soul's becoming acquainted with immateriality; when our minds contemplate the divine we are content: "the soul rests. It seeks no further. It is sated. Its vision remains all within; it is sure of its object."[100] No carnal thing holds the interest of a soul thus contented.[101]

Where Epicurus makes the contentedness of the body primary, the neo-Platonic intellectual ascent makes it irrelevant; where contentedness with the physical universe satisfies both Stoic and Epicurean, the mind trained to contemplate the divine readily gives it up. All agree that happiness is contingent on the attainability of desire and that unhappiness is due to inordinate desire for unattainable things. But where others advise us to cut desire down to size, the neo-Platonist encourages us to love something more lasting and more worth loving. The right object of desire perennially satisfies; if anything, our desire may actually be too weak!

Augustine and the Philosophers

Although many aspects of these ancient philosophers are still the subject of scholarly debate, clearly they are concerned with the disorders that afflict human desire and with the means of restoring desire to right order. This sort of therapy as it appears in the ancient philosophers is well known to scholars of the ancients, and similar analyses of desire are familiar to those who study the later writings of Augustine and the writings of other medieval thinkers. It is here at this pivotal moment, when the mind of Augustine the new Christian thinker is setting in motion the transition from the ancient to the medieval era, that we have so far been largely negligent in studying this crucial topic. The Cassiciacum dialogues are the first fruits of the philosopher-theologian who did more than any other to effect the transition from the pagan ancient culture to the Christian medieval. In these dialogues Augustine interacts with late antique eudaimonism; his Christian advice for the restoration of desire is in part a response to ancient advice on desire. He

97. Ibid., 158–59.

98. Ibid., 67.

99. Ibid., 160.

100. From Plotinus, the treatise on *Contemplation*, 3.8.6.

101. From Plotinus, the treatise on *Beauty*, 1.6.7. (1.4.7 in the treatise on *Happiness* is also helpful.)

has a valuable perspective on late antiquity, one helpful for understanding ancient philosophy and Christian theology alike.

I now turn to a summary of the dialogues' analysis of desire.

DESIRE IN THE CASSICIACUM DIALOGUES

Augustine's response to ancient philosophy emphasizes the superiority of the neo-Platonists to other philosophical schools, and *their* inferiority to Christianity. He specifically focuses on what we have come to know as the "neo-Platonic" tradition represented by Porphyry and Plotinus, whom Augustine recognizes as authentic representatives of Plato's doctrine.[102]

Let us look briefly at an illustrative example from a later work. In the 410 Letter to Dioscorus Augustine gives an overview of ancient philosophy, presenting the ethics of three ancient schools of thought in order to contrast them with one another and with Christianity, privileging the Platonist school as getting closest to the truth.[103] Each school espouses a view on the supreme good: for the Epicurean, the body; for the Stoic, the mind; and, for the Platonist, God. Stoicism has an advantage over the Epicureans; it locates the supreme good in the mind, thus promoting an *inward* turn away from carnal lusts and towards the good of the soul. Platonism locates the supreme good in a divine reality above the soul, thus promoting an *upward* turn toward God. Even so, Platonism lacks the truths of Christianity; it fails to depict God as personal and trinitarian. It also lacks the humble way that leads to God, the way of following Christ.

This response to ancient philosophy is incipient at Cassiciacum, where Augustine responds to the problems of ancient philosophy with Christian reflections on loving God and the soul. Like the ancient philosophers his treatment of desire provides all the elements of a rich medical analogy. In the next five chapters of this book I pursue the theme of desire and its renewal through each of the dialogues, devoting one chapter to each dialogue. Here I shall describe the major roles desire plays in each of the dialogues. Then I shall summarize the major insights on desire that emerge from the dialogues. Then I shall discuss the concluding chapter of this book.

102. Harrison, *Augustine*, 13. Accordingly, while there may be differences between Plato and Plotinus, these are not Augustine's concern at Cassiciacum.

103. Augustine, "Letter 118," 3.14–17.

The Dialogues and their Therapies

In *Contra Academicos*, the subject of Chapter 2, Augustine addresses the challenge of Academic skepticism. Skepticism discourages a vibrant pursuit of wisdom because it induces despair of attaining it. Despair must be combated with hope. The successful pursuit of wisdom is bound to the authority of the man who brings wisdom to us, Jesus Christ.

In *De beata vita*, the subject of Chapter 3, Augustine addresses the ancient question: How can we be happy? Associated with the question of happiness is the question of desire: What ought we to desire in order to be happy? The answer is that we must desire God, and that we must pursue God by following Christ in community with his church and by cultivating faith, hope, and charity. In *De beata vita* Augustine also presents the happy life as the activity of embodied creatures.

In *De ordine*, the subject of Chapter 4, Augustine responds to the problem of evil, saying that God's providence encompasses the universe and brings order out of evil. As a means of learning to understand order, he recommends that we pursue the reordering of our souls via a liberal arts education and Christian morality. These means of reordering our souls are also therapies to restore right desire in them.

In *Soliloquia*, the subject of Chapter 5, Augustine engages in a dialogue with his own reason. That which rightly ordered souls desire is stated most clearly here: We ought to love God and the soul. As Augustine attempts to know God and the soul in this very personal conversation, we are reminded of the need to submit to Christ's authority and to practice the theological virtues for the healing of desire. We also learn from the unique form of *Soliloquia* how Augustine seeks to draw us into the dialogues to learn what its characters learn and to have our desires reordered alongside theirs.

Augustine's Emerging Theology of Desire

Augustine's early treatment of desire makes a useful test of the right way to understand his worldview—whether as simply neo-Platonism, as simply Christianity, as quite thoroughly both, or as a sort of Platonically informed Christianity. And it is an important test, given the importance of desire to ancient spiritual writings in the genre of philosophical therapy.

What I find at Cassiciacum is that Augustine's theology of desire is under the influence of both neo-Platonism and Christianity, and that the spiritual regimen for the healing of desire is replete with aspects of both traditions. Yet that regimen is more emphatic of Christian teaching and practice, and less reliant on asceticism and contemplation, than we would expect from a neo-Platonism unchanged by its encounter with the Christian tradition. Asceticism takes a backseat to Christian prayer. Contemplation is no more important than Christian piety. Fleeing the influence of matter is not commanded so much as fleeing to Christ. And so on. Thus I think the best way to understand Augustine's analysis of desire is the way the fourth interpretation of Augustine understands his early thought: as a Platonically informed Christian approach. My findings thus strongly support the thesis that only a line of interpretation that recognizes both neo-Platonic and Christian aspects of the early writings can be correct. They also provide a lesser degree of support for the reading of Harrison, Fortin, and others over the Courcelle-O'Connell interpretation.

Recall that the therapy of desire approaches the health of the soul in terms of a medical analogy; the components to this approach are observation of symptoms, diagnosis of the underlying pathology, a therapy for curing the pathology, and an ideal of spiritual health. Augustine is no exception to this rule, as demonstrated by the repeated appearance throughout the dialogues of several major insights on the renewal of desire. However, Augustine's method of approaching the problem differs somewhat from the ancient philosophers, for he does not simply proceed empirically, observing spiritual illness and then seeking an account of spiritual health which can cure it. A devout Christian, he accepts the account of the good life offered by divine revelation and considers the health of the soul from that perspective. I shall first look briefly at symptoms and then look more closely at spiritual health, diagnosis of spiritual pathology, and spiritual healing. Following this I shall explain why the language of "therapy," while helpful, is not by itself sufficient for describing Augustine's theology of desire.

Augustine recognizes many familiar signs of spiritual pathology: anxiety and the fear of losing what we love; misery in the face of misfortunes; frenzied pursuits of money, power, and physical pleasures; the near-ubiquitous fear of death; and the desire to be glorified in the eyes of others.

As for the other components of the medical analogy, Augustine's project at Cassiciacum provides Christian answers to three questions that grow out of the ancient philosophical practice of spiritual therapy. In response to the question "What ought men to desire?" Augustine gives his perspective on spiritual health. In response to the question "What has gone wrong with their desires?" Augustine diagnoses spiritual pathology. In response to the question "How do they come to desire the right things?" he gives a Christian account of how our desires are mended.

What ought men to desire? Augustine's account of spiritual health includes several neo-Platonic insights, but Christian doctrine guides it. The happy person is one who loves God and the soul and dwells in right fellowship with God and others. Such a one's desires are rightly ordered; he does not desire material things. Instead, he loves and pursues the immaterial world; above all, he loves God and the soul, which Augustine continually reminds us are non-physical realities. Augustine does his best to teach us to contemplate immaterial reality—to understand it on its own terms, our minds free from carnal images and lusts. He presents that God whom we ought to desire as the Trinity. The one creator of the universe, the being worthy of the greatest love, is triune. We do not love immateriality as such, nor the impersonal One of Plotinus. The proper objects of our love are the Personal Three-in-One and the souls that are made in the image of that God.

What has gone wrong with their desires? Like his account of spiritual health, Augustine's diagnosis of spiritual illness includes neo-Platonic insights but is also distinctly Christian. Two insights take the forefront throughout the Cassiciacum dialogues. First, our desires go wrong in seeking to be satisfied with the things of this world rather than in the immaterial realities we should love. Second, we desire too much our own glory; in other words, pride is the disease of the soul, a root (if not *the* root) of the disorders in our lives.

How do they come to desire the right things? Augustine's prescription for the healing of desire includes some of the practices of the ancient schools. Yet, in reflecting the reality of sin, the need for grace, and the person of Jesus Christ, Augustine's portrayal of the healing of desire transcends that of the ancients. Here I shall summarize the most salient features of his early thinking on the renewal of desire; then I shall describe why this renewal is more than just a therapy of desire, but a *conversion* of desire in a rich theological sense.

To begin with, we must practice virtue to purify the soul of carnal lusts. Moreover, Augustine appeals to the neo-Platonic insight that the liberal disciplines are helpful in reordering the soul. The disciplines attune our minds to immaterial reality and have some power to cleanse our desires of carnal lusts.[104]

Much more important, however, is grace. The Cassiciacum dialogues are sprinkled with inklings of the notion of original sin and reminders that the healing of our fallen desires calls for divine grace. We need God's help, which has descended to us through the miracle of the Incarnation. Christ has extended happiness to everyone, even to those whose lack of intellectual

104. Later Augustine would come to regret the confidence he placed in the liberal arts. On this topic see below in Chapter 4 under the heading *Order of Life and Education*.

ability or training prevents them from understanding the immaterial world. The Incarnation bridges the gap between men and God even for those who can contemplate immaterial reality; for all of us are corrupted by sinful desires and need Christ's help.

The Incarnation requires a new treatment of desire. Submission to Christ's authority becomes the central component of a program for the renewal of desire. Only by following the one who came to teach us how to love can we hope to love correctly.

The authority of Christ extends to his church. The healing of desire takes place in the context of a theological community in which we must immerse ourselves and whose guidance in our lives helps to heal our affections.

The Incarnation also calls for reconsidering the relationship of our embodied life and the orientation of right desire towards the immaterial world. Although at this early stage in his literary career Augustine's analysis of the goodness of embodiment is incomplete, he already presents our embodied life as the appropriate context for healing, rather than simply as a negative influence to be spurned so our desires can be healed.

Following Christ also involves prayer. We must pray to God, who gracefully offers the healing of our desires. Prayer redirects the mind's attentions to God, and is itself an edifying pursuit of God. We must pursue healing together in community with others who prayerfully receive the same grace.

Finally, the renewal of desire requires the theological virtues. At least since Plato philosophers had considered the practice of virtue central to their therapies of desire. For Augustine the virtues include faith, hope, and charity. The path to renewed desires is the path of faith in response to the triune God and of submission to Christ and his church. We must have hope in the eventual attainment of what we seek in order to seek it diligently and fervently. And we must have charity to love God and to love our neighbor as we proceed to God.

Through doing these things our desires will be transformed, directed towards their right and fitting objects. By following this path of renewal we can hope to one day attain the object of our desire and thus be made happy. For these reasons the ancient philosophical language of *therapy* for desire does not fully capture Augustine's teaching on desire at Cassiciacum. It speaks to the fact that our souls are sick; they are not functioning properly, and need healing. We need therapy, and Augustine offers therapies in abundance. Yet at Cassiciacum therapy works in conjunction with a change in the soul's orientation better captured by the word *conversion*, for Augustine's thinking on desire has a Christian tone, a tone which displays continuity with his recent commitment to following Christ in the garden at Milan as well as with his later writings. The conversion of desire is not merely a reorientation of desire from one object to another, such as might occur in a pagan therapy. It is a *conversion* to the Christian God, on whose grace we are utterly dependent for the healing of desire; we must respond to grace by turning our desires to God.

In short, Augustine's advice at Cassiciacum for the conversion *and* therapy of desire is the work of someone who is very interested in the problems of ancient philosophy but seeks Christian solutions.[105] The conversion *and* therapy of desire at Cassiciacum links him to the spiritual practices of ancient philosophers but binds him to the doctrine and practices of the church.

In short, Augustine has inherited from the classical past a *philosophy* of desire, and at Cassiciacum he is refashioning it into a *theology* of desire. If Augustine's thought at Cassiciacum represents a "Platonism" at all, then it is a Platonism *transformed by* Christianity!

Love of God and Man

In the final chapter of this book I address an important question about the nature of Christian love and suggest an answer that is incipient at Cassiciacum. When we love both God and human beings, do we really *love* human beings, or does our love for God merely take on a human face? In other words, do we love human beings for their own sake, or simply use them to love God? With God as the true object of rightly ordered loves, what place is there for love of man?

In this chapter I suggest an Augustinian approach to this question that takes into account the essential nature of man as understood in light of the biblical doctrines of creation and redemption. Whether we can truly love man while being thoroughly devoted to God depends on whether we were created to do so. The reordering of our desires restores them to the way they were created to be. If we are created to live in community with both God and man, then we are also created to love them both, and the conversion of desire can only teach us to love them both. Moreover, if we are created to live in a holy community in which God is adored beyond anything else, then loving God above all, and doing so together, is precisely what makes us happy. In this case, the only proper way to treat each other, and hence the only way to *love* each other, is to love each other for God's sake rather than

105. In using the word "conversion" I do not intend to suggest that desire is dramatically healed in a single moment. See below, Chapter 2, under the subheading *Christ: Towards a Christian Theology of Desire.*

for each other's sake. Although this perspective is not presented explicitly in the dialogues of Cassiciacum, its building blocks are incipient in them. Thus my final chapter uncovers a region of continuity in Augustine's ethical thought that heretofore, to my knowledge, has been entirely neglected.

In sum, the thesis of this book is that Augustine's emerging philosophy of desire at Cassiciacum is neo-Platonic in some senses, especially in the broad sense that it privileges the concept of immaterial reality, yet is distinctively a Christian philosophy of desire—or a theology of desire. The Platonic idea of immaterial reality is at the core of his analysis of desire, but Christian doctrine determines the shape of the whole. Each of us should seek to know the trinitarian God, to know his own soul, to love others, and to be part of the community which knows this God. As the neo-Platonists realized, God and the soul are immaterial entities. The basic problems with our desires are that we desire things of the material world and that in pride we love ourselves too much. Various therapies for desire practiced by ancient philosophers are helpful in redirecting our desires to God and the soul and in helping us attain them, including studying the liberal arts, introspective meditation, and virtuous habits. However, in the main we come to desire these things, and to have them, through grace as the result of Christ's incarnation, through following Christ and immersing ourselves in the church, and through practicing the theological virtues. In short, rather than controlling Augustine's worldview, the concept of immaterial reality is applied to concepts he learned from the Christian tradition so that he can understand them better, and in particular to those things he most wants to understand: God and the soul.

2

Desiring Wisdom

From their very beginning a diagnosis and therapy of desire is one of the threads weaving its way through the Cassiciacum dialogues, tying their disparate elements together. In *Contra Academicos* Augustine illuminates several themes through an encounter with Academic skepticism.[1] The dialogue's central question is whether happiness requires the satisfaction of desire—whether we can be happy seeking wisdom and not having it. The answer is that happiness requires the attainability of desire. Moreover, the wisdom we desire can be attained (so happiness is possible), and the Incarnation makes it attainable. We must desire wisdom vigorously in order to attain it. Pride, overconfidence, and the despair of ever attaining wisdom choke the desire for wisdom and cripple its pursuit; undergoing a vigorous pedagogy, participating communally in wisdom's pursuit, and having hope of its attainment each nourish a robust desire for wisdom. Finally, our desire for wisdom is set in a new theological context; desire must now look for its healing to Jesus Christ, in whom the very wisdom we seek has been revealed. This entails resituating the pursuit of wisdom under the auspices of Christian authority and binding the desire for wisdom to the theological virtues.

In what follows I shall first introduce the characters Trygetius and Licentius, examine the viewpoints they represent and the arguments they give for them, and explore the significance of those arguments for a philosophy of desire (Part One). Then I shall look at the significance of our beliefs about wisdom and Augustine's efforts to cultivate Licentius's desire

1. Augustine, *Against the Academics* (referenced in text as *c. Acad.*).

for it (Part Two). Finally, I shall show how skepticism is refuted and how the Academics are replaced first by neo-Platonic insight and then by Christian teaching (Part Three).

SATISFACTION, HAPPINESS, AND THE HUMAN GOOD

Book I offers a vivid portrayal of two different perspectives on human happiness and its connection to desire and wisdom. Both views agree that humans desire wisdom, but disagree on whether we need to attain it in order to be happy. Book I introduces two characters who promote these visions, Augustine's students Trygetius and Licentius. After discussing Augustine's letter to Romanianus, I shall introduce Licentius's and Trygetius's disagreement.

Philosophy's Way Home to Virtue

The immediate audience of the dialogue is Augustine's patron, Romanianus, whom he had previously led into Manicheanism and whom he now exhorts to follow a better path to his soul's true home. In his letter to Romanianus Augustine introduces several key themes: an exhortation to philosophy; the promise that philosophy yields the stability of a virtuous life; the suggestion that we need divine help to attain virtue; and the characterization of virtue as a reordering of desire.

First, Romanianus is exhorted to philosophy. As incentive Augustine mentions that Romanianus's son, Licentius, "is now most eagerly living with me in philosophy" (1.1.4), and he exhorts the father to imitate the son in this. Augustine says he has thoroughly rejected Manicheanism (1.1.3), and encourages Romanianus now to follow him in the right direction. Philosophy will lead him "into the port of wisdom" (1.1.1), which Manicheanism had failed to do. Augustine's rejection of Manicheanism and temporary preference for Academic Skepticism (*Conf.* 5.14) are part of the background of this passage. Augustine is reaching out to Romanianus in hopes of leading him into the happy life which he himself has now found.[2] When Augustine abandoned Manicheanism he leaned toward Skepticism for a time, then became an admirer of Platonic philosophy (*Conf.* VII), and finally a Christian (*Conf.* VIII). By addressing a refutation of Academicism to him, Augustine hopes that Romanianus can take a more direct road to wisdom,

2. Kevane, "Christian Philosophy," 55. Dennis, "Three Augustines of *Contra Academicos*," 10–17.

encountering Skepticism through the passing glimpse given in *Contra Academicos*.[3] By the end of *Contra Academicos*, Romanianus will have before him both the neo-Platonic wisdom Augustine applauds as the right way to wisdom and the Christian revelation Augustine identifies with Wisdom itself (or Himself).[4]

Second, philosophy promises the stability of virtue. Philosophy's destination is virtue, "the port of wisdom" (1.1.1); this Ciceronian image links Augustine to the tradition of ancient philosophy, which seeks to secure us from life's upheavals. The metaphor is vivid; a ship at sea is susceptible to the weather; in port a ship is secured, able to survive wind and weather. A soul without philosophy is likewise buffeted by the wind and waves of misfortune, ill health, and the deaths of loved ones.[5] A soul secured by philosophy weathers the storms of life: "Virtue . . . does not allow it [adverse fortune] to snatch anyone away from her . . . ."

Third, virtue is not found without the help of "fortune," which serves a higher order. Although man is by nature "well-suited to her," access to virtue is not granted to anyone "unless fortune itself . . . leads him to it" (1.1.1). We are unable to get there on our own. Our need for assistance is first mentioned as a need for "fortune itself, be it 'favorable' or 'adverse,'" to bring us into port. No sooner has Augustine mentioned fortune than he alludes to "prayers on your behalf to the God who cares about these things . . . ." Perhaps what we call 'fortune' "is being ruled by a certain hidden order," a notion seen before in Aristotle as well as Cicero.[6] That hidden order is God's design, to whom Augustine prays on Romanianus's behalf. Fortune that seems adverse may end up returning us to wisdom. (We will return to God's role in the hidden ordering of circumstances in *De ordine*.)

Fourth, virtue is characterized as both a return to ourselves and a reordering of desire. Augustine and his friends have been praying that God would "return you to yourself" (1.1.1). He must cease being "a divine mind clinging to mortal things"[7] and learn the proper love of God: "For philoso-

3. McWilliam's "The Cassiciacum Autobiography" emphasizes the connections between Augustine's history and the events, topics, and people at Cassiciacum.

4. Neiman points out that Augustine's teaching in *c. Acad.* opposes the Manicheans as well as the Academics. Neiman, "The Arguments," 243–44. This observation is all the more poignant because the immediate audience of the text is a Manicheans.

5. Cicero, *Discussions at Tusculum* 5.2.5, *On Duties* 2.6.19. On ancient philosophy and the ravages of fortune, see above, Chapter 1, under the heading *Ancient Philosophers and Their Therapies for Desire.*

6. Cicero, *Academic Skepticism* 1.7.29. In *Physics* 2.5–6 Aristotle analyses "chance" as part of a nexus of causality.

7. *Soliloquia* (1.1.1) recounts Augustine's efforts to determine whether and in what sense the *divus animus* is divine ("this is precisely what I was struggling mightily

phy teaches . . . that whatever is perceived by mortal eyes, whatever any [bodily] sense touches, ought to be held in low regard and should in no way be cherished. And she promises to show clearly the most true and most hidden God . . ." (1.1.3). Philosophy allows us to penetrate the fog of everyday temptations—the likes of money, power, fame, and physical pleasure.[8] We focus on these fleeting parts of reality and forget the whole that gives them meaning. We forget our *telos*; we forget to pursue God (1.1.2). In short, we are sinful.[9] We must accept the aid philosophy offers in our journey home to our own good, and to God. Exhorted by these remarks, Romanianus, and we with him, are prepared to engage the Academic skeptics.

Licentius Versus Trygetius

The dialogue begins with Augustine's opening salvo: "Do you have any doubt that we ought to know the truth?" and "What if we could be happy without comprehending truth?" (1.2.5). Respectively, Licentius and Trygetius answer that we can be happy without having the truth if we seek it and that we have to know it to be happy. After Alypius recuses himself from the discussion and on the grounds that he will soon have to go into town on business appoints himself judge, Trygetius asks Augustine to define happiness. Augustine offers a definition of happiness that allows a disagreement between two students to grow into a philosophical disputation: "Who would doubt that the best of man is nothing else than that ruling part of the soul which it is fitting that the other parts that are in man should obey? . . . this part can be called mind or reason." Augustine is appealing to the notion of the sage, a central character in ancient philosophy, the man who on account of his virtue and wisdom is happy.[10] Happiness and wisdom are identical: If a man is happy, he is wise; if he is wise, he is happy. Augustine now slyly announces that *he* has been appointed judge; it is not clear *when* this happened, but he may be exaggerating Trygetius's request for a definition. Most likely he appoints himself judge in order to ensure a fruitful discussion.[11]

to know," *Sol.* 1.1.1). For now, we need only note that "a divine mind" need not mean anything more than that the mind of man either contemplates or resembles in some way the divine.

8. "People generally . . . suffer from the distemper that afflicts Boethius . . . . Like Boethius' eyes, theirs are clouded by the mist of mortal things." Silk, 26.

9. Harrison takes this passage as evidence of Augustine's early commitment to the doctrine of original sin; *Rethinking*, 185, 193.

10. Hadot, *What Is Ancient Philosophy?*, 220–31. Licentius and Trygetius are familiar with the sage from Cicero's *Hortensius*.

11. A suspicion reinforced by 2.7.17: "this disputation of ours has been undertaken for the sake of exercising you and challenging you to fine tune your mind."

The groundwork for a disputation thus laid, Licentius and Trygetius argue for their positions. Each begins by identifying wisdom with happiness. Trygetius's argument comes first: The happy man is wise; the wise man is perfect; but a man who is seeking is *not* perfect; so the wise man is not seeking wisdom. Licentius argues thus: The wise man is happy; the wise man is seeking wisdom; so the man who seeks wisdom is happy (1.3.7). His operative premise is the claim that the wise person merely seeks the truth, on behalf of which he appeals to Cicero, whom Trygetius admits is wise. Representing Academic philosophy, Cicero had claimed that wisdom is out of our reach and that, in Licentius's words, "nothing remains for the wise man except a most diligent search for the truth." Cicero had claimed that happiness without the satisfaction of attaining wisdom is possible and that a continual search for wisdom is the best life for humans. Licentius has just read Cicero's *Hortensius*, and like Augustine before him been set afire for philosophy. But his knowledge of Cicero is abbreviated and, as we shall see, somewhat confused.[12] Augustine would like to see Licentius reach the happy land of Christianity without the skeptical detour that he had traveled.[13]

Before Augustine can show Licentius that we can hope to achieve wisdom, and so free him from his skeptical chains for its pursuit, he will have to push the lads through all the rigors of a philosophical discourse. Disputation is needed to arrive at the truth and to train us in living by it. A lesson in the very wisdom they are seeking almost immediately presents itself. Under the force of Licentius's argument, Trygetius asks if he can take back a point he had granted too hastily (1.3.8). Augustine agrees, noting that "Those who are driven to debate not by a passion for finding the truth but by a puerile showing off of talent do not usually grant this." He requests that this be a rule for his students' disputation, "since you still need to be nourished and educated." He does not want agonistics to get in the way of philosophy, so he trains his pupils to prefer truth to personal victory, gently encouraging them to respond to the promise of wisdom rather than the siren-song of personal acclaim. This rule is given for the reordering of their desires.[14]

12. Dennis (11–12) says that Licentius represents Academic skepticism and Trygetius Stoic dogmatism. Although Trygetius does not say as much about his view as Licentius, this is possible; as a reply to Cicero's *Academic Skepticism*, it would be natural for Augustine to have a character supporting the Stoic position. See "The Cassiciacum Dialogues and Augustine's Ascent," 62. Licentius here, interestingly, is juxtaposed with *himself* in *De Ordine*, where he represents a dogmatism with quasi-Stoic undertones.

13. O'Donnell compares Licentius to Augustine after reading Cicero and says that Augustine wants him to reach Christianity by a more direct route. See O'Donnell, *Confessions Vol.* 3, 87.

14. The notion that happiness involves the best part of the soul governing the other parts recalls Plato's *Republic*. This incident suggests Augustine making an effort

The rule being secured, Trygetius retracts his concession that Cicero was a wise man. Licentius demonstrates his agonistic inclination and the need for the rule by rebuking Trygetius for the disrespect paid to Cicero. When Trygetius admits that Cicero may have been wise yet mistaken on this matter, Licentius blusters, "Proceed! For what do I have to lose against someone who declares himself an adversary of Cicero?" The irony is vivid; Licentius, who praises the love of truth over argumentative victory, hits his opponent with stinging rhetoric; all the while his own argument rests on an appeal to authority. Trygetius points this out with a thinly veiled insult—"I have cast off that yoke of authority"—before pressing on with his original argument, challenging Licentius to show "in what manner a man can be both perfect and still seek the truth" (1.3.9).

The challenge forces Licentius to elucidate his position. His clarification fails to refute the intuitive claim that unsatisfied desire is incompatible with happiness, but succeeds in elaborating on skepticism. There are two kinds of wisdom, divine and human. To know the truth, Licentius says, is the province of God; to seek it is the end of man, the sort of wisdom proper to him. It is, in fact, the very life according to reason that constitutes happiness. We could formalize Licentius's argument thus: The man who lives according to reason is happy; the man who seeks truth but never finds it is living according to reason; so the man who seeks the truth but never finds it is happy. The first premise was promulgated by Augustine and has Trygetius's support. The second premise is the Academic definition of the human end: "For in such a way [by seeking and not finding the truth] he is doing all that he was born to do" (1.3.9). This definition of the human good must be disproven if Licentius's argument is to be defeated.

Licentius has represented the Academics' theory of human nature fairly well. Academic philosophy is a moral outlook, not merely a set of epistemological doctrines.[15] The Academic Skeptic believes that the proper good of man consists in seeking the truth in a certain manner, namely that of one who accepts his ignorance. John Heil says, "The skeptic sees his detachment, his emphasis on the tranquility of soul, not as a turning away from the world or an abdication of human responsibility, but *as the acceptance of one's*

to keep the honor-loving part of Licentius's soul in submission to the wisdom-loving part. Given the Ciceronian background to Cassiciacum and Cicero's knowledge of and interest in the *Republic*, we can conclude the similarity is no accident. The possibility of a direct connection between Augustine's thought and the *Republic* does not concern us here. Foley, "Other Happy Life," 172–77.

15. That is, Academic Skepticism aims to achieve *eudaimonia* or *beata vita*, a happy life. Later Skepticism, exemplified by Sextus Empiricus, resembles Academic Skepticism in this regard. See Hallie, "Classical Scepticism."

proper place in nature, an immersion in the proper concerns of man."[16] As Licentius says, in seeking the truth and not finding it a man "is doing what he was born to do." Of course, one may well ask whether the Academic can consistently make this claim about human nature when he does not know any metaphysics. Licentius will face this challenge another day.[17] Now he faces a renewed challenge from Trygetius: If anyone is in error, he is neither living according to reason nor happy; "everyone who always seeks but does not find is in error"; therefore, whoever seeks but does not find is not happy (1.3.10). Having the truth we seek is necessary for happiness, not having it sufficient for unhappiness. Licentius admits that error is incompatible with happiness, but finds no answer to the claim that not having the truth is error.

Augustine steps in and recommends they each define "error." Licentius thinks it is easier to name things that count as error than to say for sure what does not. But Trygetius leaps forward with a definition clearly crafted to support his view: "To be in error is always to be seeking, never to be finding." Licentius asks for a postponement. Augustine thinks this appropriate, and the conversation ceases until the next day.

The second day's conversation is brief, beginning just before sunset; Licentius begins by defining error as "approval of the false instead of the true" (1.4.11). The definition originates in Cicero's *Academic Skepticism*,[18] and it guarantees the success of Licentius's argument that the wise man is the man who seeks the truth but never finds it, for such a one is never in error. Licentius praises their conversation of the day before as a prime example of the happy quest for undiscovered truth: "we lived with a great tranquility of mind, making the soul free from every bodily blemish and far, far removed from the fires of carnal lust, devoting ourselves to reason . . . ." He then attacks Trygetius's definition of error for not including some kinds of error (such as when someone who is *not* seeking is mistaken about something), but also for including things that are not error. He conjures up a metaphor to make his point: A traveler on the way to Alexandria who has not arrived yet but is seeking his destination is not in error; neither is the seeker of wisdom.

Trygetius in reply defines wisdom as "the right way of life" (1.5.13), a definition soon refined as "the right way that leads to the truth" (1.5.14). This only plays into his opponent's hands, for it ensures that "not only the discovery of the truth but the very quest for it will by itself make him happy."

16. Heil, "Augustine's Attack," 106; italics added.

17. See 2.7.16.

18. Cicero, *Academic Skepticism* 2.20.66.

Now Trygetius asks Augustine for help in defining wisdom, but Augustine calls a halt and puts off this important topic for another day.

On the third day Augustine gives a Ciceronian definition of wisdom familiar to the lads: "the knowledge of human and divine things" (1.5.16).[19] He expects this will stump Licentius for a while, since it means that a wise man *knows* things about God and man—just what Licentius had denied. Licentius surprises Augustine when he immediately challenges the definition as too broad (1.6.17).[20] For, he says, it suggests that Albicerius, a soothsayer, is wise, for he knew things about human matters, seemingly due to his knowledge of divine matters. Since it would be unseemly to call someone so "utterly scandalous" wise, something is wrong with the definition.

Trygetius[21] heroically defends (chapters 19–22) the definition of wisdom from this objection. Here are five highlights from his extended defense. First, Albicerius's knowledge is unreliable (1.7.19). Second, the human matters acquaintance with which constitutes wisdom are not the petty things Albicerius "knew" (such as the location of stolen money). Wisdom is knowledge of what is most truly human, namely virtue, and since virtue is the most stable thing known to man, knowledge of it is the most reliable form of knowledge (1.7.20). Third, Albicerius lacks the highest form of knowledge—knowledge of oneself. Trygetius appeals to the advice of Flaccianus—whom Licentius had cited as witness to Albicerius's knowledge—that self-knowledge ought to be gained through a study of the liberal arts rather than through divination. Fifth, divination is no special feat even when it produces accurate information, for this is likely the work of demons rather than the diviner's wisdom (1.7.20).

Trygetius's speech is redolent of Augustine's life lessons and insights from his favorite books. That demons cannot provide true knowledge, and their counsel through divination is of no account, is an insight from Athanasius's *Life of Antony* (204.31).[22] That divination's correct results are undermined by its incorrect results is the advice a wise doctor gives Augustine

19. *Discussions at Tusculum* 4.26.57; *On Duties* 2.2.5.

20. It is ironic that Licentius rejects Cicero's definition, since he had defended his own understanding of wisdom by appeal to the authority of Cicero.

21. The textual evidence leaves some ambiguity as to whether this speech belongs to Trygetius or Augustine. On this see the textual notes in King's translation, in *Against the Academics and The Teacher*, 172.

22. Augustine had encountered the story of Antony before his conversion—*Conf.* 8.6. John O'Meara thinks that the hearing of *Life of Antony* is among the *libri quidam pleni* of *c. Acad.* 2.5. See "Plotinus and Augustine." Identifying demons as the source of such "knowledge" is also part of Octavius's refutation of Roman superstition in Minucius Felix's *Octavius*, chapters 26–27.

in *Confessions* 4.3 and is also in Cicero.[23] Finally, that virtue is what is most proper to man and is stable in the face of life's storms is a Ciceronian theme well known to the characters at Cassiciacum—not to mention a clear echo from the letter to Romanianus.[24]

Trygetius follows on his oration by claiming that Licentius's wise man has less wisdom than Albicerius, who at least knew a few things (1.8.22). But Licentius is not so easily undone. The wise man, he says, seeks an altogether higher kind of knowledge than anything within Albicerius's reach, the seeking of which is better than the finding of lesser knowledge (1.8.23). When Trygetius makes one last effort to include knowledge in the definition of wisdom, Licentius extends the definition to encompass the quest for such knowledge, saying that knowledge belongs only to God, the quest for wisdom to men—a return to his conception of the proper good of man (1.3.9). Trygetius's last remark for the day returns to the intuition that an unsatisfied desire for wisdom cannot be happiness: "I wonder how you can claim that your wise man is spending his efforts in vain," that is: how a happy person can be seeking a destination he can never reach. Licentius responds:

> How is it in vain when he is hunting down such a great treasure? For he is wise by virtue of the fact that he is seeking and he is happy by virtue of the fact that he is wise. . . . he has unwrapped his mind, insofar as he can, from all the gift-wrap of the body and . . . does not permit himself to be torn apart by disordered desires but, always tranquil, he is forever straining towards himself and God, the result being that here he thoroughly enjoys reason (which we agreed earlier was to be happy), and on the last day of his life he may be found ready to obtain what he has been desiring, and he who had thoroughly enjoyed human happiness before may [now] deservedly enjoy divine (1.8.23).

The Academic quest for wisdom reaches fulfillment after death. It is embodiment that makes wisdom so hard to find; success is possible—postmortem. In the meantime, the Academic sage seeks knowledge but does not have it, tranquil and free of "disordered desires." Trygetius might have pressed his point by asking whether tranquility is interrupted by the unsatisfied desire for knowledge, but is stunned into silence by Licentius's eloquence, and it falls upon Augustine to respond.

23. Cicero, *The Nature of the Gods*, 3.14–15 (113).

24. On Augustine's preference for the liberal over the divinatory arts, see Klingshirn, "Divination."

Two Visions of the Happy Life

Book I leaves us with two very different arguments about the nature of desire and its relation to happiness. Trygetius has argued that the happy man is wise, the wise man is perfect, and the person seeking wisdom is not perfect; so the happy man is not seeking wisdom. Licentius has argued that the happy man is wise, and the wise man seeks and desires wisdom; so the happy man seeks and desires wisdom. If Trygetius is right, the satisfaction of desire is vital for happiness. The right therapy for disordered desires will be whatever treatment of desire is conducive to attaining wisdom.

But, if Licentius is right, attaining what we desire is not possible; nor is it necessary for happiness. A happy life consists in a vigorous quest for a coveted yet unattainable truth. There may be a postmortem happiness, but we hear little of its nature from Licentius. We *do* know about the kind of life this view requires and the therapy of desire associated with it. It demands a life characterized by the features Licentius has already suggested (1.4.11): a life of philosophical pursuit, devoted to reason, markedly tranquil. Although he is not explicit, we can surmise that the body's threats to wisdom consist of the dual impediments of finitude and unruly desire: the former because embodied life is finite; the latter because embodied creatures easily desire carnal things over wisdom.[25] Licentius's orations in praise of Academic wisdom reveal an incipient philosophy of desire with two features. First, we must severely cut back sensual desire, perhaps to the point of annihilation, since it is the trappings of *the body* that prevent us from getting to wisdom. Second, the desire *for wisdom* would have to be quickened. This will achieve the tranquility of the ideal Academic life, free the mind for reason's work, and prepare the soul to know the truth after life has ended. Licentius's therapy for desire has a good pedigree: It resembles advice given in Plato's *Phaedo* and is a rudimentary understanding of the neo-Platonic therapy for desire. The connection is indirect but not at all accidental. Licentius has picked up some of Plato's ideas and language via Cicero, although his understanding of them does not penetrate their face value. He sees the negative, the ascetic fleeing from bodily influence; but he does not see the positive, the ascent towards knowledge of immaterial reality.

Augustine concludes Book I (1.9.24) with a summary, reminding Licentius what he has—and has *not*—accomplished. Congratulating Licentius on his cleverness, he reminds him that Trygetius has always given an answer, and predicts that he would do so again if allowed sufficient time (as Licentius was allowed before). He makes it plain that Licentius's argument

25. Augustine responds to these disadvantages of embodiment in *b. Vita*. See below, Chapter 3.

rests on his Ciceronian definitions of error and wisdom. In this way he gently chides Licentius, warning him to avoid overconfidence while he is ahead, to cultivate humility, and above all to seek truth above victory (as 1.3.8).

In short, for the present the two arguments are equally matched. Harding's claim[26] that Book I goes to Licentius is overstated. Licentius has used superior rhetoric, and has the upper hand for the moment. But from a logical perspective the arguments have been equally defended. At any rate, what is more important is not who triumphs in the dispute, but whether their arguments lead to truth. Trygetius's argument rests on the premise that whoever is still seeking something is not perfect. In other words, if I desire something and do not have it I am incomplete[27] and cannot be considered happy. The premise is more intuitive; for who would deny that wanting something and not having it is a state incompatible with happiness? (Indeed, the conclusion of Trygetius's argument is endorsed by all parties before the question of the Academics is taken up again [*De beata vita* 2.10, 2.14].) Yet Cicero and the Academics do not accept this premise. The operative premises in Licentius's arguments are his definitions of error (as approval of falsehood) and wisdom (as the quest for truth). While they lead to the denial of Trygetius's premise, they do not themselves immediately appear problematic, and they have the endorsement of Cicero, whose status as the founder of Roman philosophy demands that they receive a careful and considered response. Since Licentius's argument depends on key Academic doctrines, the thrust of his argument falls into their care. After praising Licentius and Trygetius for their dedication to and zeal for the truth, Augustine declares this phase of the conversation over and says he will now enter the fray and himself put the Academics to the test (1.9.25).

His goals in putting the Academics on trial are pedagogical.[28] As Dennis says, Augustine is acting as a friend and Christian to Licentius and his father Romanianus.[29] As Cary says, Augustine wants to guide Licentius toward the happy life, to encourage him to be a philosopher and to find

26. Harding, "Epistemology and Eudaimonism," 260. Foley is nearer the mark, saying Book I's debate is "inconclusive." See Foley, "Cicero, Augustine," 64. See also Curley, *Augustine's Critique of Skepticism*, 65–67, and the description of Book I as "going around in circles" on 123.

27. The Latin *perfectus* connotes a completed man, a quality linguistically and philosophically inconsistent with seeking. Curley connects the notion of perfection to Aristotle's description of the perfect man as lacking nothing. See Curley, *Augustine's Critique of Skepticism*, 50–51, 47.

28. On the theme of Christian pedagogy at Cassiciacum, see Kevane, *Augustine the Educator*, 59–71.

29. Dennis, "The Three Augustines," 10–17.

wisdom, which is Christ.[30] Licentius is "a mirror held up by the author, in which a reader is invited to see himself."[31] Licentius, Trygetius, and Romanianus are *all* mirrors in which we may see ourselves. We are invited to participate in the dialogue and to learn alongside its characters. Cary adds[32] that Augustine's path to philosophy and Christ is also on display. Just as it is hoped that Romanianus will pass by some of the detours that delayed Augustine in his journey, it is hoped that Licentius will do the same. Being young and having just read Cicero, Licentius is like Augustine at Carthage in *Confessions* 3.4, and through their work at Cassiciacum Augustine hopes to set him on a direct course to orthodox Christianity, without the wanderings of *Confessions* 3–7.

We are left, then, with two arguments. One rests on the claim that unsatisfied desire for wisdom is incompatible with happiness; the other denies this. In order to determine whether happiness depends on the satisfaction of desire, Academic philosophy must be tested. The relationship of desire and happiness depends on how Academic philosophy fares under critical examination. The appeal to the Academic view leaves Augustine with a pedagogical challenge. Licentius must believe that happiness is possible so that he can go searching for it. In what follows we will see the gradual unraveling of Skeptical philosophy and the rudiments of a better philosophy of desire laid down in its place. Problems in skepticism will be exposed; Cicero's claim that happiness can be attained without the satisfaction of achieving wisdom will be exposed as insincere; Christ's role in bringing wisdom to men will be announced; and the desire for wisdom will be given new, distinctively Christian characteristics. The reader of the dialogue—whether Manichean, Stoic, Skeptic, neo-Platonist, or Christian—is encouraged to take up the road through philosophy to wisdom alongside the little community at Cassiciacum.

THE PRACTICAL CONSEQUENCES OF BELIEF

In Book II Augustine continues to talk with Licentius, while Trygetius's role is reduced; eventually Licentius drops out of the conversation and Alypius takes his place. Book II draws out the psychological consequences of the Academic view and foreshadows their undoing in Book III. Among the consequences of Academic thought is despair of reaching the truth. Despair is a sickness which infects the soul and impedes its pursuit of truth,

30. Cary, "What Licentius Learned."

31. Ibid., 143.

32. Ibid.

preventing our desire for wisdom from having its proper effect. Book II offers philosophical pedagogy as a treatment for desire; the committed pursuit of wisdom through philosophical discourse will help us resist despair, although ultimately stronger remedies are needed to heal the soul infected with despair.

Impediments to Reordered Desire

The cover letter to Books II–III discusses four impediments to the discovery of wisdom.[33] One is "the many different disturbances of this life" (2.1.1) including the stress of financial affairs such as the lawsuit Romanianus is currently enduring. These disturbances are not in themselves threats to finding wisdom; the threat is our willingness to become distracted by them.[34] Philosophy promises to provide stability in the face of such disturbances, as Romanianus has been reminded in 1.1.1. Yet this first impediment is the one that most threatens him, and Augustine prays continually (2.1.1, 2.3.8) that circumstances will turn him towards philosophy and God rather than continue to distract him. Here again is the familiar theme of reordering our desires so as to love wisdom above all.

The second impediment is a lack of intelligence (2.1.1), no serious threat to Romanianus. Augustine praises his natural abilities and says he is not concerned about this (2.1.2–3, 2.3.8).

The last two impediments are a "despair of discovery" of the truth and the delusion of having already discovered it. Each is potentially a problem for Romanianus (2.3.8). Natural abilities notwithstanding, his formal education is minimal, and he may *think* himself a victim of the second impediment. Augustine fears a little "that you think little of yourself and that you despair of your finding the truth, or that at any rate you may believe that you have found it." The main target of *Contra Academicos* is the Academics, at whom Romanianus has been angry and from whose influence he needs to be freed. *Contra Academicos* is written that he need not despair of finding the truth. Augustine worries that Romanianus may still be suffering from the fourth impediment as a result of a lingering commitment to Manicheanism, and he hints at a work (*Of True Religion*) to be composed later to

33. Burt comments on several of these impediments in *"Let Me Know You,"* 92–95.

34. On the importance of one's attitude to wealth, see Trout, "Augustine at Cassiciacum," especially 139–40. As Augustine later remarks in Sermon 167, it is often better to yield to a lawsuit, thus losing some material possession but preserving something more valuable: *time*; see Burt's remarks in *"Let Me Know Myself,"* 48–49.

help Romanianus in this regard. In the meantime, Manicheanism will only subtly and secondarily be targeted in *Contra Academicos*.[35]

In hopes of persuading Romanianus to pursue wisdom, Augustine gives an account of his own pursuit (2.2.3–2.2.6). He reminds Romanianus of his role in Augustine's journey, his moral and sometimes financial support. Augustine praises Romanianus for his virtue, thanks him, and encourages him to commit to the chase. The chase involves a *re*ordering of desire, a restoration of desire to its natural good:

> For what is philosophy? The love of wisdom. What is philocaly? The love of beauty (Ask the Greeks.) What, then, is wisdom? Is it not true beauty itself? Therefore, these two are full sisters, born from the same parent; but the former was pulled down from her place in heaven by the birdlime of lust and was penned in a popular cage. Nevertheless, she held onto the likeness of the name in order to impress upon the bird-catcher that he should not look down upon her. . . . but . . . only philosophy knows from where this philocaly of ours may deduce her ancestry (2.3.7).

This myth[36] illustrates neo-Platonic principles: that desires are too often directed towards earthly appearances of beauty; that only wisdom is truly beautiful; and that our desires ought to be directed thence.[37] Love of beauty is a confused love of wisdom, but it takes philosophy to extricate it from its ensnarement in the appearances of beauty.

The Claims of the Skeptics

Seven days pass before the conversation resumes. Licentius has taken a keen interest in Virgil, which worries Augustine; yet he comes willingly when Augustine summons him to return to the dialogue on the Academics (2.4.10). Alypius has returned and hears a recap of what has already been discussed. Now Augustine states the beliefs of the Academics:

> Now, the Academics were of the opinion that man cannot attain knowledge of precisely those things that pertain to philosophy; and yet that man can be wise and that the whole office of the wise man is on display in the diligent search for the truth, as you

35. See below, under the subheadings *The moral detriment of non-assent* and *Christ: Towards a Christian Theology of Desire*. Neiman is helpful in showing the connection between an attack on Manicheanism and Academicism, for each resists authority. See "The Arguments."

36. Tongue in cheek, Augustine refers to himself as Aesop.

37. On the identification of wisdom with beauty, see Plato's *Symposium*, 204b.

> discussed in your discourse, Licentius. Hence it follows that the wise man should not assent to anything . . . (2.5.11).

The Academics held to four principles: (1) Man cannot attain a knowledge of the things philosophy is interested in; (2) man can nonetheless be wise; (3) wisdom consists in a diligent search for the truth; and (4) the wise man does not assent to anything. But they also accept another principle, derived from the Stoics and their founder Zeno: (5) When a human being knows a truth, he knows it with complete confidence (he knows that he knows it, we might say).

An objection arose against the early Academic Skeptics, that 4 prevents one from living his life. The objection is both practical and moral, portraying the Academic sage as "someone who was always asleep, a deserter of every duty" (2.5.12). In response the Academics proffered the notion that one can live on the probable, alternately called *probabile* and *verisimile*. The beliefs on which one needs to act in life bear some similarity to the truth (they are *verisimile*), and by seeing this the wise man is able both to live and to live well despite withholding assent.

After Monica summons the group to lunch (2.5.13), Alypius casts some light on the Academic position. The New, skeptical Academy was a reaction not against Plato's Old Academy but against the Stoic incursion into the Old Academy (2.6.14). Zeno introduced 5 as a new criterion of perception, which Alypius calls a "coarse novelty": Whatever is genuinely perceived is both true and accompanied by characteristics able to distinguish it from the false. The Academics adopted this as a premise, adding a new premise to make their argument: None of our perceptions have these distinguishing characteristics; *nothing* meets this criterion for knowledge.

Academic Ironies, Lessons in Undoing Skepticism, and a Vigorous Pedagogy

When Augustine asks Licentius what he thinks of the Academics, he nearly falls into a trap of his own making (2.7.16). Asked whether "it seems to you that they speak the truth," he nearly answers affirmatively, but "a smile from Alypius" reminds him to be on his guard, and instead he says that he does not know whether they speak the truth; yet it seems *probable* to him that they do. The incident does not disprove Academicism, but it shows the need to be careful—not to promote Skepticism carelessly or without subtlety (as Licentius had in Book I). In order to avoid a contradictory dogmatic denial of all dogmas, skepticism needs to rest on probability and restrict itself to probabilistic claims.

The incident leads to a valuable exercise in critiquing skepticism, one undertaken to train Licentius and Trygetius in the rigors of a life spent in pursuit of the truth. There is an irony in the Academics' use of *verisimile.* They claim to believe what seems like the truth while not knowing the truth. They are likening the truth-like to that the likeness of which they know not. Augustine asks him: "If someone declared that your brother was similar to your father and he did not actually know your father, wouldn't he seem to you to be either crazy or idiotic?" When Augustine presses him (2.7.17), Licentius begs to be told whether his position is going to fail. Augustine advises him not to give up for fear of failure, for they entered into a disputation for the sake of intellectual training, not for the sake of winning. But Licentius, pleading his lack of formal education and doubting his qualifications, begs to be allowed to give up the struggle.[38]

Here follows a remarkable scene. To encourage Licentius to keep up the fight, Augustine appeals to his wish to see his father seeking the truth: "What if you could see your father (surely no one would guzzle down philosophy more passionately after so long a thirst than he) inquiring into and discussing these things with us?" (2.7.18). His longing to see his father pursue wisdom brings Licentius to tears. He prays: "And when, O God, shall I see this? But I should not despair over receiving anything from you."

The irony is striking. Licentius refuses to despair on his father's behalf and prays for him. His outcry is just short of oracular; when God is in the picture, there is no need to despair of anyone's seeking the truth. Licentius sounds like Augustine in his letter saying that people are not to be despaired of (2.3.8). But for all this, Licentius despairs for himself for the same reason (concern over his lack of education) that Augustine worries will hold back Romanianus (2.4.8). The irony is doubled by the fact that he who has advocated a ceaseless quest for the truth now gives up the chase at the first real difficulty. Licentius in his despair is an image of the danger looming before all Skeptics: that a despair of reaching the truth will keep them from even seeking it. The recent use of Romanianus and of Licentius's brother in an analogy suggests that Augustine has recorded this scene in order to draw out the similarities between father and son; each is beset by despair and in need of divine assistance. Augustine holds up father and son to each other as mirrors (1.1.4), encouraging the father to imitate the son in resisting despair and the son to take hold of that which he prays his father will take up: the tireless quest for truth.

38. Silk's remarks on Licentius's love of poetry in *Ord.* are appropriate here. Once many people realize "that Philosophy would be their physician, their eagerness wanes. They prefer their malady to her regimen." See Silk, 26.

Moreover, that he flags in the quest tells us something about his desire for wisdom. Something has gone wrong with his love of the truth. His desire for wisdom is impotent in the presence of despair and does not keep him on the pursuit. Augustine calls on every resource at his disposal to fan the flames of this desire and to hold him to the rigors of philosophical discourse. Keeping him focused on the truth will help him love it strongly enough that his inhibitions will not deter him. A rigorous pedagogy is a therapy with which Augustine treats Licentius's desire.

The treatment is temporarily effective. With help from those around him (including Trygetius), Licentius holds off his despair and rallies for another effort. He suggests that the person who says that his brother looks like his father "has discovered through a rumor that he is similar to my father" (2.7.19). He is trying to smuggle into the analogy information about the unknown object (Licentius's father and his analogue wisdom) so as to justify the comparison to the known object (Licentius's brother or his analogue the *verisimile*). Augustine will have none of it, reemphasizing that positing similarity between two objects while not knowing what one of them looks like is simply laughable.

Trygetius leaps (2.8.20) to his friend's aid with a strategy for positing a connection between the truth and what the Academics identify as like the truth: the *probabile*. The Academics claimed that they had *reasons* for thinking the probable to be like the truth. Augustine's riposte is the reminder that the Academics also used the word *verisimile*. At this, Licentius finally gives up. The defense of the Academics shifts to Alypius (2.8.21), who hints that he is not finished with this distinction.

Life, Morals, Soul

Alypius, suspecting that Augustine, like the Academics he opposes, is merely arguing *against* a position, asks if he is also *supporting* one. Augustine's response is strikingly clear on the significance of their dialogue on the Academics:

> . . . I do not want this disputation undertaken for the sake of disputing. Let it be enough that we playfully sparred with these youths of ours, when philosophy, as it were, was gladly joking along with us. Therefore, let the childish fables be taken out of our hands. The matter being treated is about our life, about our mores,[39] and about our soul . . . (2.9.22).

39. Latin *mos/moris*, translated by King and O'Meara as "morality."

Moments later he reveals the reasons for his interest in the topic and hints at his own position: "Do you therefore not know that I still have nothing which I perceive as certain but that I am prevented from seeking it by the arguments and disputations of the Academics? For somehow they induced in my mind a certain probability that man cannot discover truth" (2.9.23). Now he states his contention: He believes that it *is* probable that we can discover the truth.

The reference to Academicism's continuing influence on Augustine begs for interpretation. Some, including Etienne Gilson and Régis Jolivet, assume that Augustine writes the *Contra Academicos* to overcome his own commitment to Academic Skepticism.[40] This interpretation is highly suspect; not only has Augustine already committed himself to Christianity (and thereby rejected skeptical non-assent), but it is disputed whether he was ever a Skeptic in the first place. Mourant and Mosher, for example, believe that he was impeded in his journey to Christianity by the Academics without ever committing to them.[41]

Whether or not Augustine was ever a full-fledged Skeptic, he was deeply aware from personal experience of the practical consequences of skeptical belief. Despairing of ever reaching the truth cripples one's efforts to arrive there. Examples of these effects are vivid in *Contra Academicos*. The effects of Academic-induced despair linger in Augustine's heart. Romanianus, likewise, is impeded in the search for truth by his despair, and so Augustine does his best in the cover letters to help him escape its deleterious effects. Licentius is also reluctant to pursue the truth because he is convinced that he himself is unable to reach it. In their own ways all three illustrate the fatal consequences of Academic philosophy: Despair of arrival at one's destination (wisdom) prevents one from actively taking up the journey thereto (philosophy).

In addition, the status of Academic skepticism affects "our life, our mores . . . our soul." Book I lays out the question at hand in broad terms: Can we be happy without attaining the wisdom we desire? Now clarified, the question is: Given that we pursue and desire wisdom, ought we to believe that we will probably never attain it—thus casting our lot in with the Academics—or ought we to believe that we will attain it—and choose another course of life? Not only our motivation to seek wisdom, but also the mode in which we seek it, is at stake. Believing that the truth cannot be found, we will with the Academics become mired in hopeless dispute; but believing

40. For a fuller list, see Mosher, "The Arguments of St. Augustine's Contra Academicos," 51.

41. Mosher, ibid., and Mourant, "Augustine and the Academics."

that the truth can be found, we will be encouraged in the journey towards it. For Romanianus, Licentius, and Augustine himself to be freed for the pursuit after wisdom, they will have to have their chains of despair removed.

Recall also that the therapy for desire implied by Licentius would have two components: a reduction in love for the physical world and an increase in love for wisdom. Insofar as it allows despair to threaten our desire for wisdom, skepticism fails at the second component of its own therapy. Insofar as these two goals are bound together, the failure to accomplish one will no doubt detract from the other, and so it is possible that skepticism even fails in taming carnal lusts.

Foreshadowing the Mystery of the Skeptics

Augustine and Alypius proceed to uncover the curious argument which preceded: In order to know that something resembles the truth, one must know what the truth looks like; since they claim not to know the truth, the Academics contradict themselves. This argument is not above reproach. Kirwan and, following him, O'Daly have argued against this, as they call it, "argument from verisimilitude."[42] In order to know that X resembles Y, they say, I need not be acquainted with Y; I need only know a little about what it would look like should I encounter it.

Kirwan and O'Daly actually play into Augustine's hands. Augustine makes it perfectly clear that he does not intend the argument to undo Academicism. Twice Licentius attempts to refocus the argument from the problem of *verisimile* to the notion of *probabile*, and, although Augustine resists the shift in emphasis, he also urges Licentius to keep pushing for it (2.7.16–17, 2.8.20)! When Alypius assumes the defense of Academicism, he asks why Augustine is quibbling over words (2.10.24). Surely since the Academics used *verisimile* and *probabile* interchangeably it is acceptable to examine the latter, on which the Academics may fare better. Indeed, one might construe the Academic claim that X is probable as a claim that it resembles in some respect the Y that one does not know (say, in the respect of having evidence in its favor), and thus with Kirwan and O'Daly avoid the argument from verisimilitude.

Augustine responds to Alypius (and anticipates his critics) by saying that, as it seems to him, the Academics "chose these terms both in order to hide their opinion from the more sluggish and to reveal it to the more alert" (2.10.24). The Academics understood the difference between the qualities

42. Kirwan, "Augustine Against the Skeptics," 211; O'Daly, "Did St. Augustine Ever?," 161.

of *verisimile* and *probabile*. The argument from verisimilitude is a wedge to drive them apart. Through the gap between *verisimile* and *probabile* we can descry a hint of the Academics' hidden agenda. In short, the argument from verisimilitude is used pedagogically. The argument has some strength against the Academics' public claims, but its main use is to train Licentius and Trygetius to think critically about skepticism and prepare them for the revelation of what the Academics are up to.

The tactic has mixed results. We have already seen Licentius fail to keep up his efforts. At 2.12.27 he adopts the argument himself and is censured by Alypius (2.12.28) for deserting his cause. The exercise has succeeded in getting him to think critically about skepticism, but he continues to flag in his commitment to the disputation.

TRANSCENDING THE SKEPTICS

Book III will finally lay Academicism to rest. Here I shall first discuss a number of arguments Augustine gives against their position. Next, I shall discuss how Augustine unmasks the Academics and reveals their true character as closet neo-Platonists, and I shall look at the implications for a neo-Platonic philosophy of desire. Finally, I shall discuss the appeal to Jesus Christ in the dialogue's climax and three implications for a Christian *theology* of desire: the resounding affirmation of the possibility of happiness, the requirement that desire submit to Christian authority, and the importance of uniting desire to the theological virtues of faith, hope, and love.

Does a Wise Man Exist?

At the close of Book II Alypius confesses that he too is under the influence of Academicism. In part he has, like Licentius, been influenced by the authority of "great and outstanding philosophers" (2.12.30) who held that knowledge is improbable. Inducing hope of reaching the wisdom we desire is as much a goal for Alypius as it is for Romanianus, Licentius, and Augustine.

Book III begins with a protracted discussion the climax of which is an agreement between Alypius and Augustine that the wise man, if one can be found, knows wisdom (3.4.9). Augustine remarks that the issue is now "whether the wise man can be found" (2.4.10). More precisely, since it is the *probability* of Academicism that is at stake (2.9.23) the issue is whether it is probable that such a wise man exists. Alypius believes that no man can attain wisdom without divine help, and illustrates with the myth of Proteus, whom no one could capture "unless it was by a deity of some kind showing the way." I take this reference to a deity to refer to Christ. It may also refer to the church, as McWilliam thinks.[43] There is "nothing more true," says Augustine, than what Alypius has said, adding that agreement with his friend is an incalculable good, as Cicero had said in *Laelius* (3.6.13).

Three Arguments That the Wise Man Exists

Augustine moves on to establish the likelihood that a wise man exists, giving various arguments. I shall discuss three in this section and one in the next. Augustine presents the first argument as a constructive dilemma concerning Zeno's criterion. It is either true or false that knowledge requires perfect certainty; if it is true, then whoever knows it to be true knows at least one thing; but, if it is false, then the Academic project cannot even get off the ground. Either way, some knowledge is possible (3.9.18, 3.9.21).

The second argument consists of several instances of certainty. One is the law of the excluded middle. Zeno's criterion is either true or false (3.8.21), a point serving as an instance of certainty but also bolstering the constructive dilemma already given. Other cases of excluded middle counter skepticism through their content and their form; for example: "There is either one world or there is not, and if there is not, the number of worlds is either finite or infinite" (3.10.22). Another certainty is the fact of appearance; the world appears a certain way to me (3.11.24). Two other instances of certainty are the truths of mathematics: "it is necessarily true that three times three is nine and that it is the square of intelligible numbers" (3.11.25); and, mentioned briefly, the law of non-contradiction (3.13.29). Most of these truths are, in contemporary terms, analytic and *a priori*; more to the point, they have the Platonic ring of independence from the physical world. Yet, as immaterial principles do, they lend to the realms of physics and ethics a degree of stable knowledge, as these cases illustrate.[44]

To prepare us for the next argument Augustine reviews (3.7.16–3.8.17) the Ciceronian argument that the Academics are likely right because all parties award them second place, Epicureans saying they are better than Stoics and vice versa. But this fact has a different significance, for the Epicureans and Stoics would agree that the Academics, by not assenting, guaranteed they would never find the truth. Whereas the Epicureans and Stoics are "untaught" as to the nature of man's proper good, the Academics are worse, "unteachable" (3.8.17). The same charge against the Academics reappears

43. McWilliam, "The Cassiciacum Autobiography," 28.

44. Diggs, "St. Augustine Against the Academicians," 81.

in 3.15.34, where Augustine resuscitates and rethinks Licentius's analogy of the traveler. The Academics are like travelers without a map who, upon coming to a fork in the road, refuse to take either route out of fear of going the wrong way. Arriving at the wrong destination is an error, like assent to false propositions. (Stoic and Epicurean propositions are implied by the passage's proximity to 3.7–3.8; Manichean propositions are implied by Augustine's personal history and the cover letters to Romanianus.) But failing to arrive at one's destination is equally erroneous, and so is its analogue, refusing to give assent to any proposition.[45] In short, "not only does he who follows a false path err, but also he who does not follow the true one." Nonbelief is not the same kind of error as false belief, but it is just as dangerous.

The Moral Detriment of Non-Assent

Augustine offers a moral argument against skepticism (3.16.35–36), showing its detriment to morality. He chides Cicero, who was more concerned than anyone for "the morals and life of the young," for promoting a doctrine of non-assent that can have devastating results. Two interconnected reasons show that non-assent is detrimental to morality. First, in a laughable scene we imagine a young man guilty of adultery claiming that he did not *assent* to his deed, but merely claimed that it was *probable* that it was the right thing to do. Yet this is no excuse! Not only does withholding assent from crimes not excuse them, but giving assent to right action is necessary for political justice. A judge must respond to an act of adultery, murder, parricide, or the like by punishing it "as a crime that is very real" (3.16.35). Non-assent is insufficient for avoiding sin, assent necessary for doing good. By promoting non-assent, the Academics offer a tempting excuse for sin; by failing to promote assent, they fail to promote morality. For both reasons a life of non-assent is a social and political impossibility.[46]

This argument in itself requires only a modicum of assent. O'Daly claims that Augustine "argues unpersuasively that anything that falls short of ethical dogmatism undermines the basis of moral behavior," and is "worried by any attempt to question what he takes to be our certain knowledge of ethical principles."[47] Augustine may well be promoting dogmatic commitment to the evil of the crimes listed: adultery, murder, parricide, sacrilege, and

45. In the same spirit William James observes that shunning error and believing the truth are equally important goals: "The Will to Believe," 17–19.

46. Foley, "The Other Happy Life," 170–71; Curley, *Augustine's Critique*, 120–27; Topping, *Happiness and Wisdom*, 122–23.

47. O'Daly, "The Response to Skepticism," 164.

treason. If O'Daly means this, then he is wrong that Augustine's argument is unpersuasive, for any society needs some such beliefs to function.[48] But if O'Daly means a more extensive dogmatism, then he is reading into the passage. The argument succeeds in showing that assent is a requirement for morality; so we must believe that knowledge is possible; so it is likely that a wise man exists.

Summary: It Is Probable That He Exists

Different summaries of the arguments in *Contra Academicos* have been offered,[49] and there may never be a final word on the exact number and classification of the arguments. I have focused on these as Augustine's main objections to Academicism: the constructive dilemma involving Zeno's criterion, the various instances of certainty, the exposure of non-assent as error, and the argument that assent is a moral necessity. The so-called "argument from verisimilitude" and the incident of Alypius's smile (2.7.16) are arguments of a sort, but the latter fails to attack Academic teachings and the former fails to give Academicism a fair hearing. They are not used to undermine skepticism as much as to train us in undermining skepticism; they are not serious arguments, but pedagogical exercises.

As far as raw logic is concerned, what is at stake is probability, specifically the probability of the claim that there exists a wise man who knows something. Using instances of certainty Augustine shows that assent to some things is unavoidable for everyone; if we, who are unwise, know lesser truths, then it is likely that someone really wise knows the things that constitute wisdom.[50] The dilemma surrounding Zeno's criterion undermines Academic arguments, as do the expanded definition of error and the exposure of non-assent's detriment to morality; these latter two also call on us

48. O'Daly may be missing the point that we are dealing with "principally a moral rather than a logical inconsistency." Mosher, "Argument of Augustine's Contra Academicos," 100.

49. For example, in "St. Augustine Against the Academics" Diggs sees three sets of arguments: those showing that the Academics are inconsistent, those demonstrating necessary truths, and those showing that a wise man will assent to some things. Neiman also groups the arguments into three sets: those showing that the Academics are inconsistent, those showing that there are some things we must assent to with certainty, and those showing that assent to a worldview is a practical necessity; see Neiman, "The Arguments." O'Meara summarizes the dialogue in one argument: "The whole book centers around this acceptance of the incarnation: it is the argument of the book . . . One can assent to the truth, if it is found: But it is found in Christ; therefore one can assent to the truth." See *Studies in Augustine and Eriguena*, 128.

50. Mosher, "Argument of Augustine's Contra Academicos,"96–98.

to *act* as if the Academics are wrong by assenting to a great many things. Contrary to John O'Meara's claim that Augustine's text makes no serious contribution to epistemology,[51] *Contra Academicos* includes some serious rebuttals of skepticism. Alypius's smile shows the inherently contradictory nature of dogmatic skepticism, requiring that viable skepticism have a probabilistic flavor. And the cumulative effect of Augustine's arguments shatters the probabilistic claims of the Academics.[52]

However, the raw logic is not the main thrust of the text; nor is epistemology its ultimate concern: "The matter being treated is about our life, about our mores, and about our soul" (2.9.22). We are concerned with the life changes for which the undermining of skepticism calls. O'Daly,[53] Mosher, Heil,[54] Harding,[55] Dennis,[56] Neiman,[57] Curley,[58] and Topping[59] rightly read *Contra Academicos* as having an ethical and religious end. Generalizing a bit, there are two ways to go wrong in interpreting the arguments against skepticism. On one side, O'Meara treats *Contra Academicos* as "a personal work, written by Augustine to meet his own needs," and says that "it bears too deeply the traces of experience to be in any sense an objective discussion of epistemology."[60] On the opposite side, many have treated the arguments as having a narrow epistemological goal;[61] some of these claim that Augustine uses the instances of certainty to demonstrate knowledge by satisfying Zeno's criterion;[62] thus Kirwan: "In looking for propositions that compel assent and cannot be doubted, Augustine was following in the Stoic tradition."[63] While not strictly false, this remark is misleading. The Stoic criterion of knowledge is a criterion for trustworthy sense perceptions, and as such it reflects the materialistic bent of Stoicism, a target for Augustine

51. O'Meara, Introduction to *St. Augustine: Against the Academics*, 18.

52. Curley says it well: "Augustine has turned the notion of the probable against the Academics." *Augustine's Critique*, 118.

53. O'Daly, *Augustine's Philosophy of Mind*, 162–63.

54. Heil, "Augustine's Attack."

55. Harding, "Epistemology and Eudaimonism," and "Skepticism, Illumination."

56. Dennis, "Three Augustines."

57. Neiman, "The Arguments," and "Augustine's Philosophizing Person."

58. Curley, *Augustine's Critique*; see, for example, xvi of the Preface, 18, 51, and 127.

59. Topping, *Happiness and Wisdom*, chapter 3.

60. O'Meara, Introduction to *St. Augustine: Against the Academics*, 18.

61. In addition to Kirwan and O'Daly, three others are Diggs, Bolyard, and Roberts in "Augustine's Earliest Writings," 164. Mosher lists eleven more interpreters.

62. Kirwan, "Augustine Against the Skeptics," 216–18, and O'Daly, "The Response to Skepticism,"162.

63. Kirwan, "Augustine Against the Skeptics," 218.

as well as for Cicero.[64] Accordingly, in *Contra Academicos* we do not have to look far for glimpses of the strain of immaterialistic thought associated with the Platonic tradition.

In 3.11.26 Augustine mentions the Platonic tradition, saying "there are those who confess that all these things which the mind receives by a sense of the body can give rise to opinion, but they deny that it can give rise to knowledge, which they still want to be retained in the intelligence and dwelling in the mind." At 3.12.27 he asks rhetorically whether obstacles to reliable perception need trouble "him who concludes that the highest good is in the mind?" In 3.13.29 he claims that the truths of dialectic are free from bodily deception. In short, *Contra Academicos* is the emerging response of a young Christian thinker to ancient eudaimonism; his objections to skepticism hint at the neo-Platonic direction up to and through which Augustine is guiding us, and at a neo-Platonic treatment of the desire for wisdom. To this we now turn.

A Glimpse at a Platonic Philosophy of Desire

Having sufficiently refuted the stated doctrines of the Academics, Augustine acquaints us with their unstated doctrines, a revelation which points to a better philosophy and further unravels the views espoused by Licentius. Before revealing the secret, Augustine asks if the Academics really did not see the problems with their professed view, answering that "they saw it with the utmost skill and prudence" (3.16.36). Recounting the prehistory of the Academy, he describes how Plato learned first "charm and subtlety, which he wielded in moral matters," from Socrates, and later the doctrine of the immortality of the soul from the Pythagoreans (3.17.37). Plato promoted a doctrine of two worlds, the intelligible and the sensible; the former was *verum*, the latter *verisimile*; "these teachings . . . were preserved by Plato's successors and guarded as divine secrets" (3.17.38). When Zeno and his Stoical successors brought materialism into the Academy (3.17.38), the heirs of Plato went underground (3.17.39), using their method to undermine materialism.[65] So the Academics were not committed to their skepticism; they were Platonists, appearing publicly in skeptical guise so as to

64. Rist: "the Sceptical attack on the Stoic Zeno's criterion of truth—that attack which is reflected in the skeptical positions of *Against the Sceptics* itself—seems to target only those kinds of truth which . . . arise from experience of the sensory world." See Rist, *Augustine*, 53.

65. Although Augustine only mentions Stoicism in this passage, Epicurean materialism was equally a target of Academic debunking.

hide their belief in intelligible reality from unfriendly minds. Secretly they passed this belief on down to Cicero (3.18.41).

Licentius's argument from authority for skeptical conclusions is crippled, for a successful argument from authority requires that the cited authority sincerely endorse the argument's conclusion.[66] There is even a hint here of a *new* argument from authority: Cicero and other philosophers believed that satisfaction of desire is necessary for happiness; therefore frustrated desire is incompatible with happiness. For Cicero holds to the ancient distinction between material and intelligible and believes that a few "who, having cleansed themselves from all vices, have in some way appropriated a habit that is more than human" and are able to know the immaterial (3.17.38). Cicero *insincerely* suggested that the wise man only seeks wisdom. The unusual claim that we can be happy without having what we desire is left without a leg to stand on.[67] Cicero claims to believe it for pedagogical reasons, as an incentive to take up philosophy, as Foley explains.[68] Those with the acumen for understanding the intelligible realm might one day see past the façade, and those without would nevertheless be better people for having taken up philosophy.

Could Licentius appeal to any other authorities? Plato's Socrates might seem to desire wisdom yet be happy without it. But it is more likely that Socrates is satisfied to live in ignorance because, having realized the limits of his abilities, he does not desire to know more than he can. Sextus Empiricus, the post-Academic skeptic, might likewise be thought to have promoted a perennially unsatisfied desire for knowledge as the way to tranquility and happiness, emphasizing a continuing search for knowledge.[69] Yet it seems that Sextus searches for the truth and is content without it because he searches without desiring certainty. He wants only mental tranquility,[70] for which certainty is not needed and which he thinks he can attain by using his skeptical method to suspend judgment.[71] Socrates and Sextus sever the pursuit of wisdom from the desire of attaining it; dissatisfaction remains incompatible with happiness. Of course, one may argue that the desire

66. A fine discussion of the structure of arguments from authority is in Howard-Snyder, *Power of Logic*, Chapter 10, Section 2, 511–13.

67. O'Meara: "The real case against the Academics is that there were no Academics: They were only pretending; for they were Platonists in disguise." O'Meara, *The Young Augustine*, 194.

68. Foley, "Cicero, Augustine," 72.

69. Empiricus, *Outlines of Pyrrhonism* in *Sextus Empiricus*, I.1. Hallie's Introduction to this volume makes it clear that Sextus's philosophy is aimed at the happy life.

70. Ibid., I.12.

71. Ibid., 1.12–13.

and quest for wisdom should not be separated—that we cannot vigorously search for truth without *desiring* finally to attain it. We will soon see that Augustine does just this.

In the meantime we must look at the emerging neo-Platonic contributions to a philosophy of desire. The case for Academic contentedness lies in tatters, but the Academics have two insights which give way to a new teaching on the desire for wisdom. First, there is an element of truth in their exoteric philosophy. The Academics are serious about the limits of knowledge gained through the senses. The notion that natural man cannot attain wisdom about the material world was their private as well as public doctrine, since as Plato says it is only possible to achieve opinion about the sensible world (3.17.37).[72] This, of course, is why Licentius had promoted asceticism; for the Academics had publically promoted a quasi-Platonic therapy for desire along with their public teaching on the impossibility of knowledge in the physical world. (This Academic strategy, however, is not as useful in Augustine's time as it was in the days when Stoicism and Epicureanism had more influence.[73])

The second Academic insight is in their esoteric teaching. Wisdom requires an understanding of immaterial reality, which we can only hope to achieve by learning to contemplate the immaterial. While Licentius is right about the first insight, the second places it in a new light. We can grant all the challenges facing sense-perception; we can grant that knowledge is hard to attain in this life and that knowledge of the sensible world is impossible; the lesson is not that knowledge is impossible for man, but that it should be sought in the immaterial realm. In short, with the unmasking of Cicero and his ilk as esoteric Platonists, the mantle of philosophic wisdom passes to the public teaching of other Platonists, in particular Plotinus, whom Augustine mentions by name (3.18.41). Although we began by asking whether the Academics had an acceptable philosophy, the Academics lead to neo-Platonic philosophy. What we can learn from them about the desire for wisdom must now be sought from a Plotinian philosophy of desire, the central features of which are the reality and superiority of the immaterial world, and its superior position in rightly ordered desires.

72. Harding is correct about this Academic insight, although he does not address the second; "Skepticism, Illumination."

73. See Augustine's Letter 1, to Hermogenianus.

Christ: Towards a Christian Theology of Desire

Nevertheless, Augustine's purpose is not to promote Platonism, on which he barely touches as he works towards the dialogue's culmination. That culmination is the person of Christ and the miracle of the Incarnation:[74]

> . . . there is, in my opinion, a single discipline of philosophy most true[75] which—because there has been no dearth of extremely astute and learned men who have taught in their disputations that Aristotle and Plato harmonize with each other[76] . . . . this philosophy is not the philosophy of this world that our sacred [teachings] most rightly detest but of the other, intelligible world to which that most subtle reason would never call back souls blinded by the multiform darkness of error and smeared by the deepest filth from the body had not the Supreme God, out of kindness for the people, descended and lowered the authority of Divine Intellect all the way into the human body itself, so that . . . souls could return to their very selves and even gaze upon their fatherland without the bickering of disputations (3.19.42).

Wisdom is an intelligible, not a physical, reality; and through the Incarnation God has made wisdom available. Augustine implies several regions of agreement with the neo-Platonists: that wisdom is immaterial, that immersion in the physical world is spiritually blinding, and that natural man cannot hope to understand the immaterial except by contemplation. But in an act of grace wisdom has come to us, closing the gap between us and the wisdom we seek. Divine wisdom's humility makes it available to everyone,

74. On Augustine's pre-Chalcedonian yet orthodox understanding of the Incarnation, see Mallard.

75. On true philosophy, see Djuth, "Philosophy in a Time," especially pages 291–313. Madec claims that *c. Acad.* 3.19.42's "single discipline of philosophy most true" refers to Christianity but not to the Platonists. Kolbet and Evans concur. In this instance I agree with O'Connell: Augustine "clearly grants these laurels to the followers of Plato." Similarly, Topping takes *germana philosophia* in *Ord.* to refer to Platonism. Madec, "Connaissance de Dieu," 273–309; Kolbet, *Augustine and the Cure of Souls*, 93; Evans, *Augustine on Evil*, 30; O'Connell, note 18 of *Saint Augustine's Platonism*, 33; Topping, *Happiness and Wisdom*, 170.

However, *contra* O'Connell, designating Platonism "true philosophy" need not mean that in it Augustine sees virtually all truth; Harrison, *Augustine*, 19; Harrison, *Rethinking*, 22; and Curley, *Augustine's Critique*, 73, are nearer the mark; *c. Acad.* 3.19.42 requires only that "true philosophy" consist of certain doctrines of Platonism, not that "true philosophy" contain all truth. Platonism may be the "true philosophy," but it is not the true religion.

76. Nash connects several Aristotelian and neo-Platonic elements and shows how they are united in Augustine's early writings. See "Some Philosophic Sources."

not just to keener intellects.[77] What we desire is in fact attainable, and by the grace of God *radically* attainable. Finally, the quest for wisdom is placed in a new light. Following the neo-Platonists in learning to contemplate the immaterial is a worthy goal, but it is more important to respond to Christ.

There are immediate implications for our desire for wisdom. The appeal to Christ and the Incarnation calls for a rethinking of wisdom and its pursuit, a pursuit now understood to operate under Christ's authority. Desire must be fulfilled for happiness to be attained, and it *can* be fulfilled. Fulfillment requires a new spiritual therapy, submission to divine authority. Prayer is also employed as a means of reordering desire. The theological virtues of faith, hope, and love are required for the renovation of desire and are part of a successful journey to wisdom. Let us look at these things more closely.

Desire and Its Fulfillment

Satisfaction of desire is a necessary condition for happiness, and desire *can* be satisfied. *Contra Academicos*'s first lesson on desire is that Cicero's unusual claim that happiness does not require satisfaction is false. Licentius's premise that the wise man seeks a wisdom he desires and does not have has been thoroughly undone. Arguments have been offered that a wise man with knowledge exists; we have been exposed to a vigorous pedagogy that will help us make progress toward it; we have been reminded of the pressing need to believe that wisdom is possible; we have seen the authority of Cicero revealed as subtly promoting neo-Platonic insights on wisdom; and we have been given the name of wisdom Himself, by following Whom we can hope to reach wisdom ourselves. The epistemic agenda of the text is anything but "a philosophical dead-end," as one recent article has called it.[78] The same is true of the text's ethical agenda. Trygetius's premise that no one seeking wisdom is happy is vindicated, and with it his conclusion that the happy man is not seeking wisdom. We cannot be happy if we are still seeking what we desire; happiness is incompatible with dissatisfaction, as the philosophers

77. Mallard: "the picture is not of a man rousing himself to excellence by participating in divine authority, but rather the opposite: God is acting to participate downward in human life;" Mallard, "Incarnation," 88. Lactantius wrote in the *Divine Institutes* of the weakness of philosophy, and the superiority of Christianity, in bringing the masses to the happy life; see Topping, *Happiness and Wisdom*, 51–52.

78. Cessali and Germann, "Signification and Truth," 126–30. Cessali and Germann notice only Augustine's arguments for the certainties of perception and logical truth—neglecting the moral argument, the appeal to a Platonic account of reality, and the Incarnation.

are now understood to have held. Since we desire wisdom,[79] we will either attain it or remain unhappy.[80]

The second lesson is that desire *can* be fulfilled and that happiness *is* possible. The defense of the possibility of happiness proceeds in four waves. First, various lessons undermining skepticism show that our desire for wisdom can be fulfilled. We have seen Alypius's smile, the "argument from verisimilitude," and several instances of certainty. We have also seen it argued that a wise man exists and that such a one possesses wisdom. The wisdom we desire is possible, since someone has attained it. The next two waves emerge from the appearance of Platonism. Neo-Platonists such as Plotinus believed that a mystical encounter with wisdom is possible for some. The second wave is an implicit argument from the authority of such philosophers that happiness can be attained. Closely associated is the third wave, a pedagogical program for getting closer to wisdom, a program incipient in the appeal to Platonism. While Platonism does not presume that just anyone can get to wisdom, it does promise that a study in the liberal arts can help astute minds learn to contemplate the immaterial realm wherein wisdom resides. Augustine will say more of this in *De ordine*.

Christ's appearance is the culmination of the defense of the possibility of happiness. Wisdom has come to us, drawing us closer to happiness, a movement proceeding on two axes. We are brought closer to wisdom on a horizontal axis, for the chance to know wisdom now extends to the whole human race. The mental astuteness and intellectual training contemplation requires are unnecessary for knowing God; following Christ is sufficient. The acquaintance of unschooled folk with happiness is a theme to which Augustine will return in *De beata vita* and *De ordine* with the example of Monica. But the Incarnation also moves us closer to wisdom on a vertical axis. Souls caught up in idolatries and lust are not able to know wisdom; carnal desire prevents the ascent. God in mercy lowers himself to the very carnality in which we wallow; wisdom meets us in our sin and makes our acquaintance with it possible.[81] At Cassiciacum Augustine understands the

79. Augustine likely read of the natural human desire for wisdom in Cicero, *On Duties*, 1.13.

80. O'Daly suggests that Augustine has not really refuted the Academic notion of wisdom, for Augustine presumes that a wise man *has* knowledge, while the Academic thinks that wisdom is in *seeking* knowledge; *Augustine's Philosophy of Mind*, 166. To the contrary: Not only does Augustine argue against this very claim in the first chapters of Book III, but he has also showed that a man *desiring* yet *lacking* wisdom cannot be happy, which is not consistent with the notion that a wise man is a happy sage.

81. The description of movement along two axes is influenced by the three dimensions Vaught discusses in his trilogy on the *Confessions*. My horizontal axis parallels Vaught's "spatial" axis, my vertical axis the "eternal." See *Access to God*, *Encounters with God*, and *Journey toward God*.

insufficiency of intellectual acumen alone to arrive at wisdom. It is only a short time after he had lamented to Alypius: "The unlearned rise up and take heaven by storm, but we, with all our erudition . . . , see how we wallow in flesh and blood!" (*Conf.* 8.8.19). Intellectual training in the manner of the neo-Platonists is a worthy pursuit; but it is not so necessary as they would think. What is vitally important is the right response to the appearance in human history of wisdom himself.

Authority and the Renovation of Desire

The pursuit of wisdom has a new strategy and a new direction. One with a perfect knowledge of the truth has appeared on the stage of human history; it is incumbent upon us to pursue wisdom by following him. We began with Licentius's appeal to the authority of Cicero, and we end with the authority of Christ, now an important part of the quest for truth. First we will look at how Augustine realized the importance of the authority of Scripture and Christ. Then we will review how Augustine came to this authority. Christ has authority of his own and, contrary to O'Connell, wholly independently of the claims of neo-Platonism. This will lead to an examination of how submission to Christian authority renovates desire.

In *Confessions* 6.6 Augustine tells how prior to his conversion he had learned the importance of authority. History and geography tell of people and places I have never seen yet accept on testimony; even my belief that my parents are my parents depends on their testimony. Thus Augustine learned that "Unless we believed these things, nothing at all could be done in this life."[82] Manichean thought did not tolerate belief on the basis of authority and promised its initiates direct knowledge of the truth and liberation from authoritarian knowledge. Academicism also purported to resist authoritarianism. Augustine's new appreciation for the importance of authority freed him from Manichean-inspired attacks on the authority of Scripture and prepared him to trust Scripture for himself.[83]

It is not Scripture per se, but its main character, who looms large in *Contra Academicos*. We are dealing with far more than the strength of arguments from authority. Wisdom's requirement is to follow Christ. The naming of a genuinely wise man satisfies the philosopher's interest in finding a

82. The same argument appears in extended form in Augustine's *Usefulness of Belief*.

83. Neiman's commentary on this is helpful. See "Augustine's Philosophizing Person," 241–44.

guide who can show men how to live.[84] Christ grounds a new ethic and a new epistemology, each centered on his authority. Thus Augustine included the name of Christ in the dialogues so they would be full of "those healthful herbs which the Church provides" (*Conf.* 9.4.7).

But how do we get to Christ's authority? We must distinguish two different questions. One concerns religious epistemology: What justifies a decision to submit to Christ's authority? Here we cannot answer directly; Augustine does not specify conditions for justified religious belief at Cassiciacum. But another question is this: What motivates the little community at Cassiciacum to bind their lives to the authority of Christ? To this question there is an answer at Cassiciacum, and we must begin by noting that Augustine did not *turn* to the authority of Christ so much as *re*turn. As Carol Harrison says, "Augustine was not converted from paganism to Christianity. What he recounts in the *Confessions* is more a reconciliation with the Christian faith in whose shadow he had always lived and thought, than a conversion to a new religion."[85] Harrison cites *Confessions* (3.4.8, 5.14.24) as evidence that Augustine always held up new ideas to Christianity, hoping they would be reconciled and his mother's ancient faith justified.[86]

Christ's authority is much more than Platonism. To O'Connell's mind, it is little more than an effective means of accomplishing the goal of neo-Platonic philosophy. O'Connell reads Augustine as having been quite thoroughly converted to the worldview of Plotinus before he saw in Christ a chance to accomplish what Plotinus urged. Thus the authority of Christ as well as "that Incarnation, about which Plotinus himself may never have dreamt, Augustine fits neatly into the scheme of the Plotinian universe."[87] But Christ is much more than an instrument to the pagan good for at least two reasons that are evident in *Contra Academicos*.

84. Socrates describes his search for someone with expertise in how human beings should live in Plato's *Apology*. Similarly, Seneca speaks of the need for someone to guide us to the happy life; Seneca, *On the Happy Life*, 1.

85. Harrison, *Rethinking*, 22.

86. On this topic see also Curley, *Augustine's Critique*, 73. Burton's phrase "conversion back to Christianity" is suggestive; see Burton, "The Vocabulary," 141. Mourant, "Augustine and the Academics" is an admirable essay on the subject. Cary helpfully distinguishes modern notions of conversion (influenced by Protestantism) from other (neo-Platonist and ecclesial) notions of conversion which are more consistent with Augustine's "conversion" in 386; see *Inner Grace*, 64–66.

87. O'Connell, "The Enneads," 160. Another overstated remark is O'Meara's: "Augustine disagrees with [the Platonists] on only one point: their failure to see that Christ was the way of authority;" see *Studies in Augustine and Eriguena*, 156. Clark puts it nicely: "He does not point the way: He is the way." See Clark, Review, 433. Chapter 5 of Topping, is a rewarding discussion on authority; Topping objects to O'Connell's view; Topping, *Happiness and Wisdom*, 151–57.

First, Augustine always gives Christ preeminence over neo-Platonic thought. This extends even to the confirmation of neo-Platonic insights by Christianity. As O'Connell has it, neo-Platonic philosophy's insights stand on their own and provide independent justification of Christian insights. Of course, neo-Platonism gives Augustine the conceptual resources for answering objections to Christianity (*Conf.* VII), but it does not on its own authority establish the truth of Christian doctrine.[88] Augustine accepts the truths of Christianity on the authority of Christ and the church; having accepted them, he hopes to use neo-Platonic modes of thinking to understand them.[89] *Contra Academicos* 3.20.43, in fact, anticipates Augustine's later idea of believing in order to understand: "I am certain not to depart ever, in any way, from the authority of Christ, for I find nothing more powerful. But what should be accomplished by a most subtle reason . . . I trust in the meantime I shall find among the Platonists, insofar as it is not incompatible with our sacred [teachings]."

Second, the authority of Christ distinguishes itself from neo-Platonic doctrine by its accompanying treatment of desire. The call to submit to Christ's authority is also a call to allow our desire for wisdom to undergo the treatment of obeying that authority. It is a therapy for those under the influence of Academicism. Those allured by Academicism need to ally their love of wisdom to Christ. Trusting Christ is an even stronger therapy for Romanianus and others tempted by the siren-song of Manichean enlightenment. As Augustine would say later in *The Usefulness of Belief*, submission to authority renovates the heart's desires: "Here is, believe me, most wholesome authority. . . . Here is conversion from love of this world to the true God."[90] Authority renews our desires in several ways. To submit to Christ's authority for the sake of my soul's happiness is to turn away from things which beckon me with false promises of happiness and from anything away from which Christ and his church tell me to turn—the likes of money, power, fame, and bodily pleasures. Moreover, submission to Christ is an

88. Harrison is helpful on this; see *Rethinking*, chapters 3 and 4. Also see Gilson: "From the time of conversion, even when he was still filled with enthusiasm for Platonic philosophy and relied on it to help him penetrate the mysteries of faith, the authority of Christ comes first. From that time on he will never cease to point out, with increasing insistence, the superiority and the absolute necessity of Christ's authority." *The Christian Philosophy*, 29.

89. Curley, *Augustine's Critique*, 134–35. Topping, although commenting on *De ordine*, is very helpful on this theme: "philosophy . . . equips a believer to contemplate the nature of the mysteries which Christ through his Church has *already* made available. Which is to say, secondly, that the *activity* of *ratio* is contemplation. *Ratio* marches into the world less as an inventor than as an explorer." See Topping, 169.

90. Augustine, *Usefulness of Belief*, 16.34.

act of devotion to Him, turning our souls in his direction and converting our lives and loves thereto. It also entails a conversion of desire to anything Christ and his church tell me to desire. Finally, submission to the authority of Christ and church cultivates humility because submitting to authority is an admission of my inability to reach the truth on my own; trust in authority is a therapy for pride.

We must say a few more words about this last point. We need humility because pride is a crippling disorder in our desires. Already Augustine has begun to explore the Christian idea that the impulse for honor is rooted in pride, the cardinal sin and the most devastating illness afflicting our souls.[91] Alypius says of pride, "there is no more monstrous vice than that" (2.8.21) and shows Licentius and Trygetius an unexpected humility when he rejoices in being defeated (3.20.44). Pride is a significant threat to an effective pursuit of wisdom,[92] as the tale of the two travelers illustrates (3.15.34). The man who will not listen to the country "yokel" pointing the right way is "elegant" and "urbane," having "great wit." Out of his prideful sophistication he refuses the way when it is offered; the act of humility, trusting in the humble shepherd, is the first step on the right path. There are poignant lessons hidden in this passage. One is the epistemological lesson that the common sense of unphilosophized rustics who trust their perceptions is a source of knowledge, despite sophisticated Academic argumentation. Another is the picture of Christ, the good Shepherd (or the backwoods Hebrews who presented Christ to the world), pointing us to the happy life, through his lowly stature turning away the proud of heart and urging the humble on towards wisdom.[93] Curley endorses this reading of the passage, and McWilliam a similar one.[94] Seneca says that on the journey to the happy life "you are prevented from going astray by some recognized road and by questions put to local people" who know the way.[95] Augustine bids us follow, where we do not know the way, in the footsteps of the Savior who does know.

91. Later in *Free Choice of the Will*, 3.25, Augustine would identify pride as the cardinal sin which brought about the devil's own rebellion against God.

92. Foley, "The Other Happy Life," 174–77.

93. Christians in antiquity were reviled for their origins among uncouth shepherds and fishers. Caecilius in Minucius Felix' *Octavius* does so in chapter 8; Octavius replies in chapter 16. The philosophers who come to challenge Antony in *Life of Antony* 214.72–217.80 suggest a similar attitude. See also Wilken on the perception of Christians as uneducated and gullible, their beliefs unreasoned and uncritical in *The Christians as the Romans Saw Them*, 77, 92, 98. See Fortin on this as an objection against Christianity; "The 'Rhetoric' of the Church Fathers," 47–52. Also see Harrison, *Augustine*, 49.

94. Curley, *Augustine's Critique*, 122. McWilliam thinks the peasant stands for the church; see "The Cassiciacum Autobiography," 28. They are both right.

95. Seneca, *On the Happy Life*, 1.

The invocation of Christ invites a return to the rule given in 1.3.8. In a Platonic context, the rule would have the end of placing the desire for honor firmly under the rein of the desire for wisdom.[96] Keeping the impulse for honor from ruling our lives means more when considered in a Christian context. The rule is for training Licentius and Trygetius in the humility that prioritizes truth over victory. Exercising humility in disputation is an exercise in imitating the humility of Christ. However, we know from *Confessions* 9.4.7 that Augustine at this time was still to some extent puffed up with pride. Following Christ's authority is a therapy for desire, and, like most therapies, it takes some time for it to heal us.

Prayer and the Reordering of Desire

Ryan Topping shows another way desire is reordered in a manner unfamiliar to most pagan philosophers.[97] Topping argues that "the necessity of prayer figures prominently within the moral argument of the dialogue"[98] and says that prayer is "the site of his struggle to form a pious will."[99] Prayer is not only an appeal to divine grace to reorder desire. The very act of prayer reorients the will in two ways. Prayer has an intellectual aspect and an active aspect. In the intellectual aspect, prayer focuses the mind on God, redirecting our attentions "away from material goods" and towards God.[100] In the active aspect, prayer habituates the soul towards the pursuit of God; it "aids in the reintegration of the soul by a unifying act of the will."[101] Topping also explains that all readers of *c. Acad.* are invited, with Romanianus, to participate in the healing of our souls through prayer.[102]

Desire and the Theological Virtues

Contra Academicos is an interesting study in a theme hinted at by ancient philosophical doctrines. First I shall present the notion that desire, specifically the desire for attaining wisdom, interacts with its own object. Then we will look at how Augustine resituates this ancient notion in a Christian setting, reconsidering it in connection with the theological virtues.

96. See Plato, *Republic*.

97. Topping, *Happiness and Wisdom*, 100–104.

98. Ibid., 100.

99. Ibid., 101.

100. Ibid., 102.

101. Ibid.

102. Ibid., 125.

At least since Plato philosophy had been attracted to the idea that desire drives one to God, that it is the propelling force behind the soul's ascent to wisdom. This idea appears in classical texts including Plato's *Symposium* and *Republic* 490a–b, and Plotinus's *Ennead* 3.5. Our natural desire for contemplating divinity has fallen towards carnal things, but once it is more properly ordered towards immaterial objects of attraction it becomes the engine of ascent thereto. We cannot know if we do not desire to know; since desire is necessary to drive us in ascent to wisdom, a vigorous desire to know is a condition for its own fulfillment.

Part and parcel of this notion is the estimation of desire as a good thing, both a natural human inclination and the motive force for philosophical ascent. If directed to the likes of sex, money, or fame, desire can ruin a life, but it is also the necessary impetus for attaining what is good.

When Cicero calls desire natural[103] he accepts this Platonic interpretation of desire. Augustine incorporates this thought. Book I begins with the Ciceronian principle that we desire to become wise. As Heil reminds us, Augustine does not think that reason operates independently of the will.[104] We cannot know the truth if we do not love it, nor pursue it if we do not desire it.

Augustine re-forges this raw philosophical material, linking it with the theological virtues. Dennis sagely if somewhat briefly connects the theological virtues to three of the impediments to wisdom mentioned in the prologue: the distractions of life, despair, and the presumption of already being wise. These "dangers are overcome by the three theological virtues of faith, hope, and love . . . . Faith leads a person to overcome distraction when he recognizes what he truly needs; hope keeps a person from despairing that he will never find what he seeks; and, love is necessary for a person to want to find wisdom rather than remain in the darkness of false dogma."[105] He points to the treatment of the virtues in the *Soliloquies*, and in later chapters we will see further how all three virtues are conditions for a vigorous desire and active pursuit of wisdom.

There is little to say about faith at this juncture, save that resituating the quest for wisdom in the context of Christian authority places the desire for wisdom in faith's service. Submission to the authority of Christ and Scripture requires trusting them; it makes the knowledge of Scripture and church teaching a resource in the journey to wisdom; and it involves a steady belief that the goal we are seeking exists and can be obtained. Hope,

103. Cicero, *On Duties*, 1.11–13.

104. Heil, "Augustine's Attack on Skepticism."

105. Dennis, "Three Augustines," 12.

however, is the real theme of the dialogue; we will look at hope next, and then briefly at love.

Hope's centrality to *Contra Academicos* is evident from several moments in the text. Romanianus's despair is given as the dialogue's main target (2.3.8); despair threatens Licentius (2.17.18); and Augustine admits that the Academics have induced in him a despair of not attaining the truth (2.9.23). *Contra Academicos*'s message gives epistemological and eudaimonistic hope; the campaign against skepticism shows that we have reason to believe that wisdom is possible. Without hope for desire's satisfaction we are like Licentius in his despair, sluggish in the pursuit of wisdom. We must hope that we can reach our goal in order vigorously to pursue it. Augustine strives to convince Licentius and Romanianus that the truth exists and that we have hope of reaching it, thereby inspiring the hope that nourishes a vigorous desire for wisdom and its accordant pursuit.[106] Knowing that the truth exists and pursuing it ardently, they will be better able to be happy.

In the midst of Book III's refutation of skepticism Augustine mentions the danger Academicism poses to a hopeful pursuit of wisdom. Placing Stoic dogmatism in opposition to Academicism, Augustine asks which is a greater danger to the quest for philosophy:

> Is it he who says: "Listen, friend, Philosophy is not called wisdom itself but the zeal for wisdom. If you devote yourself to it, not even then, as long as you are here in this life, will you be wise, for wisdom is with God and it cannot reach man. . . ." Or is it he who says: "Come, O mortals, to philosophy! Great is the reward here . . . Come then, that you may be wise . . . " (3.9.20).

For all their materialistic dogmatism, the Stoics at least praise philosophy and encourage youths to take it up. The Academics avert the young from philosophy by telling them they have no chance at attaining it this side of the grave. The treatment for despair includes the arguments that undermine skepticism, thereby giving hope. But the real cure for despair is the Incarnation. The prescription for despair is learning that wisdom has come to us.

The Academic perspective on desire's postmortem fulfillment is not utterly rejected; but it is set in a different context and rethought. Augustine grants to the skeptics that our desire for wisdom will remain unsatisfied in this life (1.8.23). But the path to satisfaction begins now. This implies a different therapy than that suggested by Licentius's view. That therapy involved cutting back sensual interests in hope of attaining wisdom in the

106. The nourishing and cultivating of a desire stands in contrast to the Epicurean and Stoic tendencies to trim or get rid of desires; see above, Chapter 1, under the heading *Ancient Philosophers and Their Therapies for Desire*.

immaterial realm after death, but Augustine's emerging therapy for desire is to cultivate our desires for wisdom by following Christ. One element of this treatment of desire is the understanding of our desperate need vigorously to desire wisdom. Another element is the understanding that desire must be nourished by hope, the antidote for despair which sustains us in the arduous ascent towards wisdom. Some work in recent moral psychology lends a hand in showing why the likelihood of attaining wisdom is so crucial to having a vibrant hope of attaining wisdom. Analyzing the emotion of hope, Robert Roberts says that hope is defined by its construal of some state of affairs as presenting "an attractive possibility possessing a significant degree of probability" where the construal is based on a wish for its fulfillment.[107] If this is correct, then the probability that wisdom is possible also makes possible the hope for wisdom, and with it the hopeful pursuit of wisdom.[108] Although reinforced by arguments against skepticism, the climactic appeal to Christ marks Augustine's hope as a *theological* virtue acting in response to revelation. It is fitting that among the last words of the dialogue are Augustine's resolution "I am certain not to depart ever, in any way, from the authority of Christ" (3.10.43) and Alypius's remark: "Now then, mates, take that expectant longing of yours . . . and turn it into a more reliable hope of learning with me" (3.10.44).

Finally, the theological virtue of love keeps us hot on the heels of wisdom. A vigorous love for the wisdom we do not have keeps us motivated continually to strive to have it. This understanding of love's necessity for wisdom harkens back to Plato's idea in the *Symposium* that desire drives the philosopher's soul to chase wisdom. Augustine's incorporation of the ancient concept of love resembles that ancient concept in that he desires what he does not have: "I realize that I have not yet acquired it" (3.20.43). But we can descry some of the distinctives of Christian desire. The asceticism of Academics is, at best, less important than following Christ. Love is for wisdom, and wisdom is revealed in a person; love is intimately connected to Christ and the God He reveals. The love of impersonal neo-Platonic wisdom is transformed into a love of Christ and the tri-personal God. In *De beata vita* and the other dialogues we will explore this and see other ways in which Christian love is distinguished from its pagan counterparts.

107. Roberts, *Emotions*, 281–83.

108. Janelle Aijian's description of hope as making the quest for wisdom "psychologically viable" has helped me understand the significance of hope in *c. Acad.*

3

Desiring and Having God

As the Cassiciacum dialogues continue to unfold Augustine extends his response to the problems of desire which the ancients had identified—and to their attempts to solve them. In *De beata vita* he analyzes the misery that afflicts human life, commending therapies for desire's renewal mingling pagan insights with Christian.[1] Happiness requires satisfaction of desire, which in turn requires that we love the right things. This means loving what is most stable, namely God. Anyone who lacks what he desires is unhappy, and all who are unhappy are also in want. On these things Augustine agrees with some insights of ancient philosophers, especially the neo-Platonists. But happiness requires more than philosophy, which is merely the gateway to the happy life; in order to complete the journey we need God to convert our desires. Pride again emerges as the main obstacle to reordered desires. Moreover, having God involves living according to moderation, a principle applied even to contemplation. The happy life, at least for now, is embodied; and embodiment is not, in itself, in any way a bad thing; while this is somewhat of a departure from neo-Platonism, Augustine's rethinking of the neo-Platonists on this topic calls for care and subtlety, and naturally there are lively discussions on the subject in the secondary literature. Finally, prayer and immersion in the Christian community are part of the happy life and essential to the renovation of desire. A holy life, sanctified by the theological virtues, is more effective than learning for attaining wisdom and reordering our desires.

1. Augustine, *On the Happy Life* (referenced in text as *b. Vita*).

We must first look at the dialogue's cover letter to see what it says about the happy life (Part One). Then we shall turn to the argument that God alone is to be loved (Part Two) and to the diagnosis of human misery as rooted in the lack of wisdom (Part Three). We must examine the prescription for desire that emerges from these truths, considering its relation to neo-Platonism and the interpretations of Conybeare, O'Connell, and others (Part Four).

THE PORT OF PHILOSOPHY AND THE LAND OF THE HAPPY LIFE

In his cover letter to Manlius Theodorus Augustine returns to the image of philosophy as a port, extending the metaphor beyond its Ciceronian background. He speaks of a firm land beyond the port of philosophy and emphasizes God's role in reordering our desires so we can reach this land. Building on the same imagery he identifies pride as the central obstacle to happiness and hints that God and the soul are the objects of rightly ordered desires.

"If a course charted by reason and if the will itself could bring us to the port of philosophy (from which we enter into the territory and land of the happy life even now), then I do not know whether I am rash in saying, O Theodore . . . that men are going to reach it in very small numbers . . ." (*b. Vita* 1.1). Like Cicero's, Augustine's port imagery signifies philosophy's ability to secure our souls from the buffeting of life's storms (*c. Acad.* 1.1.1). Unlike Cicero, Augustine speaks of the firm land, a happy life *beyond* the port. While philosophy gets us closer to happiness, happiness lies beyond philosophy. *De beata vita*'s religious tone leaves no room for doubt that Augustine is talking about Christianity; the land of happiness to which philosophy is a gateway is the life of those who know and love God.[2]

De beata vita's opening sentence also conveys our inability to reach happiness on our own, a theme we have seen before (*c. Acad.* 1.1.1). Reason and the will are insufficient. Augustine illustrates by describing three types of people who go sailing for the happy life. Those naturally inclined to philosophy, "with a little effort and a stroke of the oars, speed away . . . and settle down in tranquility" (*b. Vita* 1.2). Second are wanderers who need God's help in the form of a storm, "a thoroughly raging tempest, a head wind that would lead them—even as they weep and mourn—to sure and solid joys" (*b. Vita* 1.2). No doubt Augustine hoped that Romanianus's

2. Mourant correctly emphasizes the preeminence of Christianity over Platonic philosophy, but errs in labeling the port itself Christian wisdom rather than the gateway thereto. See Mourant, "The Emergence," 72.

troubles (*c. Acad.* 2.1.1–2.3.9) would do the same for him. The third class of seafarers, "even in the midst of the waves themselves, remember their most sweet homeland"; some "return to it by a direct course," but others are led astray by false opinion and "drift for too long" until providential storms carry them homewards.[3]

These storms are the work of God applying to our souls a harsh surgery. Before we can have rightly ordered desires our disorderly desires must be purged; sometimes God directs circumstances to help free us from these affections.[4] The object of disordered love may be ripped away, giving temporary distress and an opportunity to learn to desire better things.[5] Or disaster may cause us to rethink what is really important. In either case, a tempest carries us, weeping at its effects, "to sure and solid joys" (1.2).[6] Augustine himself was aided by "a tempest, which is deemed to be adverse," to escape "the allurements of marriage and honor" (1.4). *Contra Academicos* 1.1.1 suggests that the return to happiness cannot be completed without divine assistance because the reordering of desire requires more healing than we can prescribe for ourselves. God must apply the restorative surgery to our souls and cleanse us from disordered affections. We need grace to reorder our desires.

The imagery gets livelier as Augustine warns against pride. Just outside the port is a great obstacle to the happy life:

> But for all of these men who, in whatever manner, are brought to the land of the happy life, there stands a vast mountain before the port itself that also causes great difficulties to those who would enter, a mountain that should be feared most intensely and avoided most carefully (1.3).

The mountain is pride.[7] The love of oneself promises to "satisfy their desires instead of the blessed land itself" and is the greatest obstacle to

3. "No one is actually healed by Philosophy or guided to *beata uita* there . . ." Silk, "Boethius' Consolatio Philosophiae," 34.

4. Burt: "The process of searching for satisfaction must begin with dissatisfaction." See Burt, *"Let Me Know You,"* 3.

5. Boethius likewise presents himself in *Consolation of Philosophy* as having loved his reputation, position, and finances too much and having his desires reordered as a result of their providential removal from his life. On the relationship of the Cassiciacum dialogues and Boethius, see Silk, "Boethius' Consolatio Philosophiae."

6. Silk, "Boethius' Consolatio Philosophiae," 31: "Such misfortune is a priceless blessing, for nothing else so draws men to Philosophy and makes them responsible to her teaching."

7. Jackson reads the mountain as representing secular philosophy; see "Augustine All At Sea," 74. Kevane draws out the connection between pride and Augustine's

rightly ordered desire. It tempts even lovers of wisdom to leave the port and return to an island in the sea rather than move up on to the land. Pride "summons to itself a good many men from even the port" (*b. Vita* 1.3), including such as the sophisticate in *Contra Academicos*'s tale of two travelers (3.15.34). But glory of oneself "has nothing full and solid within, so that it sinks and swallows up the puffed-up people who walk upon its cracking and brittle ground . . . ." The reality and danger of pride reinforces Augustine's claims about the difficulty in reaching the happy life and our need for God's help; Harrison takes this passage as evidence for her contention that "From the very beginning, Augustine identified pride as the root of humanity's fallenness."[8]

Augustine closes *De beata vita*'s cover letter with the story of his own journey towards the happy life. The account richly mingles the language of reordered thoughts with the language of reordered desires. By Cicero's *Hortensius* he "was set on fire with such a love of philosophy" that he considered sailing all the way to that port (1.4). For a while he wandered, driven by Manichean superstition. Then Academic philosophy "held the helm of my ship as it resisted every gale in the midst of the waves." Like a solid anchor, it did not lead him to port but prevented the Manichean superstition from pulling him off course. Finally, "a North Star" brought him within sight of land; this star was the dawning of the light of immateriality, for, as Ambrose said often, "when one is thinking about God one should in no way think about the body—nor when one is thinking about the soul . . . ." Still Augustine refrained from entering the port until a "tempest," a "pain in the chest," enabled him to resign from worldly ambitions. Though he is entering the port with his loved ones, he admits that he knows very little about the land itself (1.5). The land is mapped by the understanding of God and the soul, but as he does not yet possess this understanding he knows not the lay of the land.

We should read these remarks in conjunction with the insights of *Contra Academicos*. Philosophy's port is a virtuous life characterized by reordered desires; right doctrine and right love are intimately connected. Academic philosophy has an advantage over those philosophical systems infected with materialism; the port of philosophy is explicitly linked with immateriality. The connection harkens back to *c. Acad.* 19.42 where the

---

education in the schools; see *Augustine the Educator*, 58. Kolbet, *Augustine and the Cure of Souls*, in the same vein, explains that the mountain represents worldly ambition; see Kevane, *Augustine the Educator*, 89–90.

8. Harrison, *Rethinking*, 173. Brown is incorrect that "We would be rash to scrutinize" the Cassiciacum dialogues "for traces of the future bishop." See Brown, *Augustine*, 109.

Platonic stream of philosophy is described as that "single discipline of philosophy most true." The remarks concerning the immaterial nature of God and the soul also foreshadow later insights of *De beata vita*.

In sum, true philosophy brings us closer to happiness, but happiness requires more than philosophy can provide. We are unable to arrive at happiness by our own effort alone; we need providential assistance, commonly given in the form of a painful redirection of our desires. The major obstacle to happiness and rightly ordered desires is the love of our own glory. Finally, the rightly ordered desires of the happy life have something to do with the subject matter of true philosophy: God and the soul, both of which are immaterial.

WHAT IS TO BE LOVED?

From 2.7 through 3.21 we learn that happiness requires satisfaction; that we must desire God in order to be satisfied; and that in order to have God we must obey Him, live righteously, and love Him only. The opening dialogue also introduces two very important themes, one of them an analogy: Wisdom is to the soul what food is to the body. The other is that Christian piety is more effective than learning in the pursuit of wisdom and the renovation of desire.

Food for the Body, Food for the Soul

The dialogue begins on Augustine's birthday: November 13, 386, during the interlude between *Contra Academicos* I and II–III.[9] A diverse group has gathered: Augustine, Licentius, Trygetius, Augustine's son Adeodatus, his brother Navigius, his cousins Lartidianus and Rusticus, and finally his mother Monica, who will prove to be a major character. The first two chapters are a meditation on the dual nature of human beings—spiritual and physical—and on what is proper to that nature. When the company has taken lunch, Augustine asks, "Does it seem obvious to you that we are composed of soul and body?" (2.7). Navigius is reluctant, and Augustine asks him if he at least knows that he lives and has a body. When Navigius answers in the affirmative, Augustine concludes from the fact that we have a body and life that we have a body and a soul. Thus the soul is the life and organizing principle of the body. This initial definition of the soul is an Aristotelian one (found in *On the Soul* 2.1).

9. On the dialogues' chronology, see Cary, "What Licentius Learned," 161–63.

No sooner is it established that we have a soul and body than Augustine suggests that there is a form of nourishment appropriate to each, asking: "on account of which of these do we desire food?" All agree that food pertains to the body, and Augustine offers the analogy that sets *De beata vita*'s tone: "Then what about the soul? Is there a nourishment proper to it? Or does it seem to you that knowledge is its food?" (2.8). Monica agrees "that the soul is nourished by no other reality than the understanding and knowledge of things," but there is an interesting interlude before the others agree. Trygetius is doubtful, and Monica reminds him how he had been preoccupied during lunch, saying that he had been feeding his soul. The tactic fails to convince, but Augustine has a tack of his own, and uses the moment to exhort Trygetius to press on with his education, first by asking whether the souls of learned men are not "much fuller and much greater . . . than those of the unlearned?" Trygetius agrees although he thinks their minds are not empty but full of the wrong things. Augustine briefly presents the notion of evil as a privation of being, a lesson he had learned from the neo-Platonists (*Conf.* 7.12). This suggests that the souls of the uneducated are indeed empty. But for the moment Augustine is content to encourage Trygetius to continue his education and fill his mind; it is enough that knowledge is nourishment for the soul.

Although 2.7's rudimentary definition of the soul is reminiscent of Aristotle, we can already see hints of a richer notion of the soul; the soul is the life of the body, but has functions and needs independent of the body. That food is proper to the body and knowledge to the soul Augustine likely read in Cicero and may have heard from Ambrose.[10] This says a great deal about our desires. Just as we desire and seek food for our bodies, we desire and seek knowledge for our souls. Food for our souls is more important than food for our bodies because our souls are more important than our bodies. Augustine suggests "that on my birthday I ought to serve a meal . . . not only for our bodies but for our souls as well" (2.9). He hopes that his audience is already hungry for knowledge, which will be the case "if your minds are healthy." A healthy soul desires knowledge, just as a healthy body will get hungry.[11] If a soul is not healthy the only recourse is to pray for its healing.

10. Cicero, *On Duties*, 1.11–13 describes the natural inclinations of the human being, including self-preservation, procreation, and wisdom. In conjunction with *On Ends* 4.10, which acknowledges that humans consist of body and soul, we can infer that, while some of our inclinations pertain to the body, the pursuit of wisdom pertains to the soul. Ambrose speaks of the desire for "the Word" or "the Heavenly Bread" as better than the desire for earthly bread; see Ambrose, *Exposition of the Holy Gospel*, 4.20. In a text probably composed a few years after Cassiciacum, Ambrose speaks of "that satiety which knowledge brings about;" Ambrose, *Duties of the Clergy*, 2.17.92.

11. Kevane helpfully comments on this theme in *Augustine the Educator*, 86.

Only God Will Satisfy

Luckily, all present are healthy enough to eat, and Augustine has prepared a hearty meal. He observes, "We want to be happy" (2.10) and asks, "Does it seem to you that someone who does not have what he wants is happy?"[12] All agree that happiness requires satisfaction. For the reader who has read *Contra Academicos*, this principle is familiar. (Since, chronologically, we are in the midst of the discussion of the Academics, Licentius ought not to have agreed.)

We must therefore attain what we want, since we desire to be happy and not having what we want makes us unhappy. Of course, it is not guaranteed that having what we want will make us happy. Augustine playfully tests his audience with a logical fallacy: If we do not have what we want, we are unhappy; so is it the case that "Everyone who has what he wants is happy?" (2.10). Monica does not point out the formal fallacy but still arrives at the correct answer: "If he wants good things and has them, he is happy, but if he wants bad things he is unhappy, even if he has them." Augustine laughs, perhaps at the irony that her lack of intellectual refinement is coupled with such wisdom. He says, "Mother, you have utterly mastered the very stronghold of philosophy." He refers to a passage in Cicero's *Hortensius*: "to want what is not fitting—that is itself the worst misery." The best of ancient philosophy promotes this truth: Satisfaction requires desiring the right things. At the quote from Cicero Monica gives a manly shout of triumph, and Augustine perceives "from where and from how divine a source these things flowed."

Through her simple piety God has granted Monica wisdom, an insight at the heart of the Platonic tradition, which philosophers achieved through all their learning. Piety's advantage over learning in achieving wisdom and reordering our loves is a common theme for the church fathers. Athanasius's Antony has wisdom enough to stump Greek philosophers who come to test him[13] and whom he impugns for degrading God and human souls to the level of beasts and for failing to motivate rightly ordered desires. Like Monica, he beats the Greeks at their own game because of his religious discipline and piety.[14] Conybeare chides[15] the literature on Augustine for not

12. This remark parallels Aristotle's *Nichomachean Ethics* 1.4. Seneca opens his *On the Happy Life* with the same observation.

13. Athanasius, *Life of Antony*, 214.72–217.80.

14. O'Keefe and Reno explain that for Athanasius "the holiness of one's life is more decisive than learning in the interpretation of Scripture" and that "discipline of the soul must guide interpretation of Scripture." Holiness' preeminence over learning also extends to the sort of things the philosophers studied. See *Sanctified Vision*, 131–2.

15. Conybeare, *Irrational Augustine*, 64–69.

taking Monica seriously, noting Brian Stock's remark that Monica "plays no significant part in the discussion . . . ."[16] Conybeare and others[17] do well to call attention to Monica.[18] However, Conybeare associates the dialogues' undertones of inclusivity and embodiment with Augustine's supposed lack of confidence in reason. This, I think, is wrongheaded; Monica's philosophical success does not prove that something is wrong with reason, merely that piety is a more powerful source of knowledge than learning.[19] Holiness has given her insight into the nature of rightly ordered desires.[20]

But what should we desire, and what desires are rightly ordered? Licentius demands (2.11) an answer, and Augustine asks, "what should a man acquire for himself in order to be happy?" He answers that "it is something ever abiding, and it should not be dependent on fortune or subject to any accidents. For we cannot have what is mortal and unsteady whenever we want it and for as long as we want it." Schools as diverse as Epicureanism, Stoicism, and neo-Platonism understood that satisfaction depends on desiring something stable. What is not stable is either unattainable or only sporadically attainable; any satisfaction it grants may swiftly be taken away by an accident of fortune. Of course, a person may retain unstable goods through extended good fortune, but this does not make him happy. Trygetius asks whether it would not, and Augustine replies with two questions: "Does it seem to you that someone who is afraid is happy?" and "Then can someone who loves what can be lost *not* be afraid?" The answer to both questions is no, for one who possesses unstable goods will forever be fearing their loss. Such a person could only be happy, in Monica's words, "by virtue of the moderation of his mind." Happiness is contingent on the direction of desire. Desire for what fades and passes guarantees mental distress even when we are able to possess it. Thus "we by no means doubt that if someone

16. Stock, *Augustine the Reader*, 116; quoted by Conybeare in *Irrational Augustine*, 64, note 3. Stock is correct insofar as Monica contributes little to the dialectic. Here she utters a profound truth yet misses the logical fallacy Augustine dangles for his audience, forcing Augustine to repeat the logic lesson at 4.24.

17. Especially McWilliam, "The Cassiciacum Autobiography," cited by Conybeare in *Irrational Augustine*, 64, 66. McWilliam calls *b. Vita* "Monica's dialogue" and says she stands for the church: "The Cassiciacum Autobiography," 29–30. A more recent piece is Djuth, "Augustine, Monica." Kolbet comments on the significance of Monica; see Kolbet, *Augustine and the Cure of Souls*, 103.

18. For example, *Irrational Augustine* describes Monica as "cutting to the heart of the matter," 71; and notes Augustine's "epistemological inclusivity," 80.

19. This reading also conflicts with Augustine's professed trust in reason *and* faith (*c. Acad.* 3.20.43).

20. Djuth, "Philosophy in a Time," 285–87, especially 286: "The cure for the soul's perversity, then, is a life lived in conformity with God."

sets out to be happy, he should acquire for himself that which abides forever and cannot be taken away from him by any cruel act of fortune."

In identifying and naming the only stable object of desire, Augustine adds to pagan insights. Since God is "eternal and ever abiding," he concludes that "he who has God is happy." But who has God? Augustine asks for opinions, and his audience gives three answers: Licentius's "He has God who lives well"; Trygetius's "He has God who does what God wants done"; and Adeodatus's "He has God who does not have an unclean spirit" (2.12). Lartidianus and Rusticus agree with Trygetius; Monica and Navigius agree with Adeodatus. Having heard their opinions Augustine calls a halt to this line of discussion on account of the lateness of the day, suggesting instead an intellectual dessert consisting of roasted Academicism (2.13–4). For all who do not have what they want are unhappy; all who seek are in want; the Academics seek wisdom instead of finding it; therefore they are not happy. But, since all wise men are happy, the Academics are not wise.

Licentius, who has not yet profited from the lessons in *Contra Academicos* II and III, resists these conclusions but acknowledges he has no defense against them and appeals to the absent authority of Alypius (2.14–15). Pressed by Augustine to say which premise he rejects, Licentius, "laughing testily," says he rejects the claim that not having what we desire ensures unhappiness (2.15). Since he has already assented to this premise, Augustine insists (2.15) that his testy retraction be written down. "In this way," Augustine tells us as narrator, "I kept that youth all worked up between shame and consistency," still applying his pedagogy as a therapy for Licentius's desires.[21]

The day's conversation ends with an account of the Academics, given for the less educated members of the company. Upon hearing who the Academics are, Monica says: "These men of yours are spazzes!" And with that, the day's meal and dessert are complete (2.16). We still lack a definition of "having God" and clear advice on how to reorder our desires in order to have God.

Who Has God?

The next day's business is to learn who has God, and Augustine admits, "I do not know what has been prepared for you. For there is Someone Else who does not cease to provide for all men such especially excellent dishes as these, and yet we frequently cease from eating either because of weakness

21. See above, Chapter 2, under the subheading *Academic Ironies, Lessons in Undoing Skepticism, and a Vigorous Pedagogy.*

or satiety or business" (2.17). Allusions to God's hidden ordering of our affairs are by now familiar; so is the fact that we cease to pursue what God has for us on account of the weakness of desire or on account of yielding to the distractions of life. That some, sated, abandon nourishment means that our desire for God is often too weak; we are satisfied by a mere morsel when God has much more for us.

But the company must continue eating, starting with a hearty course of discovering what it means to have God. Augustine suspects that the three definitions of "having God" are one and the same (3.17). Reconciling Licentius's definition with Trygetius's is easy, for "living well is nothing else but doing the things that please God" (3.18). Augustine asks what Adeodatus means by an "unclean spirit," and Adeodatus explains that a "clean spirit" is chaste and "pays attention to God and devotes himself to him alone." So the three definitions are the same. A happy man has God. A man who has God does what God wants, lives well, obeys God, and is devoted to God alone. So a happy man does what God wants, lives well, obeys God, and is devoted to God alone. In order to become happy, then, we must learn to obey God, become fully devoted to God, and love only God.

As it turns out, however, this is a necessary but not *sufficient* condition for having God. Augustine illustrates with a simple argument: All who seek God live well and are devoted to God, but all who seek God do not have God; so some who live well and are devoted to God do not have God (3.19). A distinction soon comes to light. We can seek God and have our desires rightly ordered toward God but not have God *yet*:

> Everyone who already has God has God well-disposed to him and is happy; but everyone who is seeking God has God well-disposed to him and is not yet happy. Moreover, whoever is alienating himself from God by vices and sins is not only not happy but he does not even live with God well-disposed to him (3.21).

Sin and vice keep us from God and so from happiness. We must seek God in order to find, and we must virtuously love Him in order to seek. Seeking is not the same as finding, but it is the only way to win God's favor. We have identified the right object of desire and seen what it means to have it. We have not determined how to go about accomplishing this. We know what ought to be desired, but we do not know what sort of therapy for desire we need. We will return to therapy after we further diagnose human misery and learn whether, while all who do not have what they desire are unhappy, the converse is also true and all unhappy people do not have what they desire.

DIAGNOSIS OF MISERY

Not having what we want is a sufficient condition for unhappiness, having what we want a necessary condition for happiness. The third day's agenda is to determine whether lacking what we want is also a necessary condition for *un*happiness. We must see "whether all who are miserable are also in need," for "if . . . reason demonstrates that this is so, then we will most perfectly discover who is happy . . ." (4.23). If lacking what we desire is necessary for unhappiness, then having what we want is sufficient for happiness. Such a conclusion, coupled with the conclusion (2.11) that having God fully satisfies our desires, would guarantee that the man who has God, and *only* that man, is happy.

While they discuss happiness Augustine continues to educate Licentius and Trygetius, nudging them closer to happiness by teaching them to contemplate immaterial reality and, ultimately, God. *De beata vita* 4.24 consists of a brief lesson in logic. Trygetius asks whether, because it is true that all who lack what they want are unhappy, the converse also follows—all who are unhappy lack what they want. Augustine gently teaches Trygetius that this does not follow and repeats the lesson in different words for the others so as not to leave anyone behind (4.25).

He then praises the happiness of the wise man, who cannot be miserable, for "How will he be miserable to whom nothing happens against his will . . . . For he has his will [set on] the most certain of things; that is, whatever he does, he does only by some precept of virtue and by the divine law of wisdom, which in no way can be taken from him" (4.25). The language is redolent of Stoic and Platonic themes, and Augustine would later recant some of it.[22] Most of the speech, however, consists of a single insight compatible with Christianity, that the wise man's happiness depends on a stable object, one he will never lose and need not fear to lose. In contrast, we are asked to consider a man who wants material goods and has all he wants (4.26). Is such a one happy? Licentius shows the fruits of his education by answering that this man is unhappy because he fears the loss of his goods. Fear is incompatible with complete happiness, but we must inevitably fear that we will lose whatever we desire yet know can easily fly away.

Nevertheless, it is left to Monica to fully diagnose his misery by pointing out that he still lacks *wisdom* (4.27). As narrator, Augustine notes that this insight is "the most powerful thing . . . a great thing from the books of the philosophers," and, as character, remarks to his audience that "a mind utterly attentive to God" is better than a mind full of many ideas. Licentius

22. See below, under the subheading *Augustine's Emerging Departure from Platonism*.

intones: "For there is no need greater and more miserable than the need for wisdom, and he who does not need wisdom cannot need anything at all." So the company agrees that misery is need, need misery (4.28–30). Having what we desire is thus sufficient for happiness. The man who has God, and only that man, is happy.

Although Augustine speaks of the virtuous man's stability, he is unlike the Stoics in not taking virtue as utterly self-sufficient, but as utterly dependent on God. Wetzel reads Augustine as adopting the Stoic position that the good man's interests are self-directed and his happiness stable because his own virtue is stable.[23] To Augustine's mind the good man's interests are directed *to God* and his happiness stable because *God* is stable. Like the Stoics Augustine speaks of turning inward toward one's own virtue; however, no man's virtue is sufficient unto itself. Virtue needs God; hence an upward turn must complete the inward turn to virtue.

Themes reflecting a Stoical bent in Augustine may well come from Ambrose as much as from Stoicism. Ambrose comments on the stability of virtue in *On the Duties of the Clergy* 2.3.8 and 2.2.4–2.4.15. In *Exposition of the Holy Gospel according to Saint Luke* 6.97–98 Ambrose says that "ye too may be a rock" if built upon Christ, the Rock. Lest there be any doubt that a Christian notion of stable virtue was available to Augustine, let us recall that at Cassiciacum he had been reading from the Psalms (*Conf.* 9.4.8) and thus would have come across Psalm 15:5's words that a righteous person "shall never be moved" (KJV), a passage to which Ambrose alludes in *Duties of the Clergy* 2.2.6. These passages also call to mind the parable in Matthew 7, where the wise man is built *on* a rock—whereas according to Seneca's Stoic philosophy a wise man *is* a rock.[24]

In short, even when he uses Stoic language, Augustine is intent on loving God in the manner of his mother at least as much as moderating desire in the manner of the Stoics.[25]

PRESCRIPTION FOR HAPPINESS

We know who is happy and what it means to be happy—what it means to have God. We do not yet know how to become such a person. We know a little about what the wise man desires, but not about the treatment of desire that makes us wise. We must now explore this. We must find what kind of a

23. Wetzel, *Augustine and the Limits of Virtue*, 119; cited by Harrison in *Rethinking*, 200.

24. Seneca's, *On the Happy Life*, 27.

25. Asiedu, "The Wise Man."

man "is not in need, for he will be wise and happy" (4.30). Knowing this, we will be better able to become such a one. In the conclusion of the dialogue we will learn that having God means living according to moderation, which is described in richly trinitarian terms. I shall first study this concluding section of the dialogue and then draw out three Christian therapies for desire. Moderation is the first therapy; according to Augustine, moderation extends even to contemplation, for the human state is embodied, and happiness requires us to live a good embodied life as long as we are in the body. In making embodiment a constituent of happiness Augustine's thought is in tension with the Plotinian philosophy of desire, which considers matter to be infected with evil and tends more strongly towards asceticism; however, at Cassiciacum the reevaluation of neo-Platonism is incomplete, since Augustine talks as if embodiment is only a temporary part of our happiness. The second and third therapies are immersion in the Christian community and prayer. The presence of these three prescriptions for desire shows the relevance of Augustine's Christian faith to his emerging theology of desire and of its conversion.

Having God Is Moderation

In hopes of learning what having God is, Augustine asks what "is the opposite of need . . . ?" (4.30). Trygetius considers saying "wealth," but realizes that its opposite is "poverty." Licentius gives a better answer, "Fullness." Augustine accepts this (4.31) and shows that fullness is having due measure and is the same as *moderation* (4.32): "Whatever, therefore, is either too much or too little is liable to need because it is in need of measure." Again, "The measure of the mind, then, is wisdom," and "In life, the first advantageous principle is this: nothing to excess." In 4.33 Augustine integrates this observation with our earlier conclusions: Happiness is not being in need, which is the same as being wise, and wisdom is "the measure of the mind"; therefore happiness is also the measure of the mind. Joining present observations with the earlier conclusion that happiness is having God (2.11), it is also true that not being in need, being wise, and having a soul governed by measure are the same as having God. This is also established by a new piece of reasoning:

> what is to be called wisdom other than the wisdom of God? We have also learned by divine authority, however, that the Son of God is none other than the Wisdom of God, and the Son of God is surely God. Therefore, whoever is happy has God, which we all determined previously when we began this banquet. But

> what do you reckon is wisdom if it is not truth? For it has also been said, "I am the Truth" (4.34).

Augustine adds a trinitarian analysis of moderation, for truth proceeds from measure; *truth* is always *about* something, for what is true describes something truly. Thus truth proceeds from what it presents truly, which is measure. In the same way the Son proceeds from the Father. Moreover, "measure is learned from the truth," for it is by learning the truth of a thing that we come to know it. In like manner, God the Father is known through God the Son. Finally, Augustine refers to the Spirit: "a certain admonition that pleads with us to remember God, to seek Him, and—after driving out all distaste—to thirst for Him flows out to us from the very font itself of truth" (4.35). We have already encountered the idea that God helps us in our search for happiness by reordering our desires (*c. Acad.* 1.1.1, *b. Vita* 1.2), and here we learn that it is the Holy Spirit specifically who reshapes our desires and teaches us to thirst for God. The Spirit applies healing grace to our souls, making it possible to desire God as we ought.

Monica recognizes Augustine's philosophical language as code for Christian truth and recites a prayer from Ambrose: "Cherish, O Trinity, those who pray" (*b. Vita* 4.35). Now she ushers in another holy triad. While Augustine admits that "we are still seeking" and "not yet wise and happy," Monica says, "we must presume that we who are hurrying to it can be brought over by a firm faith, a lively hope, and an ardent charity." There is no room for doubt that Augustine's philosophy of desire is uncompromisingly Christian.[26] Happiness is presented in clearly trinitarian terms, and *Contra Academicos*'s lesson that the three theological virtues are part of the reordering of our desires is repeated explicitly.

The last word of the dialogue is Augustine's: "This measure should be everywhere kept, everywhere loved, if our return to God is in your heart" (4.36). We must love the God who is measure, measure's truth, and the admonition to return to measure; we must do so by observing measure along the way to happiness. Since measure (the Father) is known through the truth (the Son), observing measure means imitating Christ at the admonition of the Holy Spirit. For "This, then, is the full satisfaction of souls, this is the happy life: to know piously and perfectly Him by whom you are led into the truth . . ." (4.35). We must now investigate what it means to follow the authority of the Truth who became flesh (*c. Acad.* 3.19.42) to the knowledge

26. "For Monica the happy life is not a philosophical concept or ideal but a reality to be attained by the exercise of the Christian virtues of faith, hope, and charity." Mourant, "The Emergence," 71.

of the triune God. And we must first examine the embodied character of Christian happiness.

Embodiment—At Least for Now

Strictly speaking, *De beata vita* allows for no middle ground where happiness is concerned; a person is either happy or miserable, with no space in between. This taxonomy emphasizes the nature of perfect happiness, a state admitting no degree of sadness.[27] Even so, the life which is moving towards happiness is a sort of image of the happy life. That satisfaction is knowing the Christian God has enormous implications for the imperfect form of happiness which we experience now. It shows that embodiment is not a condition to be spurned; nor does the appropriate therapy for desire consist of fleeing the influence of the body. To the contrary: Embodiment is the appropriate context for healing; we begin to be healed while in the body. While in the body we begin to "enter into the territory and land of the happy life" (1.1). Happiness, such as we know it now, is an embodied activity. We can observe various strata of evidence for the goodness of embodied existence, including the initial definition of the soul as the life of the body, the banquet context of *De beata vita*, and the continued attention to bodily health and to balancing contemplation with life.

First, 2.7's definition of the soul means that embodiment is part of the soul's good. The soul is first defined as the life of the body, and the definition expands to include the immaterial life of the soul, its pursuit of wisdom. Since food is good for the body, it is used as an analogy for the soul's "food." But embodiment means that food for the body is one of the soul's concerns. Thus we can employ the analogy in reverse: Wisdom is the soul's proper nourishment and its main concern, but nourishment for the body under its care is also part of the soul's concern.

The dramatic backdrop of the dialogue illustrates, for its occasion is a birthday dinner. If we are to take seriously the form of the dialogue, its context as well as its content, then we must admit that an embodied life, complete with bodily nourishment, is a part of happiness. The disputants at Cassiciacum have in their physical and spiritual feast a glimpse of happiness, a glimpse that would be damaged by the absence of either kind of food. Moreover, this is a *birthday* celebration. Augustine is *celebrating*, not lamenting, his bodily life. If embodiment were either lamentable or morally defective, to celebrate its beginning would be a strange move indeed. By

27. However, Augustine does speak of happiness as coming in degrees in Letter 3, a 387 correspondence with Nebridius.

contrast, consider Plotinus's attitude to the body as Porphyry describes it: "Plotinus, the philosopher our contemporary, seemed ashamed of being in the body. So deeply rooted was this feeling that he could never be induced to tell of his ancestry, his parentage, or his birthplace." As a result, "he did not desire any birthday sacrifice or feast . . . ."[28]

Furthermore, the company repeatedly observes moderation by alternating periods of rigorous debate and contemplation with periods of caring for the body through food and leisure (2.16, 3.22). Augustine interprets the principle of moderation as applying even to contemplation: Discourse must come to an end "because measure itself admonishes us to mark off our [intellectual] banquet by a certain span of days . . ." (4.36). Moderation requires limiting contemplation and living a good life in the body. If contemplation were the soul's only good and embodied life not good at all, we would expect some indication that moderation's requirement is a regrettable response to the exigencies of bodily existence. But there is none; instead the thrust of the text is that embodiment is a good, albeit a finite one.[29] Again, this runs against the disapproval of embodiment characteristic of Plotinus, who says that the philosopher "will desire nothing of this world, pleasant or painful; his one desire will be to know nothing of the body."[30]

That embodiment is proper to the soul and among its proper concerns calls for an account of rightly ordered desires which does not flee from the things of the body and which even desires a good embodied life. So long as we are embodied, a banquet is part of the happy life. A degree of asceticism is called for, to ensure the body's submission to the soul. But lunch is also called for.

Living the good life in the body is both the imitation of Christ and a therapy for desire. Just as the Son helps us know the Father, so a life of moderation helps us achieve wisdom. Moderation is life according to proper measure. Because right measure avoids sensual indulgence, it trains our hearts to love wisdom more than material things so our minds can also know wisdom. But insofar as right measure limits contemplation, it requires an active life of obedience to the Wisdom that comes to us in bodily form. The body's needs should not prevent the mind from knowing God, but neither should contemplation prevent a person from living his life. We must put a limit to contemplation and live the good life in the body as Christ

28. Porphyry, *Life of Plotinus*, chapters 1 and 3, cii–ciii.

29. Bourke: "So there is no doubt that the young Augustine regarded human bodies as good parts of creation. To suggest that our bodies are evil is a perversion of Augustinism." In "The Body-Soul Relation," 437.

30. *The Enneads*, trans. MacKenna, 1.4.14, page 43.

did. For wisdom is a person; and the happy life is a personal matter, lived in community with the man who is wisdom.[31]

Augustine's Emerging Departure from Platonism

A life of moderation is an ally of neo-Platonic teaching—to an extent. Moderation keeps us from narcissism and idolatry of the material world and frees the mind for contemplation. Yet in applying moderation to contemplation itself Augustine distinguishes his Christian philosophy from the quasi-Christian neo-Platonism for which it has occasionally been taken. The prominent embodiment of *De beata vita* undercuts the interpretation of O'Connell, who argues that Augustine, with Plotinus, considered embodiment the unfortunate result of the fall of the soul.[32] In this section I shall briefly object to O'Connell's estimation of Augustine and then respond to Conybeare's reading of *De beata vita*, which I take to be something of an overcorrection to O'Connell. Then I shall outline my own understanding of the presence of the body at Cassiciacum. Finally, I shall discuss the later development of Augustine's thought, for at Cassiciacum his affirmation of the body is less thorough than it would later become.

The evidence already cited shows that O'Connell's view cannot be entirely correct. Matter is not evil, nor physical existence regrettable. Plotinus had referred to embodiment as "enchaining" and "the burial, the encavernment, of the soul."[33] However, in Augustine's view embodiment is an *imperfect* state, not a *bad* one. Indeed, the life of the church begins in the body; far from being the result of sin, embodiment's true significance is this: It is an occasion for loving God; it is in the context of embodiment that we love God.[34] Augustine has begun to craft a distinctly Christian view of embodied life. The Incarnation—the embodiment of God—ensures that redemption begins in the body. While he will soon say that "we must completely flee from these sensible things" (*Sol.* 1.14.24), his recantation in the *Retractions* of the same remark says *not* that he was wrong to believe that matter is to be shunned, but that he was wrong to speak as if he did: "I should have been on my guard lest I be thought to hold the opinion of the

31. Fortin observes that the Christian message is by its nature "inseparable from action" and is assimilated by action taking place in this world. See "Nature of the Christian Message," 35.

32. Among many other relevant O'Connell texts is *Saint Augustine's Early Theory*.

33. From the treatise on *The Soul's Descent into Body* in *Enneads*, 4.8.4.

34. Even Origen, who saw embodiment as the result of sin, thought that embodiment was important because it is the present locus of our knowing God. See O'Keefe and Reno, *Sanctified Vision*, 133–34.

false philosopher, Porphyry, according to which every [carnal] body must be fled from."[35] Over time Augustine would more deeply appropriate the implications of the Incarnation, affirming that redemption also culminates in a resurrected body. His Christian faith affects his entire worldview. The Incarnation requires reconsidering the Plotinian account of man no less than the Trinity requires reconsidering Plotinian metaphysics.[36] We are not immaterial souls in carnal prisons; the body is the true home of the soul.

Conybeare[37] is correct to call attention to the embodied character of the dialogues. She takes the significance of embodiment as evidence that Augustine is questioning the strength and significance of neo-Platonic insights. This is partly true: Augustine is rethinking the neo-Platonists. Yet he retains key neo-Platonic insights, of which two in particular loom large at Cassiciacum: the distinction between sensible and intelligible reality and the immaterial nature of God and the soul. Embodiment is all the more significant because Augustine does not reject Platonism wholesale, but accepts these core beliefs. Rethinking the neo-Platonists at Cassiciacum is not a matter of abandoning these pillars of Platonism but of adding new Christian insights to them and rethinking the old in light of the new.

Clearly the truth lies somewhere between O'Connell and Conybeare. Carl J. Vaught's distinction between finitude and fallenness is helpful, and it holds for *De beata vita* as well as for *Confessions*.[38] Fallenness is a disordered desire for finite things. Finitude itself is not the problem.[39] There are huge implications for desire. Consider the fundamental disagreement between neo-Platonism and the prominent materialisms of the day. For Epicureans and Stoics the problem is that we desire *too much* the things in this world; the solution is *to desire less*.[40] For neo-Platonism the problem is that we desire *the things in this world*, and we must learn *to desire something else*. For Augustine the problem is that we desire things in this world *more than*

35. Augustine, *Retractions* 1.4.3.

36. See above, Chapter 1, under the heading *Ways of Understanding Augustine's Conversion and Early Writings*.

37. Conybeare, *Irrational Augustine*.

38. Vaught, *Journey toward God*, 31. Also consider Augustine's remarks in the *Nature of the Good* of 404 AD: ". . . sin is not a seeking of something evil by nature . . . the deed is the evil thing, not the thing of which the sinner makes an evil use. Evil is making a bad use of a good thing." See *Nature of the Good*, 338.

39. Harrison argues that the essential goodness of God's creation, in contradistinction to the neo-Platonic notion that the material world is an emanation from the One, is a hallmark of Augustine's early thought. See *Rethinking*, chapter 4.

40. For some Stoics it seems that the solution extends as far as the complete cessation of desire; on this see above, Chapter 1, under the heading *Ancient Philosophers and Their Therapies for Desire*.

we desire God, and the solution is *to desire God more*. Augustine's affirmation of creation synthesizes elements from all three philosophical traditions. With the neo-Platonists, he asks us to love God more than the world;[41] with other schools, he does not ask us to leave this world behind altogether. The finitude of our bodily existence is a good thing. Interestingly, Augustine distinguishes his philosophy of desire from that of all three antique schools by *not* explicitly requiring that we love the material world any less than we do, simply insisting that we give God preeminence by loving the material world *less than we love God*, and ordering our love for it according to our love for God.

One might object that this is not such a great departure from neo-Platonism after all. It is true, the objection might go, that on a Plotinian metaphysics the finitude of matter is an evil, as it is the result of matter's great distance from the immaterial One; nevertheless, the reality of matter is itself a good, insofar as it *is* real. And embodiment is a good in this sense; it is *less* good, but insofar as it *is*, it is a *good*.

The objection is quite correct that embodiment is a good insofar as matter is *real*, since on a Plotinian metaphysics all reality is derived from God. The difference is in the conception of *distance* from God as itself an evil. For, as Vaught reminds us, Christianity does not label created finitude an evil. To be embodied, on a Christian metaphysics, is to be at a distance from God as the result of being *created* to be a finite good. But on the Plotinian scheme to be embodied is to be at a distance from God as the result of a falling away from God. In Vaught's language, Plotinianism does not distinguish between finitude and fallenness.

Perhaps the objection is indeed correct that this is not such a great departure from neo-Platonism after all. My point is simply that this *is* a departure from neo-Platonism—and in the direction of Christianity.

Thus it is with the soul and the body at Cassiciacum. Still, it is a delicate task to describe with precision Augustine's relationship to neo-Platonism at Cassiciacum. For our present purposes we need only make a few observations. First, for ancient philosophy embodiment and the knowledge of an immaterial reality can coexist only with a degree of tension. Yet, and second, the Incarnation does a great deal to unite bodily life and acquaintance with the immaterial God, and this unity is displayed at Cassiciacum, particularly in the dramatic elements of *De beata vita*. After discussing these things, I shall address the growth in Augustine's teaching on embodiment after Cassiciacum.

41. *Conf.* 8.2.3 recounts how, prior to his conversion, Simplicianus congratulated Augustine for reading the Platonists, who alone among the schools of late antiquity summon the mind to the immaterial world.

A good example of the tension between embodied life and contemplation is Aristotle's *Nichomachean Ethics*, Books I–IX of which describe embodied happiness. However, in Book X, chapter 7, Aristotle suggests that embodiment is an impediment to contemplation, an obstacle to our knowledge of immaterial reality. He says, "the activity of reason, which is contemplative, seems" to be the best thing for man and the happiest activity if it can be continued long enough; however, "such a life would be too high for man . . . ." Not the privilege of mortal beings, such a perfect life is fit for a god; nevertheless, we, "being mortal, . . . must, so far as we can, make ourselves immortal . . . ." Due to the limitations of our mortality we can only hope to approximate the perfectly happy life. We dwell in the tension between the active, imperfectly happy life and the perfectly happy life for which we wish. The tension is endemic to our status as rational animals, poised between the animality and spirituality the combination of which constitutes our essential character as human beings.

De beata vita responds to this tension with playful hopefulness. The Incarnation lessens the tension.[42] The immaterial God meets us in our embodied life, and it is here that we begin to know him, and that not strictly through contemplation. At Cassiciacum Augustine has an inkling of what he later wrote in *On Teaching Christianity*, saying we are meant to love our bodies, "which being related to ourselves are in need of God's benefits through us" (1.23.22). Through the Incarnation grace gives us the wherewithal to cope with the tension, lessening its detriment to happiness. We are free now to defer to the animal side, now to the intellectual side of our nature, and the give and take between these two aspects of humanity is not for Augustine the same problem it is for Plato and Aristotle. In *Contra Academicos* 2.5.13 Augustine playfully portrays the intellectual side of life giving way to embodiment when "mother—for we were already home—began to muscle us to lunch in such a way that there was no time to talk." In *De beata vita* 2.15 the bodily desire for flour, nuts, and honey is a symbol for our desire to learn the truth by overcoming Academic skepticism: "[That argument] which you are afraid of tasting is made up of these three ingredients [for its premises]—honey, flour, and nuts, so to speak." The healing of desire need not entail the asceticism of the neo-Platonists.[43]

Though the tension's severity is lessened by the Incarnation, this side of the grave it is not completely resolved. Hence Augustine says that the limitations of the body will eventually be overcome by the disembodiment

42. Fortin remarks that the Christian message overcomes Aristotle's division of sciences into practical and theoretical; "Nature of the Christian Message," 35.

43. See above, Chapter 1, under the heading *Ancient Philosophers and Their Therapies for Desire.*

of our souls. Redemption ultimately requires departure from the body. In *Contra Academicos* 2.1.2 Augustine says that "the burden of the entire body" will eventually be set aside; in *De beata vita* 4.25 he says that the happy man has no need of bodily things because his happiness resides in "the mind itself," independent of the body's influence. The separation of the soul from the body is needed to overcome the tension of our animal and spiritual nature.[44] His thought, or at least his language, has yet to mature. He later regrets these passages—because he either believed, or at least used language that suggests, that the happy life is *eternally* disembodied. In *Retractions* 1.2 he is explicit that the redeemed state of man is no less embodied than his current state. Redemption not only begins, but continues eternally, in the body.[45] Our spiritual destiny is not disembodied; indeed, our embodied state has spiritual significance. While at Cassiciacum Augustine is clearly not the foe of embodiment O'Connell would make of him, if he believes that perfect happiness is disembodied then perhaps he retains more neo-Platonism than sits comfortably within the Christian message; at the very least he has not clarified his distinctness from this aspect of neo-Platonic thought.

This does not justify a reading of the early Augustine as sharply conflicting with the later. Harrison's analysis[46] of such readings is penetrating. A strong two-Augustines thesis haunts the writings of Boissier and Alfaric,[47] who holds that the early Augustine is a neo-Platonist, not a Christian, and the later Augustine a Christian and not a neo-Platonist. While this interpretation is now widely considered defunct, a new two-Augustines thesis, the new face of the old, has arisen.[48] The new thesis is that at Cassiciacum Augustine, while Christian, is still much more neo-Platonic than he would later become; that he is optimistic about reason's ability to know God and achieve happiness; and that only in the 390s, upon re-reading Paul, does he realize the limits of reason and the corruption of the will. Brown's 1967 biography of Augustine virtually ensured that a generation of scholars would

44. The presence of this theme in the dialogue, by the way, undermines the idea that Augustine at Cassiciacum thinks we can reach a complete happiness in this life. See above, Chapter 1, under the heading *Ways of Understanding Augustine's Conversion and Early Writings*. The notion of death also imparts an eschatological aspect to the eudaimonism of the pagan philosophers. As Harding says, writing on *City of God*, Augustine maintains the eudaimonistic goal of *beata vita*, but defers its fulfillment to the eschatological state. Thus *De beata vita* 2.10's remark is not the "we want to be happy" of the Stoic, but of the Christian; see Harding, *Augustine and Roman Virtue*.

45. See also *City of God*, Book XIX, chapter 27.

46. Harrison, *Rethinking*, 14–19.

47. Boissier; Alfaric.

48. Harrison, *Rethinking*, 16, 18.

subscribe to this interpretation.[49] Harrison cites[50] Madec as its most notable foe[51] and points out that Brown himself has since admitted he was probably wrong.[52] Harrison promotes Madec's reading and argues at length for the unity of Augustine's Christian thought.

This unity is essentially what we have found, at least with respect to embodiment. At Cassiciacum Augustine's philosophy of desire affirms embodiment as a finite good, but a good nonetheless, and a genuine constituent of happiness, if a smaller one than a knowledgeable soul. This is much more than Plotinus will allow. Although in later writings Augustine explicitly treats embodiment as a *lasting* constituent of happiness, this is no sharp conflict but a developing critique of neo-Platonism and a continuing correction of ancient philosophers. Thus Harrison: "His faith would, of course, continue to grow in understanding and maturity . . . but this should not be used as a reason to write off the works before 391 as the overly philosophical ponderings of an as yet immature, over-optimistic, Christian convert."[53] Several writers have overstated the extent to which Augustine is a neo-Platonist at Cassiciacum, and while his application of the Incarnation to the happy life is incomplete, his affirmation of embodiment as a good—*and* not an evil—already sets him apart from neo-Platonism.

Community as a Therapy for Desire

In *Enneads* Plotinus treats the contemplative's ascent as his alone.[54] In *De beata vita* ascent to God is the project of the believing community. This is most clear in the drama of the dialogue. Augustine takes pains to include everyone in the discussion, seeking everyone's opinion (2.7, 2.12), slowing down to explain the Academics to the uninitiated (2.16), and acknowledging their contributions as virtually oracular (4.31), a compliment paid not to the intellectual acumen of his relatives but to their faith and piety as part of the Christian community. Christ's healing comes through the church and

49. Brown, *Augustine*, 139–50. Another instance of this interpretation is Fredrekson, "Authority and Reason, Faith and Understanding." See Harrison's comments in *Rethinking Augustine's Early Theology*, 14–15.

50. Harrison, *Rethinking*, 17.

51. Madec, *Introduction aux 'Révisions.'*

52. Brown, *Augustine*, 490.

53. Harrison, *Rethinking*, 13. A helpful piece on Augustine's developing view of embodiment is Teske, *To Know God and the Soul*, chapter 4.

54. An indicative passage is *Ennead* 1.2 on the non-social "purificatory virtues," the only virtues sufficient for ascent to the divine.

"those healthful herbs which the Church provides."[55] The community of believers who are seeking wisdom is the context of any Christian's search; reliance on the community is a mode of advancing in the journey. If, then, desire is to be renovated it must be immersed in the Christian community. This community is engaged in the activities we found to be a part of the reordering of desire in *Contra Academicos*, and those activities are portrayed in *De beata vita*. It is bound to the authority of Christ and Scripture. It is a community of those whose desire for wisdom is being quickened and whose desires for physical things are being actively submitted to the love of God. It is committed to moderation and to living a life that harmonizes the good of the body and the good of the soul. It actively pursues Monica's "firm faith," "lively hope," and "ardent charity." It is, finally, a community united in prayer, as we will consider momentarily.

We may well wonder, however, whether and to what extent community is any *more* than a therapy, or what role community plays when ascent to God has been completed. We will examine this in chapter 6.

Prayer as a Therapy for Desire

Scholars may disagree on the sincerity of religious observances in Platonic dialogues,[56] but in Augustine's dialogues prayer is unequivocal. A character who prays (Monica in *b. Vita* 4.35, Licentius in *c. Acad.* 2.7.18) or mentions prayer (Augustine in *c. Acad.* 1.1.1, 2.1.1, 2.3.8) prays to the trinitarian God who reveals himself to men through the history of the Hebrew people and through the Incarnation, the God whose authority is maintained by Scripture and the church.[57] Indeed, it is the community who prays: Augustine and his friends pray for Romanianus (*c. Acad.* 1.1.1), and Monica prays on behalf of the group at the end of *De beata vita*. The renovation of desire needs the help of God, and we must collectively seek his help through prayer.

This brings us back to Monica's insights. We have seen that desiring God is the only way to be happy and that this requires virtuous living. But

55. *Conf.* 9.4.7.

56. The ambiguity of religion in Plato's dialogues allows for divergent interpretations. Vlastos reads Socrates as testing the gods with reason and developing a rationalistic natural theology, effectively placing reason above the gods. According to Brickhouse and Smith, Socrates's reason is not above the gods. See Vlastos, "Socratic Piety;" Brickhouse and Smith, "Socrates' Gods."

57. Kevane remarks: "References to prayer abound in the philosophical dialogues and could well be made the object of a separate study. It could well be a study in contrasts, for the spirit of prayer is notably absent from the pagan philosophers, even at their best . . . ." See "Christian Philosophy," 79.

the conversion of desire requires God's help; pride must be overcome and prayers offered to God; we must imitate Christ and immerse ourselves in the life of the church. The sum of *De beata vita*'s insights on desire is this: A person with rightly ordered desires loves God, and through Christian holiness we can become such people. *De beata vita* is much more than a combination of Ciceronian and Plotinian themes. The dialogue is thoroughly Christian in form and content, in inspiration and orientation. While the therapy for desire suggested by Plato's *Phaedo* and by Plotinus is to flee the body's influence as much as possible, for Augustine the central treatment of desire is not "Flee the body's influence!" It is, instead: "Flee to Christ!"; "Flee to the church!"; "Pray to the Trinity!"; and "Practice the theological virtues!"

4

The Desire to Know Order and to Be Ordered

In previous dialogues Augustine has shown that happiness is possible and consists in community with the Triune God through the Incarnation. *De ordine*[1] has two rather obvious challenges. The first is the problem of evil: How is it that there is evil in a universe ordered by God? The second challenge is a problem pertaining to education: How is it that we can know the order in the universe? A liberal arts education presents itself as a solution to both challenges, and Augustine recommends it for Licentius and Trygetius to help them understand order and evil and contemplate God.

The dialogue's theme, order, plays several roles. First, it is a solution to the problem of evil. When the order of the universe is understood, the existence of evil in it is also understood. Second, our souls need order. An ordered soul is necessary for knowing order as well as for knowing and loving God. Third, a liberal arts education is a powerful tool for inculcating order in the soul and is a therapy for the renewal of the soul's desires. Augustine would later come to regret his overly high esteem of the liberal disciplines in *De ordine*, but even at Cassiciacum the liberal disciplines are presented in a new and Christian setting. A liberal arts education is not a *necessary* condition for inculcating order in the soul. Monica shows that Christian piety is more effective at this than any pagan therapy for desire. While the pagan philosophers identified some of the virtues of a rightly ordered soul, it is impossible to become such a person without divine aid. Pride stands in the way of rightly ordered desires. We need grace to overcome pride, and

1. Augustine, *On Order* (referenced in text as *Ord.*).

the correct response to grace is humility. The liberal arts, while useful, do not stand on their own, but are reoriented towards the love of God. Moreover, while they are helpful to some, all must follow the path of Christian piety, submitting in humility to the authority of Christ, if their desires are to be reordered. A person with correctly ordered desires possesses a perfectly stable happiness. As we are still journeying to this happiness, we must pray for God's help in finally reaching it.

In what follows I shall look at Augustine's introduction of these issues in his cover letter to Zenobius (Part One) and at the questions regarding order raised in the beginning of the dialogue through its setting and its content (Part Two). Then I shall examine Augustine's discussion of order with Licentius and Trygetius and the juxtaposition of the lads' pride with Monica's humility (Part Three). Then I shall discuss two paths of ascent to God, the liberal arts and the way of Christian piety (Part Four). Finally, I shall discuss the stability of the wise man's happiness, rooted in the stability of what he desires (Part Five).

DESIRING TO KNOW ORDER: THE PROLOGUE TO *ORD.*

In his letter to Zenobius Augustine claims that we desire, or ought to desire, to know order. In particular, we need to know how evil fits into God's ordering of the universe. In knowing order we must neither attribute evil to God nor deny his omnipotence. Augustine introduces an analogy from artistic wholes that helps us understand evil. But order must be replicated in our souls if we are to understand it. Thus the need to know God's order is also the need to know ourselves: to know the soul's nature as an immaterial substance, what order is in the soul, what order is lacking, and how it can be restored. Good habits, a good education, and meditative solitude help restore order by returning our minds and desires to the unity of order and away from everyday multiplicity and its appearances of disorder.

De ordine opens thus: "To grasp and retain the order of things proper to each, and then indeed to see or explain the order of the whole by which this world is held together and ruled—that, Zenobius, is extremely rare and difficult for men to do" (1.1.1). It is hard to know and teach order. The problem is as much with *us* as with the difficulty of the subject matter; we must be worthy to know and teach order, and we need either virtue or education. *De ordine*'s purpose is less to teach order than to train us for becoming worthy to understand and teach it ourselves. For there is a relationship between order in the universe and order in our souls: In order to *know* order we must first *be* ordered.

But know it we must, for "there is nothing that" that men of good character "more avidly long for and are eager to hear and learn about than how it is that God could care for the affairs of men when so much perversity is dispersed everywhere throughout human activities that it hardly seems attributable to divine management . . ." (1.1.1). We ought to want to know order, particularly evil's place in it—a mature form of the desire for wisdom with which *Contra Academicos* is concerned.

Evil is often explained by denying God's power to administer the universe or by attributing evil to God; "Both positions are impious, but especially the latter" (1.1.1).[2] We must avoid both extremes. There is evidence in nature of God's ordering of the universe (1.1.2).[3] Evil is not irrefutable evidence against God's being both benevolent and omnipotent. Our perspective on evil is limited: "if someone could see so little that in viewing a mosaic his eye could take in no more than the measure of one little cube, he would criticize the artisan as ignorant of order and composition" (1.1.2). An artisan whose knowledge of order vastly exceeds our own manages the universe.[4] A man who charges God with responsibility for evil is like a man who assaults an artist's understanding of aesthetics because one square of his mosaic is a bilious shade of green. We must learn to see more of the mosaic, to see the universe from a higher perspective.

To understand the universe from a better perspective, we must understand ourselves: "The greatest cause of this error is that man is unknown to himself" (1.1.3). Again, the problem lies not simply with the difficulty of the subject matter but also with us. Our ability to understand order is limited by our mental weakness and our moral disorders. In learning our true nature we also learn the nature of order. For our soul operates according to the

2. Given their doctrine that the God of the Old Testament is different from the God of the New, the former responsible for evil and the latter less than omnipotent, we can actually attribute both impieties to the Manicheans!

3. In citing this evidence Augustine cautiously, quietly agrees with the Stoics. However, while they treat order in nature as sufficient evidence for the existence of God and his ordering of the universe, Augustine appeals to it briefly, gives a Ciceronian objection to the account, and then moves on to suggest his analogy. At the end of *Ord.* Augustine has not given an account of God's ordering of the universe. This suggests that the Stoics had only a piece of the puzzle; order in nature has some strength as evidence for God's existence and ordering of the universe, but by itself does not overcome the problem of evil. See Balbus's Stoic argument in Book II of Cicero, *The Nature of the Gods*, 97 (page 82) and Cotta's reply in Book III, 63 (page 130) and 65 (page 132). Lactantius's response to the Stoic presentation of order in the universe is similar to Augustine's; see Lactantius, *Anger of God*, chapter 13.

4. Augustine strikes a helpful contrast with Epicurus, who thinks the universe operates independently of divine influence. For Augustine, belief that God orders the universe comforts us; for Epicurus, it is *non*-belief that is comforting.

same principles which guide the universe. Comparing the soul to the center of a circle, Augustine hints at what it needs to learn about itself. The key to knowledge is to know one's own soul, and specifically to recognize its immateriality. A "soul thus returned to itself" will be able to "understand what is the beauty of the whole" (1.2.3). The soul is the midpoint of knowledge, a focal point without understanding which we can understand little else. Knowing the immateriality of one's soul makes possible the ascent to knowledge. Like the center of a circle, the soul does not exist within extended space; we know it by knowing the truths of the immaterial world.

Augustine suggests three strategies by which we can know ourselves, ways of "collecting the soul into itself and holding itself there" (1.1.3). We need "the great habit of withdrawing from the senses"[5] and into the mind. We need a liberal arts education, "by which the soul is purged and cultivated" (1.2.4).[6] Finally, we need solitude (1.1.3), the discipline of solitary contemplation whose practice is illustrated in the *Soliloquia*.

The mind's path of ascent towards the contemplation of order runs alongside the heart's path towards renewed desires. For: "The soul thus returned to itself, it understands what is the beauty of the whole [*universitas*], which indeed comes from the word 'one' [*unum*]" (1.2.3). Order belongs to the whole; the seeming disorder of evil pertains to its parts.[7] The mind must be centered on the whole if we are to understand order; so also must desire be centered on the whole, for "the more the soul tries to embrace plurality, the more it ends up suffering from want." The soul's true good is to contemplate and delight in unity. In chasing after multiplicity our souls become impoverished.

The recommendation to contemplate and settle our desires on the whole rather than its parts is a Stoic trope.[8] Augustine reuses this pagan insight on how we ought to conceive of the universe. The language of unity and multiplicity also links the notion of the whole to neo-Platonic insights, particularly the immateriality of the principles by which the universe is governed and the need for a rigorous pedagogy if we are to contemplate

5. In *Retractions* 1.3.2 Augustine confirms that it is the influence of the bodily senses we must resist.

6. On the liberal arts Augustine knew and the debate over his sources, see Vessey's "Introduction" and Shanzer's "Augustine's Disciplines."

7. Evans says of Augustine's writings on evil that his view is "a man-centred view of the problem" in that it attributes evil to man rather to God. Although *Ord.* does not emphasize the origins of evil in man, it clearly shares with Augustine's later commentary the notion that evil cannot be attributed to God, but to something within the whole. See Evans, *Augustine on Evil*, x–xi.

8. Aurelius recommends considering the whole as a therapy for desire in *Meditations*, 4.40.

it. Augustine also reuses these neo-Platonic insights by melding them with Christian truth, including the understanding of order as the work of the triune God. The neo-Platonic insights are at odds with the materialism of the Stoic account of order. And the Christian insights are at odds with the neo-Platonic notion of an impersonal order governing the universe. Augustine will develop all these insights as the dialogue unfolds.

LEAVES, MICE, AND PHILOSOPHICAL INSPIRATION

De ordine's opening scenes illustrate the need for order in our souls and for the divine help that imparts order to our souls. Licentius has an insight, realizing that order encloses everything. Augustine asks him to discuss order and its apparent exceptions, hoping to show him that order is more than the necessity of material causation. Instead, Licentius reveals the disorder in his own desires. Augustine continues to train his charge in a rigorous pedagogy, which cultivates order in the soul. Order exists on two levels, cosmological and psychological. Both levels pertain to desire. We should love the order of the universe, administered by God. We love this order when our own souls are ordered. Pedagogy alone will not get us there; we need God to heal our desires.

Licentius's Distraction and Light

The dialogue's beginning is a delightful mix of literary form and dialogical content, uniting the notion of order with an example of events that seem disordered. In this scene Licentius displays both a keen insight and a distracted heart, and Augustine responds by pushing him on in the search for wisdom.

Somewhere between midnight and dawn, Augustine lies awake thinking. As narrator he informs us that he regularly spends half the night thinking in an effort to "habituate the soul to be at home with itself" (1.3.6),[9] practicing the solitude mentioned in the cover letter. He hears a strange rhythm coming from the water running behind the baths: It tends to flow at first more loudly, then more quietly, then loudly again. While he is wondering at it, he hears Licentius throw a piece of wood at some annoying mice. He asks Licentius if he has noticed the rhythm in the water. Licentius and Trygetius both say they have heard it before, and Augustine asks why

9. Augustine is obeying the advice of Ps 4:4, which he has been reading (*Conf.* 9.4.8).

they think the water makes the noise (1.3.7). Licentius offers an explanation: Some autumn leaves have fallen into the water works; they intermittently cluster, clog the flow, and return to where they started. Augustine decides to use the opportunity to teach them and asks whence wonder arises "if not an unusual thing outside of the manifest order of causes?" (1.3.8).

Licentius makes an enlightened response: "I accept 'outside of the manifest,' for it seems to me that nothing is done outside of order." Augustine, more pleased than usual with his students, congratulates Licentius and requests that he defend the proposition while Augustine challenges it (1.3.8). But Licentius asks to be left alone, for, he explains, "I have fixed my mind intently onto something else," namely love poetry, which he now begins to sing. Licentius is like a younger Augustine (*Conf.* 1.13.20), caring more for Dido's tragedy than the tragedy of his own soul. Augustine rebukes him, comparing the wall between Pyramus and Thysbe to the barrier poetry has placed between Licentius and the truth he ought to love.[10] Licentius's affection for love poetry[11] exceeds his desire for wisdom, preventing him from following through on the insight that all things are within order.[12]

Augustine's rebuke is, luckily, effective. Licentius returns to Augustine's professorial authority and to that of philosophy (1.3.9). He compares himself to the mice, saying that if he has the right to rebuke them then he also ought to submit to the rebuke of his teacher. Thus he shows that he is able to think about the order of the universe and submit to his own place in it.

Augustine rejoices (1.4.9). Trygetius agrees to the conversation and says that he favors order but would like to discuss it carefully so he can be certain. Augustine remarks that his uncertainty is probably shared by all, but Licentius says he is "utterly certain," adding that fear of finding the truth is more dangerous than the distraction of poetry. Here Trygetius rightly observes that Licentius has abandoned Academicism! He has come far since Book I of *Contra Academicos*, perhaps a little too far; his abandonment of Academicism is an overcorrection, for his confidence in order is a bit too Stoical. He will have to learn to avoid both the epistemic servility of Academicism and the overconfidence of Stoicism. The right way runs upward through a liberal arts education to Christ. Augustine hints at the end of this journey by modifying a prayer from *Aeneid* 10.875, "May God

10. Even as he criticizes the effects of love poetry on the soul of a young man, Augustine reuses poetry by making of it an allegory for the soul's plight. On reusing poetry, see *c. Acad.* 3.6.13.

11. Some connection to *Conf.* 3.1.1, where Augustine is "in love with love," may be appropriate.

12. On Licentius's disorder and Augustine's longing for him to be healed, see Silk, 24.

the Father make it so!" He explains that the worship of Apollo is utterly mistaken ("Apollo is not 'High'"!) and that it is Christ whom we must trust to lead us, "worshippers depending on piety," to the truth and to cleanse our disordered affections.

Apparent Exceptions to Order

In the next scene Augustine asks Licentius to account for the order of seemingly disordered events. Licentius's responses shows that he has a partial understanding of order: He can recognize the ordering of material cause, but little beyond that.

The leaves in the water channel are a fitting example for Augustine's query. The channel was constructed by men according to design, not so the leaves (1.4.11). Licentius claims the leaves are subject to a system of cause and effect, since the laws of nature made them fall. He says that "nothing is done without a cause" and adds that, even when things happen outside of human industry, "nature, which has produced them, is never random."[13] His words convey insight: Causality's long arm reaches down to the minutest details and can be seen in the laws of physical nature. But he has much to learn about order. He has a good eye for what Aristotle called material and efficient cause, but not for final or formal cause.[14] Accordingly, he has to think a little harder when Augustine asks about the *purpose* of things in nature that do not provide some good for men, thereby raising the problem of evil (1.5.9). Licentius recognizes the challenge, but flags in his defense of order and tries to renege his commitment to defend it (1.5.12–13). Augustine encourages him to keep up his disputation, suggesting as an analogy (1.5.14) that the very leaves in the water channel seem to resist the order that carries them along; so Licentius should not resist the order that carries him through a philosophical discussion. Though Licentius has yet to reconcile the order that tosses leaves and the order that arranges our lives, Augustine hopes that he (and we) will be well on the way to doing so after the dialogue, embracing our place in order. The incident thus shows the relationship of Augustine's pedagogy[15] and order. By training him to be steady

13. Evans attributes this remark to Augustine rather than to Licentius. Evans, *Augustine on Evil*, 94.

14. See Aristotle, *Physics*, 2.3. Cicero's Cotta in *The Nature of the Gods* criticizes the Stoic view because it treats the order of nature as evidence for providence; if the Stoic view is right, then bad things that happen by natural order (such as fever) should be attributed to providence. See Book III, 24–25 (116).

15. See above, Chapter 2, under the subheading *Academic Ironies, Lessons in Undoing Skepticism, and a Vigorous Pedagogy* and Chapter 3 under the subheading *Only*

in the pursuit of wisdom Augustine reforms his desires and instills order in his soul.

For the moment, it works. Licentius is encouraged to continue and inspired to raise an encomium on order (1.5.14), beginning thus: "Who can deny, O Great God, that You administer all things by order?" It is a good beginning, for he rightly attributes order to God. However, he needs training. The speech is explicitly dogmatic, the opposite of his earlier skepticism. He cites divination as evidence of order, reducing its operations to necessity:

> any flittering about of leaves in a field, anything that a worthless little critter does in a house, are just as necessary in the order of things . . . . Now, I pray, let no one ask me why something is done. It suffices that nothing is done, nothing is born, that is not generated and moved by some cause.

This is a quasi-Stoic view: God, via necessity, administers the universe.[16] Licentius's mind is enlightened enough to know that order governs the universe, and his desires are ordered enough to delight in the fact. But he badly misunderstands the character of order, just as his desires are in need of reformation.

Augustine gently reproves Licentius for his naïve remarks on divination, reminding him that he needs to study more:

> It appears, young man, that you do not know how many things have been said against divination, and by what caliber of men.[17] But answer me now—not whether something may be done without a cause, for I already see that you do not wish to answer it—but whether this order you have been defending seems to you to be good or evil.

This is a shrewd maneuver, possibly able to show Licentius that problems afflict his idea of order as grounded in necessity. We must distinguish the nature of things done in order from the nature of order itself. If no distinction holds between order and the things within it, then either nothing within order is evil or order is also evil. Licentius places both order and what is ordered within the bounds of necessity and thus fails to make such a distinction.

God Will Satisfy.

16. I do not consider Licentius's inspiration to faithfully represent Plotinus; see Cary, "What Licentius Learned," 148. Necessity is also a hallmark of Manicheanism; see Augustine, *Nature of the Good*, paragraph XLII.

17. We have already encountered problems with divination. See Chapter 2, under the subheading *Licentius Versus Trygetius*. Also see Klingshirn, "Divination."

If Licentius is certain that necessity governs the universe, he ought to be able to give an account of it.[18] He answers that order is neither good nor evil (1.6.15). It is in some sense beyond good and evil, although he lacks words for describing this (1.6.16). Trygetius argues to the contrary. For God loves order, and order is from God. Therefore, if evil is within order, then God loves it and it comes from God (1.7.17). Licentius answers that God loves order, but not all the things contained within order. God does not love evil; through order God overcomes evil (1.7.18). He follows with the argument that order must include evil things, for God is just; justice is "distributing to each its own"; this distribution requires a moral distinction among things; and no such distinction is possible unless some things are evil (1.7.19). Augustine now says that they will continue their discussion in the morning and promises to send a record to Zenobius, with whom he has previously discussed order. This remark re-invites Zenobius to participate in the dialogue, and it invites us to participate as well.[19]

Licentius has the last word before morning: "Something (I know not what) has at this moment shone brightly in me with a different, a far different, light. Philosophy is more beautiful, I admit, than Thysbe, than Pyramus, than that Venus and Cupid and all such loves of every sort" (1.8.21). At last he loves philosophy more than poetry, privileging it over philocaly (*c. Acad.* 2.3.7). The healing of his disordered affections is a part of order and attributable to a rich nexus of causes. Context suggests three: Augustine's stern pedagogy, Licentius's acquiescence, and the practice of philosophy. His words suggest another, divine cause, and "with a sigh he gave thanks to Christ." Joanne McWilliam correctly observes that Licentius, like Augustine before him, could not be healed without Christ.[20] Desire's conversion requires divine assistance.

The Healer of Desires

The end of the dialogue's beginning consists of a morning conversation between Augustine and Licentius followed by their pausing to watch a cockfight. The conversation suggests that only God is able to reorder our desires

18. Similarly, Cicero's Cotta says in *Nature of the Gods*, Book III, that Balbus ought to be able to explain things in the universe that do harm to man. Lactantius also faults the Stoics for their failure to account for evil; see *On the Anger of God*, chapter 13.

19. Douglass, "Voice Re-Cast," 41. Also see above, Chapter 2, under the subheading *Two Visions of the Happy Life*, on *c. Acad.* inviting the reader to learn alongside its characters.

20. McWilliam, "The Cassiciacum Autobiography," 35–36.

and that we should pray to God for this. The cockfight shows that order is an appropriate object of desire, something we ought to love.

After singing a prayer from Psalm 79:8, asking that God "convert us" (1.8.22), Licentius approaches Augustine for a personal chat (1.8.23). Having recently loved love poetry so much, he now finds it repulsive. He marvels at the conversion of his own desires, asking, "Is this not truly being converted to God?" Augustine remarks that the conversion itself "pertains to order" and asks: "what else is it to be converted, if not to be turned from the immoderation of vices and lifted up to Him by virtue and temperance?" He admonishes Licentius to yield to God's healing and the instrument he often uses, the liberal arts. For "If you care about order, . . . an education in the liberal disciplines produces lovers more lively, more persevering, and more groomed for embracing the truth; and as a result they more ardently desire, more consistently pursue, and finally, more sweetly cling to . . . the happy life" (1.8.24). The education of the intellect and the conversion of the heart are bound together. The liberal arts are meant to return our hearts to the love of God. As Topping says, "In the *De ordine*, the liberal arts are a means of the soul's reparation. The curriculum is valuable insofar as it helps to heal the soul, and sustain it on its journey toward God."[21]

God, the physician who heals our desires, administers that return. At the mention of the happy life,

> all men lift themselves up and pay attention . . . . Yet when wisdom begins to admonish them to bear with the physician and to allow themselves to be cared for with some patience, they fall back . . . . they would more gladly scratch the itchy scab of dolorous pleasures than be restored to the sound state of healthy men and to the light by enduring and submitting to the physician's warnings, which for a little while are hard . . . (1.8.24).

This sets ancient ideas in a Christian context. Pagan philosophers had long used the analogy of a physician for the soul. Doctors know the body's proper function and how to maintain its health; similarly, we ought to follow the advice of anyone who knows the soul's proper function and how to maintain its health.[22] God is able to heal our souls, although his treatment of our desires can be painful (*b. Vita* 1.4). The word "admonish" suggests the Spirit. The word "wisdom" calls Christ to mind, recalling passages such as *Contra Academicos* 3.19.42 and *De beata vita* 2.4, which advise submission

21. Topping, *Happiness and Wisdom*, 128.

22. Plato explores this theme in the *Protagoras*. Cicero continues the tradition in *On Duties* 1.136, comparing a harsh rebuke for bad behavior to surgery. Also see above, Chapter 1, under the heading *Ancient Philosophers and Their Therapies for Desire*.

to Christ for our soul's healing. Biblical passages are also in the background of this passage, such as Mark 2:17 and Luke 5:12–32.[23] The image of Christ as the great physician is the correct application of the pagan analogy.[24] Submission to God is necessary for the renovation of our desires, and thus the only way to be happy. So Augustine insisted on including the name of Christ in the dialogues so they would be full of "those healthful herbs which the Church provides."[25] Or, as Ambrose says, "So if we wish ourselves to be healed, let us in faith touch Christ's hem."[26]

Augustine now encourages Licentius to pursue the reordering of his own desires by using poetry correctly. When Pyramus's and Thysbe's desires lead to their deaths, the astute reader of poetry has "a most suitable opportunity" to "satirize the curse of" disordered desires; we should learn from poetry the dangers of disordered affections, letting the tale of sordid desire be the lesson that drives us to better desire.[27]

Our characters now proceed to the morning's business (1.8.25). On their way to the baths they notice two cocks fighting. They stop to watch and reflect, finding order in the display, which was "well-harmonized to the laws of nature and beautiful." The episode suggests that Augustine is suffering from the pleasure in animal violence he would renounce in *Confessions* 10.35.57. Yet even here he emphasizes the love of finer things. They discuss the order displayed in the fight itself, the order of their own minds as they watch the spectacle, and the order of the laws that regulate the universe (1.8.26). The thought of these laws leads them, "admonished by all this that there should be a measure to our watching," to cease. The incident contains two lessons about desire. First, we are to love the order that manages the universe more than the things in it. Second, we should conform our own desires to and order our own lives by the same order. This is just what their school will try to do as they discuss order in the remainder of the dialogue.

ARGUING ABOUT ORDER

To preserve his health Augustine leads no more disputation this day (again illustrating the lessons articulated in *De beata vita* 1.8.26). The next day brings a lively dialogue on order. Augustine begins with a remark on the

23. For Ambrose's commentary on this passage, see *Exposition of the Holy Gospel*, 5.1–15.

24. On Christ as physician in the dialogues, see Doucet, "Le thème du médecin," 447–61; cited in Cooper, "Scripture at Cassiciacum," 39–40, n. 69.

25. *Conf.* 9.4.7.

26. Ambrose, *Exposition of the Holy Gospel*, 6.58.

27. Plutarch's *How a Young Man Should Study Poems* uses a similar strategy.

importance of the topic: "order is that which, if we keep it in [this] life, will lead us to God, and which, unless we keep it in [this] life, we will not come to God" (1.9.27). After integrating this remark with insights from previous dialogues, I shall discuss the dramatic juxtaposition of pride in Augustine's students with Monica's humble faith. The one is a deep disorder of desires and prevents us from attaining wisdom; the other will heal our desires and lead us into wisdom. Then I shall discuss the order appropriate to an embodied soul. This order requires both love of the immaterial God and care for the body's needs. Finally, I shall discuss Licentius's and Trygetius's lesson that evil is a privation of good, and as such has a place in order.

Augustine wants Licentius and Trygetius to learn the distinction between order and things within it in hopes that they will be able to know order and become more ordered themselves. The journey to God reorders our lives, including both the intellectual and affective aspects of our souls. Previous lessons on Christian living and the ordering of desire are thus revealed as lessons on order. *Contra Academicos* 2.9.22 shows that right doctrine and right desires are two sides of the same coin. *De beata vita* 3.34 explicitly tells us that this coin is of the Christian currency; right thinking and right living are only possible in context of Christian community. *De ordine* shows that the restoration of mind and heart by participating in the life of the church is a restoration of *order*.

Pedagogy, Rhetoric, and Humility

After lamenting the absence of Alypius and Zenobius Augustine promises that the discussion will be written down for their sake and announces his intention to oppose Licentius on order (1.9.27). Then he asks Licentius to "sum up what this order of yours is with a definition" (1.10.28). Licentius shudders at the prospect of a definition, but then has a sudden inspiration and, after a thoughtful moment of silence, proffers that "Order is that through which all things God has constituted are guided." The definition is apt for discussing order, but it leads into an unexpected reminder of orthodoxy and a harsh exercise in training desire. The event dramatically illustrates the spiritually therapeutic value of pedagogy and of rightly ordered rhetoric; it also portrays the dangers of pride and shows how humility can help overcome pride and reorder our desires.

Augustine first asks Licentius, "Does not God Himself seem to you to be guided by order?" (1.10.29). He hopes to drive a wedge in Licentius's mind between order and the things within it. If he can learn the difference then he will be able to contemplate God appropriately, not according to the categories of things contained within order. For the relationship of order and that which is within it is different from the relationship of order and God.

Licentius answers in the affirmative. As Trygetius points out, this sets up order above God (1.10.29). Licentius suggests that this is acceptable, for the Son is sent from and under the authority of the Father. Thus God (the Son) is guided by order, and yet God (the Father) guides all things through order. Trygetius says he is confused and unsure how to respond, so Licentius presses him: "Will we therefore deny that the Son of God is God?" Trygetius suggests that "God" does not properly denote the Son, but only the Father. God (the Father) guides all things by order, and is not himself guided by order.

In his stubborn opposition to the impiety of positing an order above God Trygetius has strayed into a worse, outright heretical, impiety: the denial that Christ is indeed God. So Augustine reprimands him: "You had better pull yourself together, for the Son is not improperly called God."[28]

This attention to Christian orthodoxy represents not merely an epistemological adjustment to neo-Platonism—taking Scripture and church teaching as sources of knowledge. It is also a metaphysical correction to Plotinian thought. Plotinus's metaphysics acknowledges three transcendent divine realities: the One, Mind, and Soul. But these three are not equal: The One is superior to Mind, and both are superior to Soul. The Christian teaching that God the Father and God the Son are equally God, affirmed here by Augustine, and that the Holy Spirit also is equally God, is irreconcilable with Plotinus's metaphysics. Even scholars who tend to read Augustine as fully Christian *and* neo-Platonist recognize the significance of this.[29] What must be emphasized is that this difference affects Augustine's entire project at Cassiciacum. As Kolbet says, "philosophy at Cassiciacum became a certain psychagogy that used words (*uerba*) to lead its adherents to things (*res*)."[30] And the thing, the reality to which he is leading Licentius and Trygetius, is *God* (or, we might say, the *realities* to which he is leading them are the persons of the Holy Trinity). The *telos*, the goal, of the entire wisdom-seeking enterprise has shifted.

28. *Contra* O'Connell, McWilliam correctly takes this remark as evidence that Augustine has given up his earlier Photinianism; though not mentioning this particular heresy, Holt also takes the passage as evidence of orthodox Christology. See *Conf.* 7.19.25; O'Connell, "Alypius' Apollinarianism," 210; McWilliam, "The Cassiciacum Autobiography," 39; Holt, "Wisdom's Teacher," 52.

29. For example, Cary, *Augustine's Invention*, 59.

30. Kolbet, *Augustine and the Cure of Souls*, 92.

Now the lads' mistake is the result of pride. They have been arguing to win rather than to reach the truth, but love of victory has only led them into error. Augustine insists that Trygetius's words be written down, and Licentius agrees, delighting in his friend's humiliation. When Licentius is now scolded, Trygetius laughs. Augustine (as author) laments that they are behaving "in the manner of boys, or rather of men and of (O the horror!) almost everybody—as if indeed the case were being set in motion among us for the sake of glory!" The misplaced love of oneself is common to adults and children alike, shattering adult pretentions to have overcome the sins of childhood.[31] Augustine (as character) censures his students:

> This is not the way you act, is it? Are you not moved by the fact that we are oppressed and overwhelmed by massive piles of vice and shadows of ignorance? Is this your recent attentiveness and ascent towards God and truth over which a little while ago I, fool that I am, rejoiced? O if you would see, even with eyes as bleary as mine, in what dangers we lie, and what a deranged disease this laughing of yours indicates! (1.10.29)

The lads, oblivious to their sin, have not rectified it by pursuing truth but rather added to it by pursuing glory. Augustine expresses his grief by describing how much he laments his own sin and how "I beg God almost daily with weeping," praying for healing from his sins. He begs them not to add to his discontent with his own sins by reveling in their own, saying that if they have any affection for him and "If you gladly call me teacher, then render me the fee: be good." Here we see Augustine's rhetoric used as a therapy for the healing of desire. As Kolbet says, Augustine "would need to undermine one rhetoric by means of another rhetoric. For his students' own good, he would appeal not only to their reason, but also to their non-rational faculties."[32]

Tears force him to break off (1.10.30). Licentius, "taking it very badly that everything was being written down," audaciously asks what they have done wrong, so Augustine scolds them again for their "love of an utterly vain praise." He says that they are "trying to introduce and implant into philosophy and into the life that I rejoice at last to have embraced a pest lowest in rank yet more injurious than all the others." Licentius promises repentance but begs that the matter not be recorded. Trygetius disagrees;

31. Here we may recall what Augustine noticed in school, recorded in *Conf.* 1.9. McLynn uses a similar methodology in "Disciplines of Discipleship;" McLynn looks to Augustine's experience in school at Carthage as a source on Cassiciacum. In our own day, what scholar has never witnessed the love of victory replace the love of truth at an academic conference or in a scholarly journal or graduate seminar?

32. Kolbet, *Augustine and the Cure of Souls*, 91.

"Let our punishments remain, so that the fame which entices us may deter us from loving it with its own whip." Finally Licentius agrees. The episode evinces the profound presence of sin and its root,[33] pride, in us all. The dark love of one's own glory threatens all who would enter the land of the happy life.[34]

At the same time, however, the episode hopefully suggests several means of combating pride. One of these is submission to a stern pedagogue. The power of pedagogy to reform our desires, visible since *Contra Academicos*, is here linked to the overcoming of pride. In Augustine's own education, and in his work as an educator in the schools of rhetoric, pedagogy encouraged pride, and at Cassiciacum he is busy reinventing a pedagogy more suited to the pursuit of wisdom and of God.[35] Another approach to pride is suggested by Trygetius's actions; when administered by a wise teacher, shame allows pride to turn in on itself and have a hand in its own correction.[36] The lads' love for their own esteem teaches them that that very love is unworthy of esteem. That they understand their sin and repent of it shows there is hope for them: Order will be written in their souls yet.

Monica the Philosopher

But the only cure for this greatest threat to reordered desires is the way of life observed by Monica. When she enters and asks what has been accomplished, Augustine asks that this be recorded. Monica asks what he is doing, and whether women have ever been involved in philosophical dialogue. Augustine defends his mother's inclusion in the philosophical community. His speech shows several things. First and most obviously, it shows the inclusivity of the Christian account of the happy life. Second, it shows once again the superior ability of religious piety to bring people to wisdom and

33. See above, chapter 2, under the subheading *Christ: Towards a Christian Theology of Desire*.

34. Recall how *b. Vita* 1.3 says pride also lures men out of the very port of philosophy.

35. Holt explains how this scene shows the difference between the Cassiciacum school and Augustine's old rhetoric school. The latter was oriented to the love of praise, but the former is oriented toward good character and orthodoxy; see Holt, "Wisdom's Teacher." Kolbet notices this also; see Kolbet, *Augustine and the Cure of Souls*, 90–92.

36. Augustine was familiar with shame being turned against sensual desire. He had by now almost certainly heard how shame had once turned his mother away from alcohol (*Conf.* 9.8.18), and he may have read Porphyry's account of how a playmate's insult caused Plotinus to be ashamed of breastfeeding past infancy. See Porphyry, *Life of Plotinus*, paragraph 3, page ciii. In addition, Aristotle had explained how shame can be "an effective method for correcting youth." Topping, *Happiness and Wisdom*, 154.

reorder desire—its ability to inculcate order in the soul. Third, the piety that reforms our desires takes the form of imitating the humility of Jesus Christ.

Augustine informs Monica that "there were among the ancients women who philosophized," adding that "your philosophy is much more pleasing to me" (1.9.31). Since philosophy is the love of wisdom and since Monica loves the wisdom of the Scriptures, Augustine even asks whether he will not "gladly dedicate myself to you as your disciple?"

Conybeare takes Monica's inclusion in the happy life as evidence of Augustine's growing distrust in neo-Platonic dichotomies.[37] Although Augustine moves beyond neo-Platonism by acknowledging Monica as a "philosopher," this reading is not quite right. He has not given up the Platonic distinction between the sensible and the intelligible. Although this distinction does make philosophy harder for someone who has not received a good education, it is not by giving up the distinction that this challenge is overcome. It is through the Incarnation (*c. Acad.* 3.19.43). The Incarnation is significant, not because it leads Augustine to give up this crucial Platonic distinction, but all the more because he accepts it. Indeed, here he reaffirms that true philosophy is concerned with an immaterial world, "far removed from these eyes" (1.11.32).

One attains the wisdom Monica has through the piety that the Incarnation requires. This insight was a central theme of *De beata vita.* Conybeare correctly observes that Augustine privileges morality over the liberal disciplines as a path to God.[38] Augustine will soon recommend to Licentius and Trygetius that they pursue the liberal disciplines as a path of ascent to God. Even then, we will see that the path Monica has followed is not only a sufficient means of attaining the wisdom she displayed in *De beata vita* 2.10. It is also *more* effective than the liberal arts at reordering desires and leading one to the truth. The piety of one like Monica[39] can heal the soul in ways the liberal arts cannot. Thus Augustine praises his mother for her love of wisdom: "indeed you love it much more than you love me . . . you have advanced so far into it that already you are not frightened either by the dread of accidental harm or of death itself," an immunity which is recognized as "the supreme stronghold of philosophy" (1.9.32).

Monica's humble piety is a striking juxtaposition to the lads' pride and impiety. Pride is the direst disorder of our affections, the practice of humility the strongest therapy for disordered affections. Augustine praises

37. Conybeare, *Irrational Augustine*, 107–13, 125–38.

38. Ibid., 129, 137. Topping is correct when he explains, referencing *c. Acad.*, how the soul's condition affects its ability to know; see Topping, 124–25.

39. Or, we might observe again, Antony.

her humility, linking it to Christ's. He begins his speech by remarking that "I do not care much for the judgments of the proud and ignorant, who rush into reading books as they do into greeting men." Those who would exclude women from philosophy do so out of pride. What matters is not public acclaim but truth. Through her faith Monica has long showed herself a "philosopher" by her love of wisdom (God), whom a proud philosopher will never attain because of his love of himself. The humblest are often the greatest; such is Monica, whose humility has carried her farther than many (or all) pagan philosophers.[40]

After his speech, Monica says (1.11.33) that Augustine has never told so many lies! As narrator, he tells us the conversation was called off for the sake of his health and because they had already said too much to record. Monica's remark and the admission that the recorded speech is a reconstruction suggest we should read it with a grain of salt. I take the following aspects of the speech at face value: the privileging of the immaterial over the material; Augustine's respect for his mother's "love of wisdom"; the understanding of this love as "philosophy" in some sense; and his appreciation of her humble piety as the right way to wisdom.

However, one thing in particular calls for interpretation. There is an irony about Augustine's labeling Monica a "philosopher." The whole scene is comedic, suggesting that it is a caricature of a truth. The truth is that Monica is a philosopher in the etymological sense, for she loves wisdom, and in a teleological sense, for she is closer to the happy life than any other "philosopher." She also has no fear of death, a quality attributed to the wise at least since Plato. But Monica is not a philosopher in every sense. She is not able to engage in philosophical dialogue; her lack of formal education makes this especially difficult. More importantly, Monica's only guide for life is faith. Humbly, she trusts not in her own ability to reach the happy life but in the promise of Christ and the church to lead her there. But a philosopher's mode of seeking wisdom relies on reason alone; this being the case, a Christian cannot call himself a "philosopher" in a strict sense, and Monica is not one; but a Christian can still, loosely speaking, practice "philosophy" when he investigates God and the soul through reason, as Augustine suggests we should (*c.Acad.* 2.3.8, *b. Vita* 1.5).[41]

40. Djuth, "Philosophy in a Time," 285–86. Lactantius had also said that philosophy fails not only the many, but even the few, in bringing them to happiness; Topping, *Happiness and Wisdom*, 52.

41. In having a balanced view of Christianity and philosophy Augustine resembles various church Fathers, although some (such as Tertullian) rejected philosophy and others (such as Minucius Felix) embraced it outright; see Harrison, *Augustine*, 16. My reading of Augustine's view of philosophy differs somewhat from Holte, who takes the naming of Monica as a philosopher at face value; see Holte, "Monica, 'the Philosopher.'"

We can infer from all this that Augustine is holding up his mother to Licentius and Trygetius as an example of where they should direct their educational efforts. The disciplines they are studying are to be oriented towards the same goal Monica has pursued by another path. As the company departs, Licentius remarks that their conversation is guided by an unseen order. Augustine replies with familiar advice: "I see, and I am not ungrateful to God. And I assume that you yourselves, who notice these things, will for that very reason be better." Licentius must turn his insights on order into the reordering of his desires, especially the desire for glory. While Augustine's claim that he will dedicate himself to Monica as her disciple cannot mean he will try to be educated by her, he wants his whole school to follow the example of her faith, her piety, and her submission to religious authority.[42]

The same could be said of his readers, for we are meant to see ourselves in Licentius and Trygetius and learn the same lessons. Thus closes Book I.

The Order of the Embodied Soul

In Book II Augustine reopens the conversation about order and evil, but the discussion quickly turns to the order appropriate to the embodied soul. In this section I shall discuss the dual loves appropriate to such a soul, both of which must be stirred up in Augustine's students: the immaterial nature of God (and order) *and* a healthy embodied life. I shall also respond to Conybeare's reading of the passage.

A few days pass, and Alypius returns (2.1.1). Augustine wants to be sure that his mother is present, for her "character and soul, aflame for things divine," had so impressed him during the talk recorded in *De beata vita* (e.g., 2.10). Indeed, "her mind had appeared to me so great that nothing seemed better suited to true philosophy."[43]

Augustine addresses Licentius and Trygetius, expressing gratitude that the delay caused by their immaturity has allowed Alypius to return (2.1.2). Recalling Licentius's definition of order, "that through which God guides

42. As O'Ferrall says, Monica "exemplifies those who have come by reliance on authority to some understanding of the truths of their religion" and in *Ord.* Augustine uses "her to illustrate his new acceptance of the importance of authority in a religious dimension." See O'Ferrall, "Monica: A Reconsideration," 42.

43. This claim is tinged with irony. In isolation from its context, this remark might be taken as distinguishing *c. Acad.* 3.19.42's "true philosophy" from Platonism. On this reading true philosophy is the love of God (*b. Vita* 1.11), and Monica's religion has taught her to love God without the help of the usual Platonic strategies. On the interpretation of *c. Acad.* 3.19.42, see above, Chapter 2 under the subheading *Christ: Towards a Christian Theology of Desire.*

all" (2.1.2), he challenges him to explain whether God himself is also guided by order (2.1.2–3). Licentius admits that God and the things with him are not administered by order, though everything else is.

This being administered by order he concedes to describe as their being *moved*. Licentius quickly works himself into a muddle; for created things are without God, and therefore must be moved; but they are also with God, and so they are not moved. In need of a distinction, he is asked to define what it means to be with or without God (2.2.4). He asks Augustine to do the defining, and Augustine acquiesces.

Wanting him to help craft the definition, he asks Licentius whether things ordered by God are with God. Licentius refuses, and Augustine proffers this definition: "whatever understands God is with God." Licentius agrees. Several questions (2.2.4–5) prompt him to say that whatever a wise man knows through his bodily senses is without God, while whatever he knows through his mind is with God (2.2.5). He adds that "whoever knows only those things which the sense of the body touches" is neither with God nor with himself. Trygetius helps by suggesting that what he senses through his body he does not know, for to *know* is the province of the mind and to *perceive* with the senses that of the body.

The lads are developing quasi-Platonic notions of knowledge, of the soul, and of being with God; Augustine sets out to refine their rough understanding of Platonism. In the remainder of this section I shall accomplish three things. First, I shall show how their notion is radically immaterial and divorces the soul from its embodied activities, effectively separating the soul from itself as well as from the body—a notion with important implications for desire. Second, I shall show how, by proffering such a notion, the lads are nevertheless neglecting an opportunity to contemplate the immateriality they praise. Third, I shall look at Conybeare's reading of the passage and suggest how it might be improved.

First, Augustine shows them that their radically immaterial account of knowledge robs men of a part of their souls. For *the soul* senses *through* the body (2.2.6).[44] If the bodily senses have nothing to do with the soul, then the part of the soul that senses through the body will be divorced from the rest of the soul. Licentius quickly corrects himself, admitting that the element in man which senses through the body is a part of the soul, but a *subservient* part which ought to obey the rational part. He suggests that memory, being concerned with fleeting things, is another lower part. The wise man, who knows God (who is *not* fleeting), has no need of it. Licentius thus unites the soul, but fails to adequately integrate the human person, for he reduces the

44. Also see Bourke, "The Body-Soul Relation," 439, 443.

value of the soul to the activity of its highest part. This would imply much the same therapy for desire as his views in *Contra Academicos* 1.3.9: We must cease to desire material things and quicken our desires for the immaterial. Licentius's anthropology leaves the body uncared for. Indeed, it robs that part of the soul which is concerned with the body of its own proper function, and so will cease to care for the whole soul!

Second, Licentius and Trygetius have emphasized the need for the soul to know itself, but counseled that it do so by *escaping* bodily influence. In doing this the soul would fail to know the part of itself concerned with the body. Therefore, though Licentius has made progress in understanding that it is the soul that knows through the body, he does not know much about that particular function of the soul. Yet we should know this function. Augustine hints that the soul's own ability to sense is fit for reflection. He calls his students' attention to these lesser functions of the soul hoping they will be able to know their souls better. By denigrating memory Licentius misses an excellent opportunity to reflect on its power, a part of the soul whose function is not limited by space and time. By contemplating memory he would be able to contemplate his soul and so better learn the very immateriality to which he has dedicated himself. Cicero implicitly suggests that contemplating memory is a way of knowing the soul.[45] Augustine surely has passages like these in mind and wants his students to know their own souls by contemplating memory. In short, Licentius does not adequately understand that immateriality the knowledge of which he praises.

Third, as Conybeare reads the passage Augustine uses the episode to question neo-Platonic distinctions.[46] Augustine says in response to Licentius's theory of memory that the wise man needs memory because of "the noble and necessary disciplines" (2.2.7). Licentius disagrees: The wise man is "gazing upon God himself fixedly and immovably," so "What need does he have of memory, when we has and holds in his presence all of his things?" Augustine suggests that the wise man has an obligation to care for the lower things in his keeping, and that these "duties of benevolence" include guiding the body and "teaching wisdom itself" to "whomever he can." This duty requires that memory be present and active so it can dispense the liberal arts. According to Conybeare, Augustine puts the neo-Platonic position in the mouth of Licentius, a position he himself has held up until now. Through himself as character, he questions one of neo-Platonism's fundamental dichotomies, that of the transient and eternal. She is correct that Augustine is rejecting the radical immaterialism offered by Licentius. However, she

45. *Discussions at Tusculum* 1.24 and *On Ends* 2.34.

46. Conybeare, "Duty of a Teacher," and *Irrational Augustine*, 113–20.

assumes that Licentius's position is genuinely Plotinian. Moreover, her explanation as to *in what sense* and *why* Augustine rejects this immaterialism is unclear.

Conybeare relies on Winkler's reading of this passage as Augustine's reexamination of his earlier neo-Platonic views.[47] It is true that Licentius's account of memory is quasi-Plotinian, for Plotinus had said that memory is concerned with temporal and fleeting things.[48] However, memory is not identical to that with which it is concerned. O'Daly has responded to Winkler, pointing out that Plotinus locates memory in the higher part of the soul; Licentius is wrong in thinking memory is one of the soul's lowest functions.[49] Though memory operates on lower things it is not so low itself. This reinforces our sense that Licentius is missing his chance to contemplate the soul. It is ironic that Augustine's students, who are trying so hard to be good Platonists by praising the soul at the expense of the body, end up denigrating the soul.

In what sense does Augustine reject this account of memory? Conybeare thinks that Augustine undoes the distinction between the transient and the eternal through the notion of *teaching*, for a teacher dispenses eternal truths to those in the transient world.[50] There is no evidence that Augustine rejects this basic distinction or that he rejects the Plotinian notion of memory as the operation of our immaterial souls. He does, however, reject any idea that the material and the intelligible are not concerned with one another. The immaterial organizes the material world, as any good neo-Platonist would also know. Moreover, the soul distracted by the material can attain to immaterial truth, as the Incarnation shows (*c. Acad.* 3.19.42). And the man who possesses immaterial wisdom has a duty to care for the physical world. God himself lowered himself to take on physical form, to save souls caught up in material lusts, and to teach them the love of God.

Why does Augustine reject Licentius's account? At one point Conybeare suggests that Licentius's advice "begins to unravel when confronted with embodiment."[51] This would seem to imply that Licentius's account never had much going for it, that it would prove problematic even on Plotinian premises. Elsewhere she suggests that Augustine's move here is a response to the Incarnation, that the radical separation of the interests of the wise man

47. Winkler, "La Théorie Augustinienne."

48. *Ennead* 4.4.1–6 says that memory is concerned with the changing things that exist within time; the closer a soul is to the One, the less use it has for these things, and the less use for memory.

49. O'Daly, "Memory in Plotinus."

50. Conybeare, "Duty of a Teacher," 60.

51. Ibid., 57.

from his embodiment "ought to be impossible within Christianity."[52] This suggests that Licentius's account would be acceptable on merely Plotinian terms. This latter explanation is more likely Conybeare's sense of the passage, and it calls for a distinction. Insofar as Licentius's account denigrates memory as a lower psychical phenomenon, she has not seen where Licentius falls short of Plotinus's understanding of immateriality and accordingly does not see how his account is not acceptable on Plotinian terms. However, insofar as Licentius's account strives to abandon the concerns of embodiment, I think she is correct that Licentius's view corresponds to Plotinus's, and just as correct that Augustine rejects this view.

There are salient implications here for desire. Licentius's advice would have us remove ourselves from the care of carnal things, but Augustine advises the soul to care for the body and to teach others. While neither of these should be loved above God, desiring and seeking the well-being of each is the proper activity of the soul that knows God.[53] Even a sage cares for his body and for his friends.

Order and Privation of Order

Augustine resumes quizzing Licentius and Trygetius on order, trying to teach them the difference between order and the things within it. His students are beginning to learn that evil things within order are qualitatively different from order itself, the result of a privation of order.

Content with Licentius's definition of being with God, Augustine challenges his idea that the things the wise man knows are with God; then folly itself, being understood by the wise man, is with God (2.3.8)! The premise that the wise man understands folly is established by the claim that he must understand folly in order to avoid it. This conclusion disturbs Licentius and Trygetius, who asks for Alypius's help. Alypius suggests that the wise man need not bother to avoid folly, and so need not understand it in order to avoid it. Augustine reminds us that the wise man's business includes helping his fellowman, which requires him to know folly (2.3.9). He calls instead for a definition of folly, and Alypius steps aside so Licentius and Trygetius can give their own account. Licentius is now "totally absent," but Trygetius, itching to speak, suggests that "folly is either the chief or the sole cause of *not* understanding" (2.3.10). The definition is just what Augustine needs to teach his students something about the nature of evil. He accepts it, adding

52. Ibid., 65.

53. Conybeare correctly distinguishes Platonism from Augustine's philosophy on this point. See "Duty of a Teacher," 56.

an analogy from sensation: "no one can see darkness." He posits that "understanding is to the mind what seeing is to the sense." The analogy shows the qualitative difference between folly and wisdom and prepares us to see the difference between evil and order. Dark is the privation of light, and folly is the privation of understanding. Evil is likewise a privation of good.

Augustine gives his students a fresh challenge: If a fool guides anything, he does so either by order or not by order; if the former, then not all order is guided by God; if the latter, then something is not guided by order (2.4.11). Licentius is still "absent in every way," but Trygetius has an idea inspired by the analogy to darkness. Lacking words to articulate what he is thinking, he says that everything is enclosed in order; for order assigns even inferior things to their appropriate place. Yet, "if in lifting up and extending the eyes of the mind, he should survey all things at the same time, he will find nothing that is not ordered." Trygetius's idea does not have the same quasi-Stoic undertones as Licentius's earlier claim that order assigns all things their place (1.7.18–9). There is a hint of the idea that all things, from a perspective that sees all things, would seem ordered (1.1.2). Augustine suggests examples of the notion (2.4.12). Among these, the hangman has a hideous occupation, but serves a valuable purpose in society; some of the body parts of animals are, by themselves, ugly, but serve a useful purpose.[54] "So it is," Augustine suggests, "with all things, I believe; but they demand eyes" that have been rightly trained to see this (2.4.13).

Eyes, but also desires: We must love God in order to understand his order. Now Augustine will show how the liberal arts, useful for training the eyes of the mind to understand order, are unable without Christian faith to heal the soul of its disorders.

PATHS OF ASCENT TO ORDER

Augustine will now map out two paths by which one may ascend to knowing order and to having a rightly ordered soul. These two paths are reason and authority, and they are traveled, respectively, by those schooled in the liberal arts and those trained in Christian piety. Augustine recommends the liberal arts to Licentius and Trygetius, and encourages his mother to continue in her piety. The arts train minds for contemplation and have some power to amend our desires. But we *all* need to follow the way of Christ. As Topping explains, "The twofold method is what those who *already* accept Christian revelation may walk upon: these are not alternatives open to Platonists, but only to those who have submitted themselves to the efficacy of the

54. See Plotinus, *Enneads*, 3.2.17.

mysteries."[55] Christian piety is superior to the liberal disciplines in nearly every way.[56] It can reach everyone. The liberal arts can provide insights into virtue, but, unlike the Christian faith, they cannot make one virtuous. By faith alone Monica has reached the virtue of the happy life; she lacks only the ability to understand the obscure points of theology. No one comes so far by the liberal arts alone. Although Augustine would later attribute less to the liberal disciplines than he does now and would call his early higher estimation of them prideful, even at Cassiciacum he understands that no one is saved by the liberal disciplines. We need grace.

After introducing these two paths of ascent to God, Augustine will attempt to lead his students up the path of the liberal arts, showing them how to contemplate their own souls. Then, perceiving that his audience is not ready for the lesson, he will recommend to them the paths of ascent for which they are most suited.

Two Paths of Ascent

Continuing what is turning out to be a long speech,[57] Augustine turns to the quadrivium: "Now in music, in geometry, in the movements of the stars, in the laws of numbers, order so dominates that if one longs to see its fount, its actual innermost sanctuary, so to speak, one must either discover it in these or be led through them to it . . ." (2.5.14). By studying them one is better able to understand seeming disorder. Such evils persuade many that God's providence is limited (a reference to 1.1.1). Others do not descend into impiety but are still disturbed by the perception of disorder. For these the liberal disciplines are very helpful.

But the disciplines are not everything: "Twofold is the path we follow when we are moved by the obscurity of things: either reason, or at least authority" (2.5.16). Reason, via "true" and "genuine" philosophy, can show that all things are derived from a single "principle-less Principle." Authority teaches the Christian mysteries, that this Principle is "one God omnipotent,"[58] that this God is tripotent, and that He took on a human

55. Topping, *Happiness and Wisdom*, 170.

56. Heßbrüggen-Walter is wrong, then, in reading the way of reason as superior in nearly every way. See "Augustine's Critique of Dialectic," 187–88.

57. There is an obvious rhetorical aspect to Augustine's speeches. On the usefulness of rhetoric in persuading a person to commit to a better way of life, see Kolbet, *Augustine and the Cure of Souls*, and Di Lorenzo, "Ciceronianism and Augustine's Conception." On the importance of rhetoric in preaching Christianity, see Part IV of *Teaching Christianity* and Fortin, "The 'Rhetoric' of the Church Fathers," 50–56.

58. The designation of the universe's source of order as "one God" is more specific

body. Reason acts in the service of these mysteries by helping us understand them "as they should be understood."[59]

The Place of One's Mind

Augustine asks Licentius, who has been preoccupied, to return to the conversation and discuss the wise man and God (2.5.17), asking how the wise man's mind remains immovable when his body goes from place to place (2.6.18). Licentius accomplishes nothing before lunch beyond forcing a definition of *being moved*, a notion that requires defining what it means to be in *a place* (2.6.19). The respective places of body and soul is a topic fraught with subtlety. Licentius believes that the wise man's *body* may move from place to place while his *mind* stays with God and does not move; but he cannot give a clear account of this, for he admits that the soul is with the body. He is unwilling to say that those who are not *with* God are *without* God, because in some sense "God 'has' them," and admits his discomfort with this paradox (2.7.20). But Augustine returns (2.7.21) to the topic of order and evil. Licentius admits he cannot give an account of evil; "And nodding his head and shoulders, he said, 'We are in trouble.'"[60] Although Trygetius answered the question while he was not paying attention (2.4.11),

---

than its designation as a unitary Principle. Some Platonists may have believed in the unitary Principle but did not believe the Principle to be a personal God. Cicero may have been such a one, for Augustine would much later suggest that Cicero was an atheist (*City of God* 5.9)! Platonism might also be construed as pantheism, from which Augustine also distinguishes himself here. See Kevane, "Christian Philosophy," 73. A few years after Cassiciacum Augustine begins his *Of True Religion* with monotheism, stating that there is one God; *True Religion*, 1.1.

59. Topping argues that "philosophy never transcends authority, even for the intelligent" (168). O'Meara's wording is poor when he suggests that reason and authority are "two coordinated, although independent ways to the Father" in *Studies in Augustine and Eriguena*, 138. Reason is plainly not independent of authority in *Ord*. These words of O'Meara are more appropriate:

> Since, therefore, God is one, and is the source of authority and, ultimately, of reason, authority and reason cannot conflict on what is true. Authority and reason are two approaches to the same truth.
>
> . . . There is plenty of evidence to show that he believed: (1) that authority could dispense altogether with reason (2) that authority aided by reason was more desirable than authority alone; (3) that reason depended on some authority so that it might begin to operate; and (4) that reason could arrive at an understanding of everything taught by authority. (Ibid., 144)

60. This admission thus undercuts Cary's idea that Licentius's insights in Book I faithfully represent the Plotinian view; if they did, they would be better fit for resolving the problem of evil; see Cary, "What Licentius Learned," 148.

the admission shows that he realizes the consequences of the quasi-Stoic account he had earlier promoted, an account that cannot account for evil.

Augustine now recalls Licentius's definition of justice (2.4.11) as God's rendering to good and evil their due and asking whether God was always just (2.7.22), which would mean that evil has always existed. Even Monica agrees with this dire consequence until Trygetius suggests that God's justice is his *ability* to give good and evil their due, not his *actually* doing so.

In a final round of dialogue Augustine articulates a constructive dilemma (2.7.23). Since "evil was born" at some point, either it was born within order or it was not; if it was, then God is responsible for evil; if not, then something is outside of order. Licentius is silent, but Monica says nothing is "outside of God's order" because evil, itself not born from order, is taken up into order, driven there by God's justice. Again Monica shows herself capable of insight. We may recall the cover letter's analogy from art. A great artist can take an ugly square and incorporate it into a beautiful mosaic, or a great musician can take a horrible sound and incorporate it into a beautiful song. So also God can integrate evil into a beautiful universe.

Throughout this conversation Augustine has had at least three goals: to train his students in dialectic for the betterment of their souls; to encourage them to reflect on their own souls and their relation to God; and to help everyone understand the problem of evil. Unfortunately, these goals meet with only modest success. Augustine perceives (2.7.24) "that all of them were most zealously seeking God (each according to his own strength)," but realizes they are not observing order in the conversation. Accordingly, he introduces a new topic: Instead of *solving* the mysteries of order, he will now teach how we can *learn to solve* the mysteries of order.

Order of Life and Education

Several things will become apparent as Augustine and Alypius discuss the order of life and education. First, in order to understand order, one's morals as much as one's mind must be trained. As we have seen before (1.2.3), the renovation of the mind and the renovation of the heart go hand in hand. *Both* must be ordered if we are to know order. The reordering of life involves aspects of virtue known to pagan philosophers, but also requires uniquely Christian virtues. Second, Augustine at Cassiciacum has a higher view of the liberal arts than he would later find appropriate. Even here, however, there are salient differences between Augustine's theology of desire and mere neo-Platonism. For, third, grace is needed in the form of the divine intervention taught by Christian orthodoxy; though the philosophers were able to learn a great deal about what an ordered soul looks like, they failed to accomplish it. Fourth, the liberal arts are helpful in reordering our mind and our desires; but, finally, following the path of Christian piety (Monica's path) is necessary and more effective than the liberal disciplines.

We begin with the remark that there is "a certain lofty discipline" which promises to those who rightly love God and souls an absolutely certain explanation of the problem of evil (2.7.25). "This discipline is the very law of God, which, remaining always fixed and firm with Him, is transcribed, so to speak, onto wise souls so that they know how to live better and more sublimely insofar as they contemplate it more perfectly through understanding and guard it more carefully through living" (2.8.25). The order of God is replicated in the wise man's soul, contemplated in his understanding, and lived in his life. It enjoins us "to follow at the same time a double order, one part of which pertains to life, the other part to education."[61]

We must distinguish the discipline Augustine promotes from the liberal disciplines. The way up to God includes the liberal arts, but should not be identified with them. It is the command of the Christian God, and it is as much moral as intellectual. There is a common misperception that Augustine is promoting the liberal arts as a sufficient means of intellectual ascent to perfect contemplation of God. For example, Stefan Heβbrüggen-Walter compares Augustine's thought at Cassiciacum to the Stoic philosophy of religion, saying he thought that through dialectic alone we can learn all the truths about God we want to learn.[62] We are reminded of Brown's earlier idea that Augustine at Cassiciacum wanted to ascend to knowledge of God using arguments derived via the liberal disciplines.[63] The arts by themselves, however, are useless without morality—and not just pagan morality, but a uniquely Christian morality.

Augustine elaborates on the order of life first, showing strategies by which our desires can be reordered (2.8.25). These include modes of training in virtue which pagan philosophers also recommended, but also a number of biblical practices. We must avoid sensual indulgence and thinking too much of the body; avoid sloth, sleep, and the games; and pride and the pursuit of vain praise. These habits turn our desires towards God, making us more fit to know order. Moreover, in our relationships with others we must practice love. We should avoid immoderate anger and hate for others' sins, using even punishment for the offender's own good. We must serve

61. On the relation of order in life to cosmic order, see Topping, *Happiness and Wisdom*, 218–19.

62. Heβbrüggen-Walter, "Augustine's Critique," 194.

63. Brown, *Augustine*, 148.

others with joy and obey the Golden Rule—"Let them do to no one what they are unwilling to undergo"—and pursue friendship. These various injunctions call for personal and communal treatment of the disordered soul. Some were recommended by the pagans, but others are clearly biblical. This passage is rich with scriptural references[64] and culminates in a clear call to Christian living: "Let them worship, think of, and seek God, supported by faith, hope, and charity."

Now we come to the order of education, an order the student must pair with the order of life. Education aims for a rational understanding of things, but it begins with authority (2.9.26). This is the authority of Christ and the church (*c. Acad.* 3.19.43 and *Ord.* 2.5.16), which has precedence over reason in that it gives reason the truths she seeks to understand. However, reason has a sort of preeminence over faith: "Authority is first according to time; reason, according to the reality." Once the liberal arts have made reason "firm and fit after the cradle of authority," it will be able to reach a deeper understanding of the mysteries. Those who disdain the liberal arts or are not intellectually fit are limited to "authority alone" and are not able to be perfectly happy in this life. Their only hope is to live well now and be able to understand the mysteries after they have left the body. One paragraph later, citing the authority of the incarnate Christ, Augustine suggests that Christ wants us "to fly up to the understanding" (2.9.27). I have already discussed the possibility that Augustine believes in a disembodied afterlife at Cassiciacum,[65] but there is another concern here. Augustine seems a little denigrating to those who, like Monica, are diligently following the order of life but lack education. Perhaps he is attributing a little too much to his own intellect. Perhaps this mistake is among those of which he was thinking when, in *Retractions*, he says that when he wrote these books he "was still puffed up with the usages of secular literature"[66] and that he "attributed a great deal to the liberal disciplines about which many saintly persons do not know much—some, in truth, know them and are not saintly . . . ."[67]

64. Foley footnotes Matt 7:12, Matt 20:28, Gal 5:20 and 21, and Eph 4:21–5. The words "a quiet life" also call to mind 1 Thes 4:11.

65. See above, Chapter 3, under the subheading *Augustine's Emerging Departure from Platonism*.

66 Augustine, *Retractions*, Prologue, 3.

67. Ibid., 3.2. Similarly, *Conf.* 4.16.31 and 12.27.37 discuss how the lowly language of Scripture leads the humble of heart into truth while Augustine at a young age, a clever but arrogant reader of Aristotle, fell short. Two helpful sources exploring Augustine's submission of whatever is valuable in these arts to the Christian Scriptures are Burton and Pollman, "Augustine's Hermeneutics!?" Augustine's continuing project of rethinking pagan insights called for a reconsideration and resituating of the liberal arts.

There are at least two implications for the healing of desire. First, a better understanding of the Christian mysteries is a proper, indeed a necessary, object of correct desire. Second, the healing of desire swings somewhat towards neo-Platonic therapies for desire, wherein the liberal arts are central. Augustine at Cassiciacum retains aspects of neo-Platonism which do not fit perfectly within a Christian worldview; even so, it is crucial to recognize the difference between Augustine's analysis of desire and a simply neo-Platonic analysis. The inclusion of Christian humility, faith, hope, and love in the renewal of desire separates his use of the liberal arts from neo-Platonism. Although Augustine's treatment of desire develops and solidifies into a more thoroughly Christian treatment as he matures, the fact is that at Cassiciacum the process is already well under way.[68] Indeed, he displays more than a touch of Christian humility in his portrayal of Monica at Cassiciacum, whose simple piety gives her insights as good as any pagan philosophers reached after years of liberal studies.[69]

Other factors distinguish Augustine's view of the liberal arts from neo-Platonism.[70] Alypius says that Augustine has laid out for them "A grand image of life," but immediately laments our inability to live up to this image: "if only those words were as easy to imitate as they are wonderful to hear!" (2.10.28). He does not understand how the soul "proclaims these celestial things to be divine and utterly true while it is hearing them, yet comports itself differently in its desires." We may *know* what is just and right, but we do not *desire* it.[71] For this reason we need grace. Only Christ or someone with God's help can live rightly. The corruption of human desire is deeper than ancient philosophers understood, and the solution is God's mercy. The situation is much more urgent than any pagan philosopher knew, for our desires are deeply corrupted by sin, and we are incapable of saving ourselves. But Augustine is also more hopeful than any pagan philosopher could be, for the transforming work of the Holy Spirit makes possible the renovation of desire so that we can pursue the happy life.[72]

68. O'Donnell strikes a good tone: "on the one hand, already Christian, on the other hand, not entirely satisfactory . . . ." *Confessions, Vol. 3*, 85.

69. See Djuth, "Augustine, Monica," 252: Augustine "recognizes in these works that Monica's love of wisdom at Cassiciacum was far more mature than his was on account of his pride in learning, and that God had a way of making this evident to him through the aid he bestowed on Monica and the quickness with which she grasped the truth."

70. Heßbrüggen-Walter, for example, assumes O'Connell's reading and takes the orientation of the liberal arts in *Ord.* as fundamentally Platonic, intended to achieve knowledge of and union with God.

71. Alypius's words may be influenced by Romans 7.

72. The remarks of Wilken are helpful on this topic. See *The Spirit of Early Christian Thought*, 18f, 275.

Augustine modestly admits that these precepts are not his own, but come from "the books of great and almost divine men."[73] He praises Alypius for following the precepts better than he has! Few live by these precepts, though many may live thus incognito, who will likely "become known by some illustrious deeds" (2.10.29) as Victorinus was (*Conf.* 8.2.5) and perhaps as Augustine himself when he resigned his position as teacher of rhetoric (*Conf.* 9.2).[74] He gives one final remark before moving to another topic, saying that "divine assistance" has gracefully extended this reordering of desires "through the whole of mankind more widely than many think."

Deeming enough said about authority, Augustine begins a lesson on reason and the liberal arts. He means to teach Licentius and Trygetius about their souls, to help them become accustomed to reflecting on their souls, to learn wisdom, and to love what a wise man loves, namely God and the soul. Through reason a wise man "understands God and the soul itself," but Augustine is not wise yet (2.10.30). He reminds them of their nature as human beings, rational animals superior to beasts because of rationality but inferior to the divine because of mortality (2.10.31). The soul has lapsed into a fall of some kind,[75] wherein it clings to mortal, material things and neglects the divine, immaterial things it was created to love. By returning our attentions to these things, the liberal arts are meant to correct this fundamental disorder in our desires.

To help his students contemplate reason, Augustine praises it, beginning with its manifestations to the bodily senses. Reason makes itself known via the ears through the harmony of sounds (2.10.32), via the eyes through the proportionality of parts (2.10.33). The pleasure we take in harmonious sounds or well-proportioned sights also partakes of reason: Not only does the soul operate our very bodily senses (2.2.6), but our perception of material things mingles with our perception of the principles of reason. By pondering the fact that our pleasure in material things depends on reason,

73. Who are these great men? Augustine may well be speaking of the best of pagans, no doubt including Plato and Cicero. But, given the presence of explicitly Christian virtues among the precepts, we cannot rule out the possibility that Augustine is also speaking of Christians such as Ambrose.

74. Holt extends this point by arguing that Augustine's manner of teaching in *Ord.* is a new manner of teaching, a Christian pedagogy that displays a new Christian life. See Holt, "Wisdom's Teacher."

75. What kind of fall? One persistent interpretation is that Augustine holds to the neo-Platonic view of the soul's preexistence, prenatal sin, and subsequent fall into a carnal body. See O'Connell, *Saint Augustine's Platonism*, 3. For my response to this issue, see above, Chapter I, under the heading *Ways of Understanding Augustine's Conversion and Early Writings.*

Licentius and Trygetius will learn to love reason more than those material things. Contemplating reason is a therapy for directing our loves to it.

Reason also makes industry and art possible (2.10.34). It appears in deeds, for it tells us "to do nothing rashly;" it also appears in speaking and delighting, the respective provinces of two liberal disciplines (2.12.35).

Augustine now tells the story of the liberal disciplines as the story of the maturing of reason.[76] Grammar began with the naming of things, naming being the activity of reason (2.12.35).[77] Grammar birthed other disciplines, including the copying and calculating of things too abundant to name (2.12.35) as well as history, the discipline which records things worth remembering (2.12.37). Reason now sought to understand the power by which it had created these arts (2.13.38). Thus dialectic, "that very discipline of disciplines," was born. Through dialectic we can know knowing itself. But knowing produces the duty of teaching, which requires rhetoric, through which the fruits of the liberal arts are distributed to those not trained in them (2.13.38). Dialectic liberates those who study it, and rhetoric liberates the souls who do not, stirring up their desires to a love of the truth.

Reason longs to know God: "From here, reason wished to take itself to the happiest contemplation of the divine things themselves" (2.14.39). Thus "it sought steps" by which it could ascend to knowing God. The lower steps involve reflection on reason's power in the sensible world and human affairs. One such reflection is particularly meant for Licentius: Poetry operates by measure, proportion, and number, for it is the product of reason (2.14.40). Poetry should never be sought in itself, but considered as evidence of its artificer and used as a means to the contemplation of higher things.

The subsequent steps of ascent include the liberal disciplines of the quadrivium. Reason understands that numbers "rule and perfect the whole" of a rhythm or a cadence (2.14.41). Thus we must study music, a discipline that participates in both "sense-perception and understanding." Geometry melds sense-perception and understanding, using the sense of sight (2.14.42). Geometry shows us "that nothing which the eyes see can in any way be compared to what the mind discerns," thus helping us contemplate the immaterial. Astronomy also helps us understand eternal principles, for "dimension and numbers dominate" the motions of stars.

Knowledge of immaterial reality is needed to know one's own soul (and vice versa) (2.16.44). So, also, are a virtuous life and right desires. For "whoever is either still a slave to desires, gazing eagerly at perishable things,

76. The personification of reason here is a preview to the *Soliloquia*, where Reason has a speaking role. For this insight I am grateful to Cary, *Augustine's Invention*, 91–94.

77. In treating language as derived from reason Augustine may be drawing from Cicero's remarks in his *Republic*, 3.1.

or is someone who, now avoiding those things and living chastely, does not yet know" (2.16.44) or understand the difference between the material and the intelligible, is doomed to err when reasoning about his soul. In training us to contemplate the immaterial, the liberal arts free us to love them; they reorder our loves by showing us worthier objects of affection than sensible things. To attain the happiness we seek we need to know ourselves (1.1.3), and for this we desperately need minds trained for contemplation and hearts turned toward God. As for knowing God, the mind trained by the liberal arts will be better able to know about God what a mind can know—what God is *not*. God "is better known through not knowing," for example through knowing that God is *not* in time and space, existing in no place such as our physical experience knows. The nod toward apophatics distinguishes Augustine from the raw intellectualist he is sometimes taken to be, attempting to ascend to a knowledge of God through arguments. Augustine would hardly have promoted the idea of knowing God through a cloud of *un*knowing if this portrayal were the whole story.

Augustine has presented two paths of ascent to God. Each is desirable. A liberal education gives the soul knowledge of things it must have to be happy, training the mind to contemplate immateriality. Music helps us see the power of immaterial principles to structure and organize our experience in the material world, reminding us of the superiority of the immaterial. Grammar and dialectic train us to know the power of reason and the laws, independent of space and time, by which it operates.[78] Mathematics, geometry, and astronomy lead the mind upward to the immaterial realities above the mind. Mathematics helps us understand evil, which appears as a disunity in experience, because it shows a unity behind the multiplicity of everyday affairs.[79] Rhetoric helps us lead others in the same contemplation. The disciplines lead us from the contemplation of material objects outside the mind, through the contemplation of the mind itself, to the contemplation of immaterial realities above the mind, and, ultimately, to God. In short, as Cary says, "By the end of *On Order*, Licentius has before him a whole curriculum of education in the liberal disciplines, which is aimed at acquiring the philosophical wisdom—the possession of truth—in which happiness consists."[80] We must know the immaterial realm in order to understand evil, and the liberal arts help us do just that.

78. Foley, "Cicero, Augustine," 25.

79. Augustine also uses the text of *Ord.* to illustrate order uniting diverse elements. See Foley, "Cicero, Augustine," 74. Plato also used the dialogue form to illustrate order, though today this aspect of the Platonic dialogue is somewhat neglected. See Howland, "Re-Reading Plato," 193–94.

80. Cary, "What Licentius Learned," 156. I cannot agree with McWilliam's remark that "it is not the account of the education of the young men, but rather the story of

But the final word on the two paths of ascent privileges the second path, Christian *mores*. This path is superior for two reasons. First, as Monica shows, one can ascend farther by this path alone than by the liberal disciplines alone. Second, the moral purification of one's life cannot be accomplished by the liberal disciplines.

Augustine encourages his mother to "not let the fact that we need some things from these [disciplines] for what we are seeking deter you" (2.17.45). He praises her exemplary life, saying that her "mind, far removed from all trifles," is "already emerging from the body's great fall . . . ." It will eventually be much easier for her than for most to attain the knowledge for which the liberal arts are necessary. Hardly needing the "body" of grammar, its words, Monica will easily grasp its "soul," the eternal principles to which a study of grammar leads. Christ opens up happiness to all. Monica is the archetypical example of one who lacks liberal arts training yet becomes happy by following Christ. She cannot do philosophical theology or describe order and evil's place in the universe, "matters most obscure and yet divine"; but she is capable of loving and being satisfied in God. Ancient philosophers worked long and hard for the mysteries, the truths of the Christian faith (2.17.46), which Monica has cherished for years.[81] Augustine asks her to "guard, firmly and cautiously, that faith of yours which you have seized through the venerable mysteries."

After several remarks on the things a soul trained in the liberal disciplines learns about God and himself (2.18.47–2.19.49), Augustine shows that the path of Christian *mores* is better than the liberal disciplines, for their ability to reform us is severely limited. A neo-Platonic education can reorient the mind, but the reformation of desire requires grace. A heart fraught with carnal love may accompany a mind that knows immaterial reality; Augustine himself (*Conf.* 7.18–8.11) has recently been in this in-between state, and he laments this condition:

> To the soul that carefully regards the force and power of numbers, it will seem exceedingly unworthy and exceedingly lamentable that it is through its own knowledge that a verse flows well and a harp plays in tune, while its own life and its very own self are following a wayward path and, dominated by lust and

---

Augustine's conversions and his subsequent reflections, which provides the underlying coherence of the Cassiciacum writings." Indeed, it is both. See McWilliam, "Cassiciacum Dialogues," 141.

81. Holte: "his mother sometimes had the ability to catch, intuitively and immediately, the same truth that he and his pupils needed many sessions to establish, using a complicated chain of arguments." See Holte, "Monica, 'the Philosopher.'"

> accompanied by a most shameful racket of vices, are dissonant (*Ord.* 2.19.50).

The order that obtains in a righteous man's soul mirrors the order known through the liberal arts, and so the arts can show a person the state of his sin. But they are not able to heal it; this requires the imitation of Christ.[82] In short, *De ordine* is not the work of a Christian recycling pagan schemes of education; it is the first efforts of a young Christian to *renew* pagan education, to accomplish its transforming encounter with the Gospel. As Kevane remarks, Augustine's philosophy of education resituates education in the context of Christian metaphysics,[83] and, along with Christian *doctrine*, Christian *practice* as well.

Of course, that there is an ascent fueled by a liberal arts education to an understanding of immaterial reality is a theme in common with neo-Platonism. Yet neo-Platonism's insights, even insofar as they are correct, are not for everyone—and the crucial point to recognize is that *this is ok*; they suffer little from it, or not at all. Another crucial point is that even the correct insights of neo-Platonism *are not enough* for the soul that ascends towards immaterial reality and does not follow Christ. Thus Augustine mingles neo-Platonic insights with Christian theology, the former transformed by the latter.

THE STABILITY OF HAPPINESS

The dialogue concludes with reflections on the wise man, whose happiness is perfectly stable, immune to any buffeting. To help us understand happiness Augustine contrasts the things enclosed in the physical universe, which are themselves located in space and time and thus subject to change, with the wise man's soul, desires wholly directed to God and thus immune to change. The stability of his perfect happiness is rooted in the perfect stability of the object of his happiness. Poised between the state of the wise soul and the ephemeral physicality we should not desire are we, wandering souls learning to desire God. The final recommendation to become a happy person is a recommendation to pursue the reordering of our desires with prayer. In the conclusion to this chapter I shall first discuss the stable happiness of one who loves God's order. Then, after comparing Augustine's

82. Clark says of Christ, "He is the way even for intellectuals." See Clark, "Review," 433.

83. Kevane, "Christian Philosophy," 76. Several articles in Pollman's and Vessey's *Augustine and the Disciplines* underplay this point.

and ancient portrayals of happiness, I shall discuss the motion of our souls towards happiness.

Augustine has suggested to his students a contrast between the place of things in the physical world and the "place" of the wise man's soul. In 2.6.18 we are told that the wise man's body moves, but his soul does not. In 2.19.51 Augustine unveils this abstruse theme a little more clearly:

> in this sensible world, one should intensely consider what time and place are so that what delights in a part of place or time may nevertheless be understood as far inferior to the whole of which it is a part. . . . what offends in a part offends for no other reason than that the whole into which that part wonderfully fits is not being seen. But in the intelligible world any part is as beautiful and as perfect as the whole.

This is *De ordine*'s final mention of the notion that evil things are part of an ordered and beautiful whole—though not all can see it. We ought to know this whole, the knowledge of which is the aim of a liberal arts education. Augustine wants us to understand that things within a place are within space and time: material things. But space and time themselves are enclosed in an ordered whole. Things within order are subject to the rules governing space and time, and thus they are subject to change; hence the wise man's body moves from place to place within it. Things not enclosed in this order (including order itself) are immune to such changes, and nothing enclosed within order is to be loved; we should love order itself, the knowledge of it, and the God who administers it.

The wise man loves what is immune to the ravages of temporal and spatial change and so is secure in his happiness. Augustine quotes Virgil: "Of the wise man alone can it most truly be said, 'He, like an unmoved rock in the open sea, resists'" (2.20.54) all the storms (*c. Acad.* 1.1.1) of life, remaining happy through them. We are allowed a glimpse at this soul's delight in God: "But when it has composed and ordered itself and has rendered itself harmonious and beautiful, it will now dare to see God and the very Fount itself from where all truth flows and the very Father of Truth . . . . How serene! How happy!" (2.19.51). The unmoved rock is an image of one perfectly happy because his desires are satisfied. Only one who knows and loves God can be a rock.

The portrayal of the wise man's happiness as imminently stable has some affinity to various pagan philosophers. Cicero had said that virtue makes us immune to the buffeting of fortune.[84] Epicurus's happy person is no longer the victim of unsatisfied desires and, consequently, ceases to pur-

84. This is the argument of *Discussions at Tusculum*, Book V.

sue anything. His restful state replicates in human fashion the impassible state of the gods; as Cicero's Epicurean spokesperson Velleius says, "nothing is blessed if it is not restful."[85] He remains contentedly free of all cares. Seneca describes the virtue of Socrates as resembling a rock on which waves incessantly beat without affecting it.[86] Plotinus says of the soul that contemplates the One, "the soul rests. It seeks no further. It is sated. Its vision remains all within; it is sure of its object."[87]

Conybeare reads this passage as going against the grain of the dialogue, a last look back at the pagan ideal of perfect happiness: "Yet it is this very notion of fixity—the immovability of wisdom, of the divine, of the things that last—and the wise man's less than simple relationship to it which Augustine has been questioning in *De ordine*."[88] There is no indication that Augustine questions the immovability of God, and the perfect man's relationship to God is equally stable, as Augustine probably learned from the Psalms and may well have heard from Ambrose.[89] But Conybeare is partially correct; as *De beata vita* says, none of us is yet perfect, so our relationship with God is not fixed. We are still on the journey. As such we undergo a sort of motion. Strictly speaking, "motion" is superimposed on "place" and conveys a change of location in a spatial field. But there is an immaterial world more real than anything in extended space, as suggested to Zenobius (1.1.3). This suggests a different notion of "place," and a different sort of "motion," metaphorical senses of the terms which denote more *real* things than do the literal senses of the terms. The soul's "place" in this immaterial world is marked by its relation to God, and accordingly those changes in the soul which mend its damaged relation to God constitute a form of "motion" towards God. The conversion and healing of desire—learning to understand order, learning to love it, and becoming more ordered—is a sort of motion, a change in the soul that restores it to its proper place. While we undergo this motion we have neither the wise man's stability nor his perspective on order; hence *De ordine* never attempts to explain *how* evil fits into the whole,

85. Cicero, *Nature of the Gods*, 52.

86. Seneca, *On the Happy Life*, 27.

87. From the treatise on *Contemplation* in the *Enneads* 3.8.6. Also see 1.4.4 and 1.4.12–13 from the treatise on *Happiness*.

88. Conybeare, *Irrational Augustine*, 138.

89. See above, Chapter 3, under the heading *Diagnosis of Misery*. Conybeare is right that Augustine does not accept the notion of stability *as the pagan philosophers understood it*. Plotinus's defense of the wise man's stability in the treatise on *Happiness*, the *Enneads* 1.4, paragraph 13 is based on his soul's fundamental disinterest in bodily affairs, a disinterest we have seen Augustine does not promote.

claiming only that it *does*, and telling us what sort of training will prepare us to understand it.

Thus we must pursue this wisdom with vigilance and "a supreme commitment to the best *mores*" (2.20.52). We must also seek the reordering of desire with earnest prayer: "Let us therefore pray, that there come to us not riches or honors or things of this sort . . . but those things which make us good and happy." Although each should pray for wisdom for himself,[90] prayer is a communal activity. Augustine tells his mother that he credits her prayers for the reordering of his own desires, and asks her to pray for them all. The ascent to reordered and satisfied desires is prayerful and communal. *De ordine*'s conclusion unites the dialogue's form and content. The disputation ends, and, "with everyone filled with joy and hoping for much," the company begin the journey home from the meadow, guided by a lamp (2.20.54). The lamp-lit path home symbolizes the state of their souls; they are not happy yet, but a light shows them the way. That light is the light of Christ and of the Christian *mores* that the company must follow in order to be happy. The notion of light also suggests the liberal arts and their promise to teach the soul much. As usual, the dialogue form is meant to invite us to join Licentius and Trygetius as they follow these paths toward wisdom.[91]

In sum, the wise man loves the order of God, and as this order cannot be destroyed, neither can the object of the wise man's desire be destroyed; hence his happiness is complete and unmarred. We must pray for this happiness and for the grace to love God's order; that is, we must seek God for the conversion of our desires. We must also be diligent, all of us, to follow the path of Christian piety and, some of us, to study the liberal arts for the healing of desire. Augustine's personal efforts at this diligence are the subject of *Soliloquia*.

90. Prov 8:17 and Jas 1:5.

91. Topping, *Happiness and Wisdom*, 129–30.

5

Desiring God and the Soul

In *Contra Academicos*, to spur our desires towards God, Augustine demonstrates the possibility of attaining wisdom. Pride is identified as the greatest barrier to knowing and loving God, and the authority of Christ and the church is identified as the cure for it. In *De beata vita* Augustine calls God the proper object of desire, again warns against pride, and advises prayerful Christian community as the path towards happiness. In *De ordine*, again identifying pride as the threat, Augustine recommends two paths of ascent to God. The liberal arts are helpful for teaching some to contemplate God's immaterial nature, but we must all follow the path of Christian orthodoxy and orthopraxy.

In *Soliloquia* Augustine gives us a clearer understanding of what rightly ordered souls desire, namely God and the soul. He also suggests a number of lessons about the conversion of desire to the love of God and the soul. Reason helps us know God and the soul through reflection on immaterial and immortal things. It also helps us uncover the sordid desires that hinder our ascent. In this ascent one must closely monitor one's own desires and thoughts, but must also surrender absolutely to God's help. We are not able fully to know the sorry state of our own souls, and we need God's help to diagnose and heal our sinful desires. Accordingly, prayer should support the ascent to knowing God and the soul. We need the Trinity's help; but at the same time we must participate in the healing process by practicing the therapies of faith, hope, and charity. As an aid in knowing and loving God and the soul, Augustine offers an argument for immortality based on the soul's knowledge of immortal truth, and he encourages us to follow him in his ascent. In short, the conversion of desire is initiated by and depends on the trinitarian God; it calls for vigorous reason united with a prayerful Christian life.

In what follows I shall discuss the identity of *ratio*, or Reason (Part One). Then I shall discuss Augustine's prayer in the first chapter of *Soliloquia*, a passage mingling the renewal of desire with prayer and with the life of each member of the Trinity (Part Two). Next, I shall examine Augustine's attempts to know God and the soul in Book I (Part Three) and Book II (Part Four) of *Soliloquia*. Finally, I shall clarify the role of desire and the means of its conversion in *Soliloquia* (Part Five).

WHO IS REASON?

The unusual form of *Soliloquia*, no less than its content, welcomes analysis for insights regarding the happy life.[1]

> For a long time I had been turning over within myself many different things, and for many days I had been assiduously seeking my very self and what was good for me (or, if you will, what evil I should avoid), when suddenly it spoke to me. I know not whether it was I myself or something else outside or inside of me; for this is precisely what I am struggling mightily to know (1.1.1).[2]

These words introduce Augustine's interlocutor. But who is *ratio*? Is *ratio* identical to Augustine? Does it speak from within or without? Although Augustine candidly admits his ignorance of these questions, this ambiguity has occasioned surprisingly confident opinions about *ratio*. After discussing them, I shall outline my own opinion on *ratio*'s identity and discuss several significances.

Theories on *ratio*'s identity fall into two general categories.[3] The first category has it that *ratio* is Augustine's own reason, thus either identical with him or with a component of his person, speaking from within. The other category has it that *ratio* is God and speaks God's own words; *ratio* speaks from above. Conybeare seems to take the first theory for granted in her *Irrational Augustine*, assuming that *ratio* is either Augustine's own reason or a

1. Miner reads the dialogue with close attention to the dialogue's form and drama in "Augustinian Recollection."

2. Augustine, *Soliloquies* (referenced in text as *Sol.*).

3. Van Fleteren provides a helpful summary of the uses of the word *ratio* in the Cassiciacum dialogues. See "Authority and Reason," 42–43.

personification of universal Reason.[4] TeSelle agrees.[5] A theory in the second category may identify *ratio* with Christ or with the Holy Spirit. These are the approaches of Cary in a 1998 article and Olivier du Roy, respectively.[6]

None of these interpretations is either thoroughly correct or thoroughly mistaken. Augustine's confessed ignorance of *ratio* suggests that he himself has questions about its identity and, so to speak, its location. A working synthesis of these theories is possible. The ambiguity surrounding *ratio* ensures that, whatever it is, it serves as a bridge between God and the soul. It is intimately related to and intermittently acts on behalf of each. When Augustine talks to *ratio* he is literally talking to himself, but God is also talking to him—intermediately, through *ratio*'s voice. Yet *ratio* is not God. The non-identity of *ratio* with God is established by 2.7.14 where Augustine speaks in the first person using *ratio*'s voice: "I most peaceably (in my opinion) and advantageously decided to seek the truth with God's assistance, by means of being questioned by my very self and giving answers to myself."[7] All the same, the faculty of reason makes it possible to distance oneself from oneself, and hence *ratio* in this passage quickly lapses into addressing Augustine in the second person.[8]

Cary, in 1998, says *ratio* is "the same Inner Teacher, which a few years later Augustine explicitly identifies as Christ, the Wisdom and Virtue of God," pointing to *De magistro*.[9] Cary's interpretive instincts are good, for *ratio* is connected with Christ, and a fuller account of its locus and role would indeed have to take *De magistro* into account. Yet I believe *ratio* to be a personification of Augustine's own reason. It is not the inner Teacher,

4. Conybeare, *Irrational Augustine*, 144–50.

5. TeSelle, *Augustine the Theologian*, 77.

6. Cary, "What Licentius Learned," 161, and du Roy, *L'intelligence de la foi*; cited in Van Fleteren, "Authority and Reason," 43, n. 49.

7. I will return to the topic of Reason's non-divinity later under the subsection *Interpreting the Argument*.

8. In the power of a person's reason to be separate from person himself Tertullian saw a parallel to the Son's relation to the Father: "Because human thinking involves a back and forth within the mind, it is plausible, argues Tertullian, to speak of a kind of second person within us;" Wilken, *The Spirit of Early Christian Thought*, 98–99. The possibility of a trinitarian subtext to Augustine's relationship to reason is intriguing, but I have not come across any literature exploring the possibility.

9. Cary, "What Licentius Learned," 161. More recent writings of Cary are less committed on the identity of Reason. In his 2000 *Augustine's Invention* he suggests that Reason may be either Christ or the divine higher part of the human soul of which Plotinus spoke, or both (77–80). He adds that Augustine may well have not been sure himself who Reason is. In his 2008 *Outward Signs* he says simply that Augustine may have been "toying with the idea of identifying this inner teacher with Christ," and elaborates on the non-godly characteristics of Reason (99).

but it *hears* from the Teacher and communicates His word to Augustine. So, while I am nearer to agreement with Conybeare on the identity and location of *ratio* (and accordingly I shall henceforth refer to it as "Reason"), I am nearer to agreement with Cary's earlier article on *ratio*'s function.

Thus the ambiguity surrounding Reason revolves around the very mystery which Augustine, as he says in his first sentence, seeks to understand. The mysterious appearance of Reason raises the dialogue's theme, the knowledge of God and the soul. Moreover, Augustine's presentation of its appearance suggests a lesson about desire, namely that we should yearn to know God, the soul, and their relationship.

The dramatic introduction of Reason's voice is only the first instance of the things we can learn from the form of the dialogue. Two other insights are associated with Reason's place as a bridge between God and the soul. First, Augustine's dialogue with his own reason resembles a typical Stoic means of ascending to wisdom and cleansing one's desires. Second, Reason's ability to hear from God and relay its lessons to Augustine is reminiscent of lessons from Epicureanism.

The first insight springs from considering Reason as Augustine's own reason. Its position within his soul shows that he is talking with himself in a manner recalling Stoic self-treatment. The Stoic philosopher treats the diseases in his own soul by conversing with himself, as Marcus Aurelius in his *Meditations*. Augustine examines and reminds himself what he ought to believe and desire in a similar manner. The lesson is that, if we wish to know God and the soul and to be happy, we must keep watch over our thoughts and desires.

But self-therapy only goes so far. Only a healthy soul can heal the sick soul. In *Soliloquia* "the ailing soul is not called upon to make the journey alone but is in the hands of a competent philosophical physician and guide."[10] When we consider that Reason's advice comes from somewhere outside Augustine, we see that the form of *Soliloquia* mirrors an aspect of Epicurean therapy. Epicureans did not pretend to heal themselves, but engaged in philosophical therapy under the direction of a mentor,[11] believing that for a person's soul to be healed he needs help from his master. But there is a striking difference between Epicureanism and *Soliloquia*. Epicureans treated Epicurus as their sainted savior. Augustine's therapy is linked to a better friend and savior. Desire can only be healed through conversion to Christ.

10. Silk, "Boethius' Consolatio Philosophiae," 37.

11. See, for example, Nussbaum, *Therapy of Desire*, chapter 4; Hadot, *What Is Ancient Philosophy?* 123–24.

In sum, Reason is not God, but it acts as a bridge between God and the soul. It shows our need to be circumspect. But circumspection, for the Christian, must be more than Stoical. Our souls are not able to sufficiently monitor and heal their own thoughts and desires. The soul must be converted to and remain in communion with God in order to understand the truth and be healed of its disordered loves.

AUGUSTINE'S PRAYER: THE TRINITARIAN QUEST FOR REORDERED DESIRES

From the moment it begins to speak Reason seems bent on helping Augustine. First it encourages him to write down anything he finds to overcome the weaknesses of memory. Then it advises him to "Pray for health and for obtaining what you desire," and to record the prayer (1.1.1). In recommending prayer Reason shows that it submits to God. The recommended content of the prayer also shows something about desire and its satisfaction; Reason is referring to spiritual as well as physical health. The process of reordering one's desires must be infused with prayer if it is to succeed. So also the quest for satisfying desire must be prayerful.[12] Reason reinforces the importance of the individual soul's relation to God, for it recommends "complete solitude." However, Reason also suggests that one of the advantages of writing is for the reading of "a few of your fellow citizens," a reminder that seekers of God should hear from one another as a help in the search.

The prayer, consisting of praise and petition, unites themes from the previous dialogues with an explicitly trinitarian theology; several themes Augustine would explore in later writings are incipient in the prayer. He praises the Father for creating and ordering the universe. He praises the Son for being the source and substance of true happiness. He praises the Spirit for being able to lead us to happiness. He asks the Father to hear his prayer. Speaking of the Son's work, he asks for help returning to the place from which he has run. He also asks for the help the Spirit can provide. He attributes to God the power of reordering our desires and illustrates his belief that our pursuit of right desire must be prayerful. He also shows how the reordering of our desires involves each member of the Trinity.

12. Cary rightly takes this passage as evidence that "Augustine is never without a doctrine of grace." He correctly claims that Augustine in his earlier writings seeks divine help to get the wisdom he desires (*Inner Grace*, 26). Cary's view that Augustine in the early writings "does not fully recognize the need for divine help in the moral life" (27)—i.e., that he does not seek help to also *desire* what he ought—is not correct. For this is precisely the health for which Reason advises Augustine to pray.

First, Augustine praises the Father, calling him the "Founder of the universe" and "O God, through whom all things, which by themselves are not, strive to be" (1.1.2). He acknowledges the Father's power to create out of nothing; God "out of nothing did create this world." He acknowledges the goodness of creation, for God "makes no evil," and we all perceive the world "to be most beautiful." This reaffirms *De beata vita*'s treatment of creation as a finite good, in itself having no existence but graced with goodness and beauty from its creator. God makes no evil, and "shows that evil is nothing to the few who take refuge in that which truly is." Through God "the whole, even with its perverse side, is perfected." Thus Augustine reaffirms *De ordine*'s lessons, and hints that evil as such lacks being. There are, then, two themes in this praise offered to the Father: his creative power and his re-creative power, the one to create and order the universe *ex nihilo*, the other to take up evil into the order of the whole and to "be the Father of our awakening and our illumination."

Now Augustine praises the Son, "O Truth, in whom and from whom and through whom all the things which are true are true" (1.1.3). The Son is "Happiness, in whom and from whom and through whom all those who are happy are happy." He is "the Good and the Beautiful." The Son is the one "from whom to depart is to die, to whom to return is to revive, in whom to dwell is to live." *De beata vita*'s lessons are rehearsed: Christ is happiness. In Him we must seek satisfaction. We must seek Him through the theological virtues, for "faith excites us, hope lifts us up, charity joins us" to Him.

Augustine next praises the Spirit, an active member of the Trinity, described fifteen times as the one "through whom" the universe is administered and souls return to God, "through whom" only we can do good (1.1.3). The Spirit reorders our desires: "O God, who dost convert us . . . through whom we thirst for the cup which, when drunk, quenches our thirst forever . . . who dost convict the world . . . who dost purify and prepare us for divine rewards . . . ." There could be no clearer attribution of the healing of desire to the work of God. While the Father is the source of all that is to be loved, and the Son is to be loved by our converted hearts, the Spirit must convert us; thus Augustine asks, "graciously come Thou to me."

The petitioning section of the prayer also begins with the Father, whom he asks to "come Thou to my aid" (1.1.4). More praises are mingled with the requests. In these Augustine reiterates the order by which the Father guides the universe, praising Him as the source of order. As *De ordine* affirms, God is not responsible for evil; he maintains order in the universe and takes evil up into order. This God Augustine asks to "Hear, hear, hear me."[13]

13. There is even a hint of *Free Choice of the Will*'s explanation of evil as grounded in the freedom of creatures. Augustine prays to God, "by whose laws the soul's choice is free . . . ."

In the next section of the petition, Augustine mentions his partly healed affections: "Now do I love Thee alone, follow Thee alone, seek Thee alone" (1.1.5). Yet he asks: "heal and open my ears . . . . Heal and open my eyes . . . ." He asks God to "Receive . . . Thy fugitive." The theme of running from and returning to God is prominent in this passage and suggests the story of the prodigal son. Although directly petitioning the Father, he is speaking of Christ. For God's role in this passage is that which Christ attributes to himself as the one who rescues those who have run away. Augustine confesses the importance of reordered desires, saying: "I know nothing except that fleeting and perishable things should be spurned and that certain and eternal things sought after," but he also confesses that he knows not "how one may come to Thee," asking for whatever will help him come. Most important are three things: "Increase faith, increase hope, increase charity in me."

Finally Augustine begs for the Spirit: "Thee do I solicit, and again do I ask Thee for the means by which Thou art solicited" (1.1.6). Only the pure, who seek God rightly, can achieve wisdom, but we need God's help to seek Him rightly: "every man hath sought rightly whom Thou hast made to seek rightly." We need right desire to see God, but we need God to have right desire. So he asks for healing: "if there is a desire in me for something superfluous, do Thou cleanse me and make me fit to see Thee." He trusts his body to God, and begs regarding his soul "that Thou convert me completely to Thee" and make him "a perfect lover and recipient of Thy wisdom . . . ."

Clearly prayer is essential to the pursuit of happiness. We must pray both for reordered desires and for the attainment of what they seek. The prayer's trinitarianism gives the lie to the old Alfaric reading of Augustine as insincere about his Christian commitment, for he mingles trinitarianism with the quest for rightly ordered desires. All three members of the Trinity are involved in converting our desires: the Father as the creator and re-creator of the desiring soul, the Son as the one we ought to love, and the Spirit as the active administrator of the process of renewal. If we are to know God, we must pray to the Trinity for the conversion of our desires and for help in attaining them.

TO KNOW GOD AND THE SOUL

In this section I shall first discuss Augustine's claim that God and the soul alone are to be loved. Then I shall discuss Reason's efforts to circumscribe the knowledge of God. Then I shall discuss how faith, hope, and charity reorder our desires, making it possible for us to love God and the soul as we ought. Next, I shall discuss the diagnosis of Augustine's sin, emphasizing his limited ability to know the disordered desires in his own soul and his need to hear from God in order to be healed. Finally, I shall look at Book I's concluding reminder to trust God alone for the healing of desire.

What Healthy Souls Desire

Augustine's dialogue with Reason begins immediately after the prayer:

> Augustine. Behold, I have prayed to God.
>
> Reason. Then what things do you want to know?
>
> Augustine. All those things for which I prayed.
>
> Reason. Briefly summarize them.
>
> Augustine. I yearn to know God and the soul.
>
> Reason. Nothing more?
>
> Augustine. Nothing whatsoever (1.2.7).

The theme of the dialogue and the object of Augustine's prayer, briefly summarized indeed, is the knowledge of God and the soul. This knowledge would be the sum of the wisdom sought in *Contra Academicos*, the benefit of the relationship with Christ sought in *De beata vita*, and the end of the liberal and spiritual education promoted in *De ordine*. God and the soul are also the objects of rightly ordered desire. In asking for cleansing from desire for what is not eternal, Augustine is asking for help in loving God and the soul, for these things are eternal, and healthy souls desire to know them.

Remarks on Knowing God and the Soul

Reason now plies Augustine with questions comparing knowledge of God and of geometry. There are three themes to these questions: that knowledge of God is through the mind rather than the senses; that knowledge of God is better than knowledge of geometrical figures or anything else that is known through the mind; and that knowledge of God is to be supremely delighted in.

Reason first asks Augustine how he can be sure that, were he to know God and the soul, it would satisfy him. Augustine says it would, for there is nothing that would compare to this knowledge. He says, "I love nothing but God and the soul, neither of which I know" (1.2.7). Reason asks whether this means that he does not love his friends, and Augustine replies that he does love them for the sake of their souls. Indeed, the better they use their souls the better he loves them. Augustine explains that he wishes to know the souls of his friends through his own soul, not through his senses, and that he wishes to know God the same way (1.3.8). Significantly, he says that the knowledge of the Platonists is not enough, for even if what they said was true that does not ensure that they knew God (1.4.9).

Reason presses him to describe something he knows in the manner in which he desires to know God. Geometry serves, for Augustine says he knows a line and a sphere with certainty that defies Academic skepticism. While the senses helped him learn, he knows them through his mind. He tells Reason he is content to call this "knowledge," and does not fear the Stoic restriction of knowledge to what he is not, the wise man.

An interesting interlude follows. Augustine asks Reason to "proceed; I want to see where you are going with this inquiry." It replies, "Don't be in a hurry, we are at leisure—only listen attentively . . . . I am striving to make you more joyful about things over which you may fear no loss, and here you are ordering us to rush in headlong as if this were some paltry affair." Augustine bows to this rebuke, which reminds us to seek the truth at a workable pace. Moreover, Reason shows its interest in reordering Augustine's loves; it wants to make him "more joyful" over things in which he ought to take joy.

Reason now asks about lines and spheres (1.4.10), but the questioning is meant to draw out the relationship of geometrical knowledge and knowledge of God. Reason reminds him that it has asked him not about what he *knows*, but about what he knows about *knowing* God. So now it asks "whether it is good enough for you to know God in the way you know that geometrical ball—that is, to have no doubt about God as you have no doubt about it." Perhaps geometry affords a clue as to how we should hope to know God: with absolute certainty. Yet Augustine maintains that there are differences between knowing God and knowing geometrical figures. He names a difference of disciplines and a difference of delight (1.5.11). God is not known through the discipline of geometry, and the knowledge of geometrical figures does not cause Augustine to rejoice in the way knowledge of God would cause him to rejoice. Reason agrees that he will rejoice "much more" in the latter, adding that the knowledge of God is better than the knowledge of geometrical figures in the same way looking at the sky is better than looking at the earth. This comparison is derived from the old Platonic analogy of the cave, and considers geometry in much the same way: as a study of non-physical reality knowing which is training for knowing the divine highest reality.[14]

14. Plato, *Republic*, 514–15.

In sum, knowing God is not a sensible activity, and in this respect it resembles the knowledge gained through the liberal arts. But knowledge of God is better by far than any knowledge gained through the arts, and accordingly we should desire and delight in knowledge of God.

Faith, Hope, Charity

But how shall we achieve this delight? In the next three chapters Reason and Augustine discuss the things that heal our souls so we can know God: faith, hope, and charity. In this section I shall first summarize this presentation of the theological virtues as the means of desire's renewal. Then I shall discuss their ultimate end, delight in God. Then I shall explain how this delight completes or corrects some interpretations of *Soliloquia* offered by scholars.

Reason now explains what is needed to see, that is to understand, God: healthy eyes, the act of looking, and the act of seeing (1.6.12). To see God we need "eyes," or "a mind free from every bodily blemish, that is, a mind that is now removed from and has been purged of the various lusts for mortal things." Faith accomplishes this purgation. Trust in God and in the truths of Christianity purges the mind of diseases so it can see God. But we are in danger lest we despair so much of seeing God that we do not even look. Hope, as we saw in *Contra Academicos*, is the cure to despair, which fits us to look for God, to seek the knowledge of Him. Finally, we shall never see God if we do not love Him. A mind that believes with faith and hopes for healing but does not love God seeks and never finds. Thus we need charity.

Again, we need faith that we can be happy by seeing God; hope that we will be happy upon seeing God; and charity, by which the soul "longs [*desidero*] to see and enjoy [*perfruor*]" (1.6.13). Yet charity while we are *seeking* is different from charity when we have *found*. Reason says:

> Now looking is followed by the very vision of God, who is the end of our looking, not because it no longer exists, but because it has nothing further towards which it may strive. And this is truly perfect virtue, reason reaching its end, from which follows the happy life.

Now charity is a seeking of wisdom. It is the desire for God. But its purpose is to be satisfied in God. Once the vision of God is attained and as long as it continues, we cease to desire God, and charity in the form of desire ceases. Then we *delight* in God; charity is not canceled but fulfilled in the form of delight. Love and desire overlap, for one should love the God one does not fully have. But desire and love are not identical: Desire, as a yearning for what one does *not* have, ceases; but love, which begins as a desire for something one does not have, is fulfilled as *delight* in having. Reason asks "whether these three things are still necessary to the soul after it has reached the point of seeing God" (1.7.14), answering that faith and hope are not necessary; but charity remains and increases. "For when the soul has seen that unique and true beauty, it will love all the more."[15] Reason adds that faith and hope must remain in this life, for the body prevents us from holding on to the vision of God.

The desiderative element of the passage and the emphasis on desire's renewal through the theological virtues pose two problems, one minor and one more significant, for some claims about the purpose of *Soliloquia*. Van Fleteren believes that Augustine's intention at Cassiciacum was to outline a path of ascent to a perpetual intellectual vision of God and that in *Soliloquia* he now "begins to apply himself to this program" of ascent.[16] Similarly, Cary remarks in one of his earlier articles that at Cassiciacum Augustine's "aim is to get beyond mere transitory glimpses of truth and attain a stable possession of it such as characterizes the wise man."[17] This requires liberal arts training the others at Cassiciacum do not have, and thus Augustine in *Soliloquia* must pursue this path on his own.

The first problem is a minor one, and that is that this sort of analysis of the purpose of *Soliloquia* is not, in itself, complete. The project of *Soliloquia* is an intellectual one, but also deeply affective. Reason praises faith, hope, and charity not as modes of thought, but as practices that heal the soul's affections in preparation for the vision of God—a vision approved by Reason as true, but also *delighted* in. These virtues administer the conversion of desire.

Of greater concern is the idea that the Cassiciacum dialogues are dedicated to achieving a perpetual vision of God in this life.[18] The text is subtle here, but I think this reading is mistaken based on what Reason says in 1.7.14. From the first several sentences of the passage we can get this conditional proposition: *If the vision of God is perpetual, then faith and hope no longer remain.* From the next few sentences we can get this conditional proposition: *If we are in this life, then faith and hope remain.* It follows that *if we are in this life, then the vision of God is not perpetual.* We should also

15. Similarly, Anselm says: "Let me seek you in desiring you; let me desire you in seeking you. Let me find you in loving you; let me love you in finding you." From *Proslogion*, ch. 1, pg. 6.

16. Van Fleteren, "The Cassiciacum Dialogues," 60.

17. Cary, "What Licentius Learned."

18. Such as Cary and others argue. See above, Chapter 1, under the heading *Ways of Understanding Augustine's Conversion and Early Writings*.

note the reasons given for the absence of faith and hope in the perpetual happy life. Faith is not needed when God is seen directly, and hope is not needed when the soul has God: "Why is faith necessary when now it sees? Likewise, why hope, since now it holds?" Towards the end of 1.7.14 identical or similar reasons—the soul's *not* seeing without the "interruption of falsehood" and its *not* possessing what it desires—are linked to the need for faith and hope *in this life*. So I think the perpetual beatific vision and this life do not overlap.

Now it is true that in *Retractions* 1.4.3 Augustine regrets the degree of happiness *Soliloquia* had attributed to the soul in this life; for at Cassiciacum he had written of the soul that, "when it understands God, it is now happy." In my view the young Augustine thinks that in the vision of God a complete happiness is possible in this life, *but only temporarily*. (His idea of such a vision of God is no doubt shaped by his vision of God recorded in *Conf.* VII, and would soon be shaped by the experience at Ostia in *Conf.* IX.) The mature Augustine thinks that no happiness in this life can be complete. In short, at Cassiciacum the vision of God in this life is a state of *complete but not perpetual* happiness, but later on Augustine thinks that happiness in this life is *neither complete nor perpetual*.

The reason the happy life is not perpetual is that in this life our desires are not fully healed. *Sol.* 1.7.14: "unless it [the soul] fixes its eye with unbounded love and never ceases from looking, it will not be able to remain in that most happy vision." Similarly, in *Conf.* 7.17.23 we learn that the weight of sinful desire had put a stop to the vision of God Augustine experienced prior to Cassiciacum. For vision of God to be perpetual, the gaze must be steady; but the gaze is steadied by a steady love, and this we do not have in this life. For this same reason, the imperfection of our desires, we need faith and hope in this life, to help us love God in imperfect fashion until our desires are healed—and, ultimately, to heal them. And in order "that it may be healed," the theological virtues are "always necessary" in this life. As early as *b. Vita* 2.11 we were told that desire must have a stable object, or else happiness will be unstable; but it is just as true that desire must also be stable, or else happiness will be unstable.

Diagnosis of Sinful Desires

In the next scene Reason questions Augustine to see if his desires are properly ordered for ascent. Augustine confesses some sins, but Reason identifies a number of sins of which he is not aware. He will find that his desires are not set so thoroughly on God and the soul as he thinks they are. God alone knows the true state of a person's soul, and we must turn to God in order to be healed; the conversion of desire needs God's help.

The Sins Augustine Knows

Reason says: "But why do we delay? We should be getting on our way. Yet let us see that which comes before all else: whether we are healthy. . . . Do you love something besides the knowledge of yourself and God?" (1.9.16). Based on his current feelings, Augustine feels he could answer no. But he opts for caution and admits he does not know for certain, remembering that he has before thought himself free of disorderly desires and then been surprised by one of those very desires. Nevertheless, he thinks he has only three desires for non-eternal things, the loss of which could hurt him: to be free from physical pain, to live, and that his friends live. He admits that his desires are not yet perfect.

Reason asks about various desires that have plagued him in the past (2.10.17). Augustine says he has not desired riches for fourteen years, when he first read Cicero.[19] He has not desired honors since his recent conversion. He says he does not desire a wife. He does not know whether a wise man should seek marriage in order to have children, but in any case he will not trust *himself* with sex. He says he only desires such food as is needed for health.

Reason says, "You have made much progress!" but immediately adds, "And yet, the things that remain are hindering you a great deal from seeing that light" (1.11.18). It now questions him more closely. It worries that he is not ruling his unruly desire but merely "lulling it to sleep"; it wants to be sure that he is not only content without the objects of disordered desires, but would not rejoice to have them if they were offered (1.11.19). Augustine maintains that he has made progress. For, if he would delight in these things at all, it would not be for their own sake but for the use he could make of them for attaining wisdom. Reason accepts this account, but continues to test him. Through further questioning Augustine says that he desires his friends and his own life for the sake of attaining wisdom, not for their own sake (1.12.20), saying the same of his desire for freedom from pain (1.12.21).

19. There is no clear contradiction with Augustine's recollection in *Conf.* 6.6.9 that he wanted honors, money, and marriage at this time. Augustine may well have wanted riches these past years as a means to some other end: perhaps for attaining wisdom or honors. Russell suggests another reconciliation of the passages: After reading Cicero Augustine resolved to not pursue riches, but his resolution was conditional on attaining the truth, which took a long time. See Russell, "Cicero's Hortensius."

Now Reason reveals why it tests Augustine's desires. It compares wisdom to a woman who will not give herself to just any man, but only to one devoted to her. "Will the most chaste beauty of wisdom show herself to you unless you are on fire for her alone?" (1.13.22). The sexual imagery suggests the degree to which Augustine at least hopes to overcome the unruly sexual desires that, as *Confessions* tells us, had plagued him for so long. These desires must be either redirected toward God or eradicated so love of God can take their place. Claiming his desire for wisdom is already pure, he asks why he continues to wait in agony for wisdom. Reason explains that each person's journey to wisdom is matched by his own abilities (2.13.23). In a way, there is more than one path to God.[20] "Each person, in fact, comprehends that unique and most true good according to his own health and strength." We are not permitted to see wisdom until we are ready. A slow ascent is required for many; we must learn to see immaterial things below God before we are able to see *God*. Reason again calls on the Platonic cave analogy, saying that one long kept in the dark needs time for the eyes to adjust before he can look at the sun. With this observation, Reason calls off the discussion for the day in order to preserve health.

The Sins Reason Knows

On the next day Reason continues to test Augustine's desires. Augustine will learn that he was not as aware of his sin as he thought. He knew of small disorders in his loves, but Reason will make him aware of much worse. As Silk says, "His vision is clouded by mortal shadows, he is held fast by earthly longings, and he is tossed by passion."[21]

Augustine invites Reason to lead him, even if the way is hard, to a reordered soul: "Please give me that order . . . . Lead me, guide me—wherever you will, through whatever you will, however you will. Command whatever hard, whatever arduous things you want . . ." (1.14.24). Reason says, "we must completely flee from these sensible things,"[22] for the wisdom we desire is given only to one whose desire is only for wisdom: to "the kind of man whom no earthly thing delights in any way." It now unearths hidden sins,

20. Augustine is not suggesting a religious pluralism such that one can reach God without Christ. Rather, he is emphasizing the different abilities of each of us to contemplate God, and the different relationships different people have with Christ. See *Retractions* 1.4.3; also see Van Fleteren, "Authority and Reason," 54.

21. Silk, "Boethius' Consolatio Philosophiae," 38.

22. In *Retractions*, 1.4.3 Augustine regrets these words, too much in the spirit of Porphyry; we must not love carnal things more than God, but we must not denigrate the matter God created.

for "the soul is often deceived . . . the result being that it considers itself healthy and boasts about itself; and because it does not yet see, it complains as if it were right for it to do so" (1.14.25). This was Augustine's state a few days ago, boasting of spiritual health and complaining that he did not yet have wisdom. His health is not as strong as he thinks, his own heart opaque to him.[23] Reason reminds him where his desires had gone last night: So recently after professing no desire for sex, he had found himself longing for a woman's embrace. This happened "so that the most hidden physician"—a reference to Christ[24]—could teach him about his disordered desires.[25]

This is compelling evidence that Augustine believes we cannot heal ourselves. We are blind to our own disorders, unable even to diagnose ourselves unaided. We need God to diagnose and heal our desires. God is performing surgery on Augustine's soul, with Reason as his instrument. This episode is like yet unlike Marcus Aurelius's self-treatment; for Reason is in the service of Christ, working for the healing of his soul.

The treatment is painful, but it succeeds in pushing Augustine to surrender more to the healing of Christ: "Be quiet, I beg you, be quiet! Why do you torment me? Why do you dig so much and go so low? . . . from now on I promise nothing, I presume nothing, lest you ask me any more questions about those things. . . . Let Him do as He pleases . . . . I now commit all of myself to His mercy and care" (1.14.26).

Book I's Conclusion

Despite his professed submission to the healer's authority, Augustine still tries to lay down his own terms for the healing process, asking for a short cut

23. Cooper comments that this episode shows how aware Augustine (Augustine the author, that is) was of the disorders in his loves at Cassiciacum. See Cooper, "Scripture at Cassiciacum," 35. Seneca had mentioned that our own vices are often opaque to us in *Tranquility of the Mind* 1; in *Seneca: Dialogues and Essays*, 115.

24. The reference, by the way, shows that Reason is not identical to any member of the Trinity. So will the next words Reason and Augustine exchange, in which they speak of Christ in the third person. This passage cuts against Cary's claim in *Augustine's Invention* that Augustine's eventual strategy, only developed later, was to recommend contemplating God via an "in then up" movement. As an inward movement, the soul learns to contemplate its own immaterial nature; this we saw Augustine recommending in *Ord.* But as an upward movement the soul learns to contemplate the God from whom it is distinct. I differ from Cary's claim that at Cassiciacum Augustine thought of the soul as divine, not clearly distinct from God—that he had yet to learn of the upward movement, 85–89.

25. Augustine, who has pointed out to Licentius his need for the soul's physician (see above, Chapter 4, under the subheading *The Healer of Desires*), here admits quite candidly that he also needs the physician.

(1.14.27). Reason suggests ending the first book for the sake of his health, but he insists on "some tidbit about the vicinity of the light on which I am intent" (1.15.27). In response Reason discloses a rudimentary argument for the immortality of the soul (1.15.27–29). We want to know the truth; truth exists, and whatever exists is somewhere; but the truth is not in a *locus*, for only mortal things exist in a "place," and the truth is immortal; therefore, there are immortal things.

This rudimentary argument previews Book II's argument for immortality. By reassuring him that they exist, the argument instills confidence in the immortal things Augustine desires somewhat and strives to desire more. Augustine agrees to ending the conversation for now, saying they will reflect on these things in silence later (1.15.30). As they cease their conversation, Reason advises Augustine to thoroughly commit himself to God's care and to serve Him rather than try to be his own master. For God "will not stop lifting you up to Himself, and He will permit nothing to happen to you unless it is good for you, even if you do not know it." Reason counsels us to trust in God, not ourselves, for the healing and satisfaction of desire.

ARGUMENTS FOR IMMORTALITY

On another day, agreeing to continue their work, Reason recommends that Augustine pray "as briefly and as perfectly as possible" (2.1.1). The prayer is stunning in its simplicity: "O God, ever the Same: may I know myself, may I know Thee." The remainder of Book II is the locus of an unusual argument for the immortality of the soul, meant to help us know both God and the soul. I shall first present the argument. Then I shall discuss its interpretation, emphasizing its role in both reordering and satisfying desire.

The Central Argument

The argument is preceded by a discussion in which Augustine tells Reason how much he wants to know and understand God and his soul. Above all, he wants to know whether he is immortal (2.1.1). This takes some doing, some meandering through subtle ideas. The argument for immortality is developed through a series of arguments, some of them not particularly impressive.

Twists and Turns

The first argument establishes that truth always exists, and meets with no resistance: The truth outlasts the world; for if the world exists it is true that it exists, and if the world does not exist it is true that it does not exist (2.2.2).

The second argument is: Sense-perception and understanding both pertain to the soul, although the latter also pertains to God (2.3.3); falsity also cannot exist without a soul, for falsity needs a soul to be mistaken about the truth; yet falsity always exists because the truth is so hard to find (2.3.4); therefore the soul is immortal.

This second argument is unimpressive. That truth is hard to come by can only ensure that falsity exists *if* souls already exist, so as to be able to get caught in falsehood. If there were no souls seeking truth, truth would not be hard to come by; so the argument only shows that as long as souls exist, souls exist. Augustine calls the argument a "leaden dagger," an instrument of false material that fails to cut (2.4.5).

Luckily, Reason suggests the premises of a new argument resting on truth rather than falsehood. If falsehood does not exist, all things are true. Since neither truth nor falsehood can exist without the soul, this premise secures the soul's immortality.

But there are two worries with this argument. First, as Augustine says (2.4.5), it does not show that any individual soul exists; it only shows that *some* soul or souls exist at any given time. Perhaps there is an eternal succession of mortal souls. We need to anchor immortality in *each* soul, not in the category of things that are souls. Second, there is a problem with the notion of truth. As Reason explains (2.5.7), the operative definition of truth is whatever is as it seems, and all things that seem are perceived. Since only souls have sense-perception, the things they do not perceive do not exist. This includes the inside of any opaque object, the inside of the earth, or anything hidden in darkness. Thus Augustine tries to define truth as "that which is" (2.5.8). But this definition excludes falsehood from existing at all. Augustine is flummoxed at this point (2.5.8), so Reason reminds him to pray for help (2.6.9). He does, asking: "With Thee as my guide, may I return to myself and to Thee."

Reason suggests another effort to define falsity (2.6.10). Augustine struggles to do this (2.6.10–2.8.15). He says that falsity is what partakes of similarity to the true, and then that it is what partakes of *dis*similarity to the true, and finally that it is what partakes of both. Each definition encompasses everything in the universe, and thus fails to distinguish what is true from what is false. Reason, refusing to believe "that we have implored divine aid in vain" (2.9.16), finally gives a definition of falsity: whatever we perceive which "strives to be something and is not" (2.9.17). Falsity is whatever is less than it should be, whatever partakes of more non-being than is suitable for its nature. Here is a definition that can ground an argument for immortality; the insight leads to reflection on what truly is, and the final form of the argument begins to emerge.

The Argument Emerges

The false is that which partakes immoderately of non-being. Clearly the true is that which exists to the degree appropriate to it, and that which is most true is that whose existence is eternal—the very things we have been striving to love and to understand in the Cassiciacum dialogues. If immortality is to be demonstrated, the argument will have to be based on its connection to these immortal things. In this way, also, the riddle of truth, once solved, can link immortality to an individual soul, not just to the category of things that are souls.

Accordingly, the groundwork for the argument is laid with a discussion of the liberal arts, those disciplines which help the soul get to know eternal things. We must first lay the groundwork for the argument. The liberal disciplines are true (2.11.19), and whatever makes them disciplines makes them true (2.11.20–21). It is also agreed that that by which all other things are true is true in and through itself (2.11.21). Finally, if anything is necessarily in a subject it can only exist if the subject exists (2.12.22).

The argument is summarized in 2.12.22–2.13.24. If anything is in a subject necessarily and is eternal, then the subject is also eternal. The disciplines (dialectic is emphasized) are in the soul necessarily. The disciplines are true. But truth is eternal, and so the disciplines are also eternal. Therefore, the soul also exists eternally.

Augustine cautiously voices two concerns with the argument: that some premise may have been conceded rashly and that it is strange that a discipline which many have not studied is in their souls eternally (2.14.25). Reason agrees to address the first concern (2.15.27), but the second will be put off for another book (2.19.33), which Augustine in fact never wrote. Augustine and Reason revisit two premises, confirming that the truth is eternal; even if truth passed away, it would be true that it had passed away (2.15.28). The claim that the disciplines are true is confirmed by considering geometry (2.17.32–2.19.33). Bodily shapes exist by partaking of the perfection of geometrical figures; their existence is thus imperfect; they strive to be. But geometrical figures themselves are perfect and do not strive to be. Thus they meet the criterion of truth. Since geometry studies these things, truth is in geometry. Moreover, the discipline of dialectic *is* the truth; for a discipline is true through its ability to get to the truth, but this ability is its use of dialectic; thus dialectic is truth, and is true through itself (2.11.21).

Interpreting the Argument

We must now interpret this argument. First, I shall briefly highlight its neo-Platonic and its Christian aspects. Second, I shall examine the argument's substance and respond to Cary's claim that the argument is meant to establish the ontological unity of God and the soul. Third, I shall contrast my understanding of the argument's purpose with Conybeare's. At least one of the argument's purposes is to heal our desires.

Platonic and Christian Aspects of the Argument

The argument is neo-Platonic in that it treats being as coming in degrees; things have a lesser degree of being in accordance with their distance from absolute being. Moreover, the soul is an immaterial reality; this, too, is a neo-Platonic notion.

The argument also has Christian characteristics. In particular, an object's degree of non-being is not treated as bad, nor is its distance from absolute being. A definition of falseness as that which is at a distance from the true was *rejected*. Falseness rather is understood as the distance an object has strayed from its own place. This corresponds to the Christian understanding of creational goodness. If God created an object with a lesser degree of being than himself, that did not make it bad; what was bad was its falling away from the place God assigned it to. What is in common with neo-Platonism is the understanding of evil, badness, or falseness as a *lack* rather than a *substance*, as Augustine had learned from the neo-Platonists themselves (*Conf.* VII). What is different from neo-Platonism is the understanding of evil, badness, or falseness not simply as a lack in a thing, but as a lack of what God *intended* for a thing.

Does God Depend on the Soul?

We could produce a formalized version of the argument:

1. If X is necessarily in Y and X is eternal, then Y is eternal.
2. The disciplines are necessarily in the soul.

3. Truth is necessarily in one of the disciplines.
4. Truth is eternal.
5. So truth is necessarily in one of the disciplines and is eternal. (from 3 and 4)
6. So one of the disciplines is eternal. (from 1 and 5)
7. So one of the disciplines is necessarily in the soul and is eternal. (from 2 and 6)
8. So the soul is eternal. (from 1 and 7)

The premises of the argument successfully demonstrate the conclusion. That truth is necessarily in one of the disciplines is established by 2.11.21's conclusion that dialectic *is* truth. We must remember that Jesus Christ, also, *is* the truth (*b. Vita* 4.34). Accordingly, it falls to the careful reader of Augustine to ask the very important question: *Can this argument really mean what it appears to mean, that God is ontologically dependent on the soul?* Moreover, *did Augustine* intend *for it to establish that God is ontologically dependent on the soul?* Unfortunately, I must answer *yes* to the first question, but I answer *no* to the second question.

Since Jesus Christ is God, and since he is also truth, and truth is necessarily in dialectic, and dialectic is necessarily in the soul, God is necessarily in the soul. The sort of necessity we are talking about is such that, if God is necessarily in the soul, God cannot exist if the soul does not exist: "what is in a subject inseparably cannot remain if the subject itself does not remain" (2.12.22). So God is dependent on the human soul. (Cary, in *Augustine's Invention of the Inner Self*, explains this aspect of the argument rather well.[26])

Now there are only two ways to understand the dependence of God on the human soul. Either God is ontologically inferior to the soul, or else God depends on the soul in the way a thing depends on itself for its own existence, in which case God and the soul are the same being. Either of these alternatives is, of course, inconsistent with orthodox Christian theology; they impart divinity to the soul. (The former alternative is also inconsistent with neo-Platonic thought, as Cary notes.[27])

But did Augustine actually intend to promote any such doctrine? I think not. After presenting Cary's view that this is just what Augustine intended, I will explain how I think the argument was meant to do something quite different, explain why I think the text of the *Soliloquia* goes against Cary's view, and comment on why Augustine's argument goes so far awry.

26. Cary, *Augustine's Invention*, ch. 7.

27. Ibid., 102.

According to Cary, it is no accident that Augustine's argument seems to merge God and the soul. In a 1994 article, Cary takes this argument as evidence of Augustine's residual Manicheanism, a residue he is converting into neo-Platonist concepts.[28] Says Cary, Manicheanism, along with Stoicism and Platonism, conceive of the soul as divine and a part of God. Part of the soul is unfallen, unsullied by sin, an "oasis of untarnished perfection."[29] While the other two philosophies conceive of God and the soul in materialist terms, Augustine's goal in *Soliloquia* is to establish the divinity of the soul—and its oasis of perfection—on neo-Platonist, that is to say immaterial, terms. Accordingly, *Soliloquia* argues that God is the truth contained in the soul—God is literally *in* the soul, as a constituent to it. This is Augustine's "Manichean optimism." In his 2000 *Augustine's Invention of the Inner Self*, Cary still understands the argument as a movement towards neo-Platonism and Christianity and away from Augustine's earlier, materialistic conceptions of the divine soul. He claims that the argument "clearly implies the divinity of the soul" and entails the immutability of the soul, "at least in its higher or rational part."[30]

The argument for immortality is indeed neo-Platonic, and assumes the incorporeality of the soul,[31] and indeed Cary is right that it entails God's dependence on the soul. Nevertheless, I do not think Augustine means to establish God in, and dependent on, the soul, nor that the soul is ontologically God. The argument suggests that dialectic—and truth itself and God along with it—is contained within or limited by the soul, as if it needed a human soul to survive. But this is not the direction in which the broader dialogue points. The whole point of exposing the flawed definition of truth as grounded in human perception was to *avoid* making truth dependent on the soul. Accordingly, Augustine's analysis is not meant to drag the truth down to the level of the soul. The argument is meant to pull the soul up to the level of the truth. The truth, something immortal, will not deign to be known by what is mortal; since the soul knows the truth, it is immortal. The disciplines are not meant to tether the truth down to the soul. They are meant to be the soul's connection to the truth, raising it up to immortality. Cary actually agrees with this, saying that Augustine's argument is "designed to show that the soul is dependent on Truth for its being, life, and immortality—not the other way around!"[32]

28. Cary, "God in the Soul," 98–100.

29. Ibid., 72.

30. Cary, *Augustine's Invention*, 100.

31. Norris, "Immortality," 445.

32. Cary, *Augustine's Invention*, 103.

Despite thinking that Augustine's argument fails in his own goal of maintaining the ontological superiority of truth over the soul, Cary thinks its implicit merging of God and soul is intentional. But this runs against the grain of the dialogue, particularly the literary elements. If this is Augustine's goal, then the character of Reason would have to be perfect—indeed would have to be Christ himself! But it is not the case that *Soliloquia* tries to establish that the soul has an "oasis of untarnished perfection."[33] If this were the case, then we would surely not see Reason itself asking "whether we are healthy" (1.9.16) and then see the soul—including both Augustine *and* his Reason—diagnosed as rife with sinful desires (1.9.16–1.14.26). We would also not see Reason seeking instruction from other men (2.14.126). Moreover, if the argument were meant to establish that God is present in the soul in such a way as to guaranty the soul's divinity, then the fact that Reason speaks of Christ in the third person (1.14.25) is strange.

So why would Augustine propagate an argument with such a startling entailment (the divinity of the soul) if he did not mean to? This passage of *Soliloquia* is subtle, and it is difficult to be certain; nevertheless, I suggest this explanation: *Augustine simply did not realize the ontological and theological problems of this argument at the time he made it*. As a result, he crafted an argument which dwells in some tension with his otherwise consistent characterization of himself and of his own Reason as not being God.

It is worth noting that Augustine does not seem to have his mind entirely made up on what sort of argument he is after. Before noting the textual evidence for this, let us first note that there is a very different sort of argument lurking in the vicinity of the main argument:

1. If X is necessarily in Y and X is eternal, then Y is eternal.
2. The disciplines are necessarily in the soul.
3. A discipline necessarily has truth.
4. Truth is eternal.
5. So a discipline necessarily has something which is eternal. (from 3 and 4)
6. So a discipline is necessarily in the soul and necessarily has something which is eternal. (from 2 and 5)
7. So the soul is eternal. (from 1 and 6)

33. Augustine may well think that God is "in" the soul in a different sense, namely as the inner teacher described more thoroughly in *De magistro*; see above under the heading *Who Is Reason?* where I suggest that Reason in *Sol.* is in communication with the inner teacher.

In *this* argument we make use of the same sort of necessity—where X is in Y and X cannot exist without Y—but also of another sort of necessity—where X is in Y and *Y* cannot exist without *X*. The first sort of necessity binds the disciplines to the soul; they cannot exist without it. The second sort of necessity binds the disciplines to the truth; they cannot exist without it. But *it* may be able to exist without *them*; accordingly, in *this* particular argument the conclusion is *not* guaranteed by the premises. (Statement 7 does not follow from statements 1 and 6.) The argument would thus fail to establish the immortality of the soul, and would not make truth dependent on the soul.

Now the logical difference between this argument and the one Augustine uses arises from the third premise. But the possibility of this very premise, and of the very different argument which uses it, is suggested in 2.18.32, where Augustine says that either "those things which are taught in geometry dwell in the truth itself or that the truth dwells in them." Again, in 2.19.33: "whether geometrical shapes are in the truth or the truth is in them, no one doubts that they are contained in our soul . . . ." Here Augustine seems committed to the claim that the discipline of geometry necessarily has truth, but he is unsure whether it has truth because truth is in it (and thus truth depends on it) or whether it is in truth (and thus it depends on truth).

Cary remarks that "specifying the sense in which Truth, Reason, or Discipline is 'in' the soul is a tricky conceptual problem that Augustine is not equipped to solve yet. That is, I suspect, the most important reason why the third book of the *Soliloquies* was never finished."[34] I tend to agree. The issue is clearly whether, on the one hand, the eternal reality which is in my soul is dependent on my soul (which is both bad religion and bad metaphysics), or whether on the other hand it is independent of my soul, in which case the argument fails to establish personal immortality. Augustine's mistake is the former; Cary thinks it was intentionally done and resulted from Augustine's immature understanding of Christianity and of neo-Platonism. I think it was *not* intentionally done, for the results of the error cut against the rest of the dialogue, and in any case it is not entirely clear that Augustine meant to rely on precisely this argument. We can have Cary' explanation that the root of the problem was a poor understanding of metaphysics, yet without the additional charge that he did it on purpose.

We must now examine how confident he is in this argument, and what desiderative use he makes of it.

34. Cary, *Augustine's Invention*, 101.

What Sort of Proof is the Argument Meant to Give?

Conybeare's reading of this argument[35] is multileveled. At one level, she takes Reason as being quite serious about the argument, using it to prove immortality beyond a reasonable (if any) doubt. On another level, she sees *Augustine* involved in an "interrogation of reason" in which he exposes problems with Reason's ivory-towered rationality. The simplest response to this approach is to point out that it is altogether out of form. Typically, the philosophical dialogue (at least since Plato) relies on a relationship between a character who leads, corrects, and teaches and a character (sometimes two characters) who is led, corrected, and taught. Such are Socrates and Glaucon, Augustine and Licentius, and Reason and Augustine; Reason has the literary role of the teacher or the master, not of the student or the follower. Augustine's questioning of Reason is portrayed as a sign of weakness on his part, and he generally yields to rebuke for doing it.

Conybeare's reading adopts *both* extremes where a balanced reading is called for. At one extreme she reads Reason's perspective on the argument as overly confident, overlooking Reason's caution as well as its occasional playfulness; at the other extreme she thinks Augustine overly suspicious of it. Reason does not present the argument as establishing its conclusion with perfect certainty.[36] The objection based on souls that have not studied the liberal disciplines is explicitly set aside for another writing project (2.20.34), and Augustine tells us that without an answer to this question he will not be satisfied (2.19.33). Reason, tolerating this caution, should not be taken as promoting the argument with overconfidence. The second extreme is also a mistake, for Augustine does not in the end suggest that the argument in its developed form is flawed.

A balanced interpretation of the argument is that Reason and Augustine both take it seriously as evidence for the soul's immortality, but do not consider it irrefutable proof. The argument is meant to show the strong likelihood of immortality and so comfort Augustine when he is worried; it is given as a formidable argument, but not as a perfect or final proof. It is not a panacea for the soul that longs for knowledge, but a medicine that puts it on the way to recovery and soothes its discomfort.

Related to this, the argument may be described as having two purposes pertaining to desire.

35. Conybeare, *Irrational Augustine*, ch. 5.

36. Here again I find myself in disagreement with Cary's characterization of Reason as a "perfect intelligence" who "speaks with unshakeable certainty." Cary, *Augustine's Invention*, 79.

First, it mends desire by encouraging it in the pursuit of God. Augustine says in response to the argument, "I hear, I am recovering my wits, I am beginning to go over these things in my mind" (2.19.33). The argument is designed to instill confidence that the desired objects, God and the soul, exist eternally and are worth pursuing. It helps Augustine overcome the fear of death that encroaches on his newfound happiness, strengthening his resolve to know God (2.20.36).[37]

Second, the argument is meant to ease the thirst of a soul longing to know God and itself by giving it a better notion of their existence and immortality: a bit of the knowledge we crave. It does not quench, for the knowledge one seeks requires the long program of morals outlined in *De ordine* and, for Augustine at least, will require more extended study of the nature of God and the soul.

DESIRE IN *SOL.*

Now I shall clarify the place of desire in *Soliloquia*. First, I shall discuss what knowing God and the soul means to a Christian and contrast it with two other worldviews, Stoicism and neo-Platonism. Then I shall discuss three aspects of the renewal of desire that have become apparent in *Soliloquia*: the Trinity's work in renewing desire; the human response to this work, participating in the renewal of desire through a life of faith, hope, and charity; and Augustine's invitation that we follow him as he pursues this path.

Knowing God and the Soul

The Christian invitation to love God and the soul invites comparison with other worldviews. Cicero had made the happy life a function of the philosopher knowing himself in relation to his own virtue,[38] but Augustine makes the happy life a function of the Christian knowing himself in relation to God. Some similarities with Stoicism and neo-Platonism make the contrasts all the more significant. The Stoic, if he desires anything, desires that his own soul be in good relationship to the universe. As a Platonist, Cicero may have seen in Stoicism a rudimentary form of the goal that motivates the neo-Platonic mystic, to achieve contemplative unity with the divine. When

37. On the argument's purpose of instilling hope, see below, under the subheading *Our role in the renewal of desire*.

38. Cicero's version of this notion in *Discussions at Tusculum* (Book V, chapter 14) has a decidedly Stoic bent. Aristotle has a similar notion in his idea of the great-souled man (*NE*, IV.3).

Augustine desires to know "God and the soul," he is responding to the Stoic and neo-Platonic notions. In naming these the proper objects of desire, Augustine agrees with both perspectives. Nothing is more important for the soul's happiness than that it be in right relationship to God; nothing is more to be desired. Augustine also sides with the neo-Platonists against the Stoics in arguing that we must think of God and the soul in immaterial terms; knowledge and desire must turn to incorporeality. The penultimate moments of the dialogue, a few words on the incorporeal ideas that undergird perception, reinforce this. Augustine asks Reason about the difference between "a true figure" and a phantasm (2.20.34). Reason explains briefly (2.20.34–35) that the mind of man has some grasp or recollection[39] of the immaterial principles by which we perceive, such as the properties of geometrical figures. Liberal arts training helps some souls know these principles by which we know everything else. But knowing them requires knowing God,[40] to know whom is the goal of our efforts.

This is not merely a Stoic or neo-Platonic meditation on God and the soul. The usual differences are at play. Desiring and knowing the soul in relation to God take place in a trinitarian and incarnational setting. We know a triune God distinct from the universe He created. Knowing Him is the privilege of every believer. It is a personal process initiated by a personal God, colored by personality (this is nowhere more evident than when Augustine bares his soul in *Soliloquia*), and with implications for life with other persons. While many early Christians had agreed with the Stoical advice to remove the emotions,[41] Augustine recommends that desire for God be quickened. The resulting account of the journey to God is that the journey is driven by desire and culminates in delight in God.[42] Moreover, many of the "external" things for which the sage of ancient philosophy has no regard are components of the happy life, as we saw in *De beata vita*.

The Renewal of Desire

Soliloquia teaches us several things about the healing and renewal of desire. First, it shows that the trinitarian God is active, indeed the main actor, in converting our desires. Second, the renewal of desire on our part involves cultivating the three theological virtues. Hope specifically is revealed as a

39. On Augustine and recollection see Miner, "Augustinian Recollection."

40. See O'Meara, *Studies in Augustine and Eriguena*, 141–42.

41. Wilken, *Spirit of Early Christian Thought*, 295–97.

42. In sharp contrast is Seneca's remark that virtue is sought without regard to the pleasure it provides. See Seneca, *On the Happy Life*, 9.

motive for the argument for immortality. Third, the form of the dialogue suggests that Augustine is inviting us to follow him in the ascent to reordered loves and knowledge of God.

God's Role in Renewing Desire

The healing of desire involves the activity of God and man. God works to renew our desires. The healing of desire is the work of the Trinity, the conversion of desire an act of grace. It remains only to be said explicitly that this theology of desire is unapologetically Christian, neither simply neo-Platonism nor a neo-Platonism untransformed by the Gospel.

Our Role in the Renewal of Desire

We are also called to be active in the healing of our desires. It is incumbent upon us to respond to grace by turning to God; as Augustine says at 1.1.5, "teach me how to come to Thee. I have nothing except my will . . . ." Three members of the Trinity act to heal our minds and hearts, and we must cultivate three theological virtues in response. While pagan philosophers have recommended four virtues for the healing of desire—wisdom, courage, justice, and moderation—Christian theology prescribes an additional three. Faith binds us to the source of our healing and purifies our minds of false beliefs, clearing the way for true beliefs and pure desires. Hope combats despair, helping us pursue God and keeping desire for God strong. Charity longs for the object of pursuit and joins us to it when we reach our destination.

The dialogue's final words invite us to revisit the purpose of the dialogue. Reason observes that Augustine is afraid of death and tells him: "Be of good heart. As we can already feel, God will be present to us in our seeking, the God who promises after this body something that is the greatest happiness and the greatest fullness of truth without any lying" (2.20.36). This remark again suggests either that a perfect and perpetual vision of God in this life is impossible, or at least that it is exceedingly rare and difficult. Augustine replies, "May it be as we hope!" We have seen that the argument for immortality is meant to encourage Augustine in his ascent, though it is not entirely foolproof. It encourages by inspiring hope.[43] *Soliloquia*'s end

43. In contrast to Epicureanism, which seeks to extirpate hope in the afterlife in order to remover our fear of it, Augustine seeks to nourish hope in the happy life.

shows how concerned Reason is that Augustine will flag in his pursuit of wisdom; but, with hope, the pursuit will continue.

Following Augustine

The unique form of *Soliloquia* suggests a final lesson. We have already noted that the other dialogues invite the reader to participate in their action, to ascend alongside their characters.[44] This is even more true of *Soliloquia*. Its form encourages us to ascend alongside Augustine. Augustine inserts himself into his own story of ascent. The author participates with himself in the journey toward Wisdom, showing us the way to go. We also should be in dialogue with ourselves, cautiously scanning ourselves for sin and cultivating the theological virtues. But, since Augustine is following Christ, we must also follow Christ. We are meant to follow Augustine as he follows Reason, itself following Christ, toward God. The form of the dialogue is *participation*, and this is also its rhetorical challenge, for the drama urges us to participate as well. This insight also invites the reader to revisit the three earlier dialogues to see how he may more fully participate with them in the healing of desire.

44. See above, Chapter 2, under the subheading *Two Visions of the Happy Life* and Chapter 4, under the subheadings *Apparent Exceptions to Order* and *Monica the Philosopher*.

6

The Love of God *and* Human Beings

In previous chapters I have uncovered many lessons about desire—about its proper object and its renewal—in the dialogues of Cassiciacum. In this chapter I shall discuss the place love for human beings occupies in the overarching love of God. Does a wholehearted love of God leave any room for the love of human beings? In *Soliloquia* 1.12.20 Augustine seems to say no:

> Reason. But, I ask you, why do you desire that the men whom you love either live or live with you?
>
> Augustine. So that together we may harmoniously inquire into our souls and God. For the one who first touches upon a discovery may easily and without effort lead the others to it. . . .
>
> Reason. Then you do not desire their life or their presence for its own sake, but for the sake of finding wisdom?
>
> Augustine. I completely agree.

This remark suggests that for Augustine all love of men is subsumed in the love of God—that the pursuit of God does not honor men but only uses them for God's sake. This is a worrisome thought, for it suggests that loving humans is logically incompatible with loving, really loving, God.[1]

1. Two similar but distinct worries are in the area; one, that loving God is psychologically so consuming that it leaves no time or energy for loving human beings; two, that loving God provides no motive for loving human beings. Although I shall not address these fears in this chapter, they are small worries for the Augustinian, who must acknowledge the biblical command to love one another. This command is a motive for

Anders Nygren suggests this line of interpretation when he writes, "Love to neighbour thus occupies an insecure position in Augustine: in principle there is no place for it in his scheme of love . . . ."[2] Nygren explains his view that love for other human beings is for Augustine a mere function of other loves, namely our love for God and for ourselves,[3] and goes so far as to claim that Augustine's writings on love are infected with the Greek notion of *eros*, a notion he describes as "egocentric."[4] Oliver O'Donovan's similar interpretation of *On Teaching Christianity* has more recently been quite influential. O'Donovan sees "an outstanding tension" between the command to love both God and neighbor and "the monist principle that God alone is to be loved."[5] On such a reading love for Augustine reduces the neighbor to a tool; the Christian's love for others is an instrument in his personal quest for happiness.

But is this correct? We must answer carefully. It is all too easy to reason, with Nygren, as follows: Everything is either a means or an end; Augustine cites God as the only legitimate end of rightly ordered affections; therefore, human beings are not ends; therefore, they are means; whatever is a means has no intrinsic value; whatever has no intrinsic value is not to be loved; therefore, human beings are not to be loved in Augustine's ethics. The reasoning proceeds from a strong distinction between ends and means and allows the *prima facie* reading of passages such as this one from *Soliloquia* to categorize human beings as either one or the other, and never both. Augustine appears to endorse this methodology when he says, "what is not loved for its own sake is not loved" (*Sol.* 1.13.22).

All the same, I believe this approach is flawed. It is not the only way to reason about the relationship of God and man in properly ordered desires, and it is not clear that it is the best way. An alternative approach is to reason from the natural good of human beings. In this chapter I shall show that there is reason to believe that love of God and neighbor are fundamentally a harmony—given the Christian understanding of human nature and its divine origins and purpose, as well as the Incarnation and redemptive work of Christ. The good life for which we are created and redeemed is a life that loves God as part of a community. I also aim to show that the Cassiciacum dialogues contain the rudiments of this perspective, a perspective that is

---

loving the neighbor, resolving the second worry. Insofar as love to God involves obedience, this command ensures that a measure of the time and energy spent in loving God is spent in loving the neighbor, resolving the second worry.

2. Nygren, *Agape and Eros*, 553.

3. Ibid., 549–55.

4. Ibid., 179.

5. O'Donovan, "*Usus* and *Fruitio* in Augustine," 383.

in tension with the approach used by Nygren and suggested by the above passages in *Soliloquia*.

I shall first offer a few remarks on the methodology with which one approaches this question and on the usefulness of looking closely at the natural good of human beings in order to analyze their proper desires (Part One). After considering several pagan perspectives on man's natural good (Part Two), I shall outline a Christian perspective on human nature (Part Three). Finally, I shall show how the Cassiciacum dialogues contain the rudiments of this perspective and make a few remarks on how Augustine's continuing work develops this perspective (Part Four). In these findings we thus have a glimpse of the direction in which Augustine's ethical thought develops after Cassiciacum. We also have a little more evidence for the general continuity of his ethical thought.

TELEOLOGY AND COMMUNITY

Here I shall give three remarks. First, we should be wary of the assumption that the difference between ends and means is a strict dichotomy. Second, we must consider the natural good of man in order to understand the proper place of love for man, for his nature determines *how* to love him rightly, and this has a bearing on the place of love for man vis-à-vis the love of God. Third, to determine Augustine's views on the love of God and man we must look at his understanding of man as he was created to be, for man's nature is rooted in his creation by God.

To begin, a strict distinction between ends and means is not ubiquitous in ancient thought. In Book II of Plato's *Republic* Socrates suggests that some things are good both for their own sake and for the sake of their benefits; such a thing is justice (357b–358a). Aristotle in the *Nichomachean Ethics* (Book I, chapter 7) states that we seek happiness for its own sake, but we seek the virtues both for themselves and for the sake of happiness. Analyzing, comparing, or contrasting these remarks would be the task of a lengthy study;[6] for our purposes it is sufficient to note that for Plato and Aristotle it is not the case that everything is either a means or an end but not both. Accordingly, we should not dismiss out of hand the possibility that human beings are both ends *and* means for loving God. The modern mind

6. Interestingly, Plato treats things desired for their own sake *and* for the sake of something else as better than things desired for their own sake, but for Aristotle it is the reverse. An important article on the passage in *Republic* is White, "The Classification of Goods." On Aristotle's classification of goods and its distinctness from Plato's, see Lear, *Happy Lives*, 31–34.

may find it difficult to consider this possibility, accustomed as it is to thinking that people are not ends unless they are ends in themselves and that a person who is not treated as an end in himself and is "used" as a means is also *abused*. Bourke suggests that this mentality is due to the influence of Kant.[7] At any rate, it is not grounded in ancient thought and may prevent us from understanding Augustine.

Second, we must consider our natural good. Philosophical therapy is teleologically oriented. When reasoning about the places of God and man in rightly ordered affections we are reasoning about the affections *of humans, for humans*; so we need to understand the human end. In seeking wisdom we seek the life that is best for us because it is the life we are meant for. We should love God but not man only if loving God *is* our end but loving man is *not*. We must, therefore, investigate whether it is our end to love God but not one another; we must ask whether the good life for which we are meant is a *communal* life.

Third, considering our natural good is especially important for interpreting Augustine, for whom ascent to God takes place within the context of the creation-fall-redemption narrative. The place of our love for God and human beings is illuminated by our understanding of the human good, and for a Christian this good is known through the biblical narrative. Augustine describes the happy life we are seeking as a *recovery* of happiness that was once our due, a state we lost. Ascent is a *re*turn to something; what that something is determines what place man has in rightly ordered desires. Investigating the good life entails investigating the *original* good life. We must therefore ask whether God created men to love one another. If we find that men are created to dwell in community with God *and* with each other, then we will most likely find that love of God and love of men are, when fully realized, different names for the same way of life. We must also ask whether man was created *to be loved for God's sake*, for if so then loving God above man is the fulfillment, not the abuse, of man. In short, we must reason from Augustine's understanding of human teleology, keeping in mind human nature as created by God and in process of redemption thanks to the work of Christ.

The realization that biblical teleology determines the parameters of human happiness allows us to dispense with the notion that love of God does not satisfy human desire. Martha Nussbaum remarks that at the heart of Augustine's philosophy of desire is the idea that God's ethical norms are distant from human life; "the central structural idea remains: the idea of the

7. Bourke, "Joy in Augustine's Ethics," 33.

radical independence of true good from human need and desire."[8] Again, she says that Augustine "speaks of the progress of the soul as an ascent of love and desire from the earthly to the heavenly, an ascent that strips away and leaves behind the merely human in love."[9] In loving God as the true good we flee from what is good *for humans*. This is a deeply flawed understanding of Augustine, for by making the true good independent from human need Nussbaum's Augustine would remove human need from true good. To the contrary: Because we were created with the purpose of obeying God's norms, living by them satisfies our deepest needs and desires. Loving God as the greatest good *is* the good *for humans*.[10] It remains to be seen whether and to what extent this purpose is communal. After a brief look at the pagan perspective on the human purpose I shall turn to the Christian perspective.

PAGAN PERSPECTIVES ON THE COMMUNAL HUMAN SELF

Various moments in pagan philosophy present themselves as relevant points of comparison to Augustine's understanding of the human design and its communal character. Although there is no exact ancient equivalent for our English word "community,"[11] we can observe that there are two sides to the ancient understanding of community, and that there is a sort of tension between them. On the one hand, ancient philosophers thought of the human person as having a political nature, for by portraying human nature as requiring justice they make the individual's good a political good. On the other hand, they believed that we are happiest in contemplating the divine. Man's political end is never fully integrated with the doctrine that the best are those who contemplate immaterial reality. This is evidence that the prospects for a communal relationship with both God and men are at least as good, and probably better, in Augustine's thought as they are in pagan thought. After looking at the importance of justice in Plato's and Cicero's thought I shall discuss the fundamentally non-political character of philosophical ascent in several ancients. Then I shall look briefly at two notions that have potential for lessening or resolving the tension; one of these is friendship, and the other is the idea of a universal community of rational creatures.

8. Nussbaum, *Therapy of Desire*, 18–19.

9. Nussbaum, *Upheavals*, 529.

10. *Conf.* 1.1.1: "our heart is restless until it rests in you."

11. Fortin, "The Patristic Sense," 61.

Consider Plato's and Cicero's defenses of justice. In the *Republic* Plato responds to Thrasymachus's claims that justice is unnatural and that acting on self-interest without regard for the needs of others is natural. The *Republic* situates justice within the bounds of human nature while construing injustice as bad for the soul and powerless to make us happy. By making justice natural Plato ensures that acting on behalf of the community is good for each of us. The good of the community is a component of the individual's good. Thus the *Republic* treats the human person's end as bound up with other human persons. Cicero reaffirms this lesson in texts Augustine likely read, including the *Laws*: "nothing is more vital than the clear realization that we are born for justice, and that what is just is based, not on opinion, but on nature."[12]

However, this doctrine pertains to man's political activity, and it is unclear whether and how it pertains to his contemplative activity. The noblest of humans is meant to contemplate, and the works of several ancient philosophers suggest that this goal is not in harmony with man's political nature. In the *Republic* contemplative pursuit is held in tension with man's political nature: The philosopher is compelled to govern the city (519c–520d). Life in the city is concerned with the mundane affairs of the physical world, concerns which hinder contemplation. The tension is evident in the Aristotelian school as well, as evidenced by the contrast between the theoretical end of man described in Book X of the *Nichomachean Ethics* and the political ethics described in Books I–IX.[13] This is also true of Cicero, who if he is indeed a Platonist agrees that contemplation of the immaterial realm is best for man. His promotion of this goal is hidden, for publicly he promotes the political community as man's highest end: "there is no greater blessing than a well-ordered state."[14] But man's political nature and his contemplative purpose cannot be in harmony because the political realm encompasses mediocre and bad men who are a hindrance to contemplation. Finally, in a revealing passage Plotinus separates the "civic" virtues from the "purificatory" virtues, which free the soul from the body's influences.[15] The

12. Cicero, from *Laws* 1.28 in The Republic *and* The Laws, 107.

13. See also Hadot, *What Is Ancient Philosophy?* 77–81.

14. Cicero, from *The Republic* 5.7 in The Republic *and* The Laws, page 83. See also Harding: "for the early Cicero it is civic virtue, as opposed to the contemplative life, that most benefits the soul;" Harding, *Augustine and Roman Virtue*, 39.

15. *Ennead* 1.2. The virtues here called "civic," by the way, are technically the virtues uniting the different parts of the soul in *Republic*. But given the *Republic*'s political application of these virtues and the strong connection between city and soul, it may be inferred that the contemplative and purificatory virtues are at least as far removed from the communal virtues as they are from what Plotinus calls "civic."

soul needs the purificatory virtues to ascend to contemplative unity with the One. The political nature of man is no help to his contemplative goal. Thus, the desire for immaterial reality and the desire for the good of one's neighbors are not unified.[16] In sum, although the philosophers practiced community,[17] we do not see community thoroughly integrated into their accounts of the very best life. Pierre Hadot explains that ancient thinkers as diverse as Aristotle, Pyrrho, the Stoics, and Plotinus were marked by the "tendency to strip ourselves of 'the human.'"[18] They held up their idea of a moral exemplar as thoroughly independent and happy in himself.[19] At a minimum, community is not necessary for such a person; at the most, one must cease to desire the good of others in order to become such a person.

Cicero comes close to uniting our contemplative end with our political character when he bases community among humans in their shared reason. "Reason," being "common to us all," unites us all.[20] Every human being, having an equal share in reason, should be treated well; Cicero's claim is no doubt influenced by Roman expressions of the Stoic idea of cosmopolitanism.[21] The notion of community among all rational creatures is significant because it connects, at a fundamental level, our communal and our contemplative nature, each being based in reason. Perhaps the reason which unites the masses in political association can also unite them in the highest activity of reason, contemplation of immateriality. But if he believes this Cicero does not explicitly say so (at least as far as I can tell), and we can only wonder whether he means for the communal aspect of our nature to be united in this way with our contemplative end.[22]

16. Rist in *Augustine*: "the love of human persons seems to have no privileged status in the Platonic tradition. At the very least that tradition is ambivalent about the relationship between love of persons and love of the higher non-personal realities which should mould the lives of the persons themselves;" Rist, *Augustine*, 160.

17. Hadot, *What Is Ancient Philosophy?*, 220.

18. Ibid., 211.

19. Ibid., 221.

20. Cicero, *The Laws*, 1.28, 107.

21. On cosmopolitanism see Kleingeld and Brown, "Cosmopolitanism." For sources on Stoic cosmopolitanism see Nussbaum, "The Worth," and Berges, "Loneliness and Belonging."

22. It is also not clear that Stoic cosmopolitanism can harmonize contemplation with the love of others. Indeed, it is not entirely clear that Stoicism promotes a genuine love of others; as Harding reads them, the Stoic performs his duties to others out of self-interest. Doing good for my fellowman is good for me, but the wellbeing of my neighbor as such confers no good on me. The good man's happiness remains independent of whether others are well; if I am virtuous I will be happy even if my fellowman is unhappy. Harding, *Augustine and Roman Virtue*, 49–50.

Finally, one aspect of ancient philosophy in particular presents itself as avoiding this tension. This is friendship. In *Nichomachean Ethics* Aristotle considers three kinds of friendship; he argues that the best friendship is the one in which friends love each other for their own sake, wishing each other well for their own good and not for the sake of pleasure or utility (Book VIII, chapters 2–4). The best of people make the best of friends because they have a mutual admiration and affection for each other's virtue (Book IX, chapters 4.8). Moreover, the happiest man lacks no good thing, including friends, for a friendship is a great good in life and "since man is a political creature" (Book IX, chapter 9). If the contemplative virtues are among the good things which the happy man does not lack, it would follow that the true friend can share the activity of contemplation. Thus, while community in the sense of a political bond with the mass of men is not needed for a happy life, community with a few friends who share the highest good is needed. Similarly, Cicero defines friendship as "a complete identity of feeling about all things in heaven and earth."[23] This definition, coupled with the definition of wisdom as knowledge of human and divine things, shows that mutual wisdom for Cicero can establish friendship. This reinforces the idea that our communal nature is bound up with our contemplative nature, for the latter completes the former. To the degree, then, that the best man has friends, man's political nature is united with his contemplative nature—but just to that degree, for the mass of men are excluded from this sharing of the good.

In sum, ancient philosophers believed that all men are by nature meant to participate in political community. This ensures that personal happiness is bound up with caring for one's neighbor. However, the same philosophers also believed that the happiest among men is the one who contemplates the most effectively. Such a happy man may share his happiness with his friends, but not with the rest of men. It appears that they never completely reconciled these two facets of human nature.

CHRISTIAN PERSPECTIVES ON THE COMMUNAL HUMAN SELF

Perhaps the ancients had scant resources for doing this, but Christian thought has done better. In this section I shall discuss the consequences of looking at a biblically teleological account of human nature. Then I shall show how the Christian mysteries, the Trinity and the Incarnation, suggest that the love of God and man together comprise a harmony. Next, I

23. Cicero, *Laelius*, 187.

shall look at suggestive passages wherein Lactantius responds to the Ciceronian notion of the community of rational creatures and Ambrose discusses Christian friendship; both explicitly unite our knowledge and love of God with the community among men. After summarizing these claims, I shall examine this perspective in several of Augustine's later works.

The inclusion or non-inclusion of love for human beings in the love for God depends a great deal on the end of man and on whether that end is communal, and on what sort of community it is; hence an understanding of God's purpose in creating man is needed. Let us expand on this notion, for there are at least two consequences of considering our creational end. First, as noted above, if the good life for which human beings are created is a life of community with God and other humans, then the loves of both are included in that life. There is reason to believe that this is the case. Genesis records the creation of two humans who lived in fellowship with each other and God, talking together with God (Genesis 3:8). The human person is communal, created for mutual fellowship with God and others, for in our original community he fellowshipped with God and other human persons.

Second, if man is created to love God above all then it is incorrect that in loving man only for God's sake we misuse the man. In loving man for God's sake, rather than his own sake, we are only doing what we are meant to do. In *being loved* by one another for God's sake, not for our own sake, we are *being loved* as we are meant to be loved. Using someone for God's sake is his proper use, not his *mis*use.

The key is in integrating *love* with *teleology*: Love for X is defined by the good of X—by X's nature and purpose.[24] Hence if a Christian ethicist insists that we love men for the sake of God it need not mean that men are nothing in the grand scheme of things, for they are necessary means of one another's love of God. And it certainly does not mean that humans are used or manipulated in the love of God, as Nygren reads Augustine. To the contrary, we are *fulfilled* in loving and in *being loved* by each other each other *for God's sake*. The phrase "for the sake of" calls for interpretation. Loving people "for the sake of God" can mean that people are mere means in my personal pursuit of God, of no value in themselves; but it means something very different if man's essential nature is to exist in a loving community headed by God. In loving God, and loving each other because we love God,

24. In itself this line of argument is incomplete, as it does not preclude the possibility that God created us to use one another and to be miserable in being thus used. This possibility is easily avoided with the premise that God had our good in mind when he created us to love him best—that God wants us to be happy in being good; this premise is eminently plausible, pious, and Augustinian.

we only do what we are meant to do; in so doing, we are happy.[25] Christ commands us to love our neighbor as ourselves, assuming that we do indeed love ourselves.[26] The command does not do away with love for oneself, but renews it by binding it to the love of neighbor. Similarly, when Christ commands us to love God he does not do away with the love of neighbor, but renews, perfect, and completes it by binding it to the love of God.

Two Christian doctrines in particular suggest love for God *and* humans. An ethic that combines our communal end with our divine end is incarnational in three ways. First, as a result of the Incarnation this way of loving is revealed by Christ to the Apostles, and through them to us. Second, a love for both God and humans resembles a love of Christ, who is both God and man. Finally, this love also *imitates* Christ, who loves both God and man. Such an ethic is trinitarian because the persons of God exist as a community of love which, through the actions of each divine person, draws us to participate in God's own life. The union with God articulated in Christian thought is quite different from a pagan paradigm in which a philosopher might hope to be united with the One through contemplation. The desires of the individual are not part of the highest good for the neo-Platonist; for Plotinus the contemplative mystic transcends his humanity along with its desires.[27] But for the Christian, since the divine Persons are not alone, we should not expect to be alone either while we ascend to God or even after we reach the summit of our ascent.

The church fathers did not neglect the opportunity to promote a way of life based on the community of humans with God. In chapter 14 of *On the Anger of God*, Lactantius continues where Cicero does not, saying that the community for which human beings are meant is a community of human beings knowing and loving God together. Referring to Cicero's suggestion that the communal nature of men is based on a common reason,[28] Lactantius states his agreements that we are made for justice, that is for communal

25. Adams interprets *Teaching Christianity* 1.29.30 as arguing that, since we do love both God and neighbor, we can desire the wellbeing of a community that includes ourselves and the neighbor, with God at its head. Adams endorses this perspective but calls it incomplete, saying it does not give us a reason to love the neighbor in the first place. But the biblical teleological perspective gives a reason: To love God and the neighbor for God's sake is the natural good for ourselves and the neighbor and is, accordingly, the happy life; Adams, "The Problem," 113–15.

26. We need no command to love ourselves; *Teaching Christianity* 1.22.22–1.24.24.

27. Hadot, *What Is Ancient Philosophy?*, 211, citing *Enneads* 5.3 and 6.7. Also see *Ennead* 4.4.2, on the absence of personality in a soul which possesses a vision of immaterial reality.

28. *Laws* 1.28, page 107; also see above under the heading *Pagan Perspectives on the Communal Human Self.*

living, and that community encompasses all men. Then he goes on to say that this community of men is a community that knows God and that we ought to love each other on this account:

> If God, therefore, designed man to be a worshipper of Himself, and on this account gave him so much honour, that he might rule over all things; it is plainly most just that he should worship Him who bestowed upon him such great gifts, and love man, who is united with us in the participation of the divine justice. For it is not right that a worshipper of God should be injured by a worshipper of God.[29]

Several features of Lactantius's remark illustrate what we have discussed. First, the human good is rooted in a human nature which is oriented towards a particular end. Second, our nature is communal. Third, the community for which we are meant encompasses both divine and human relations. We are meant to know and love God in community with each other. Fourth, the love of man is subordinated to the love of God. This subordination does not prevent their being united, but is the very condition for that unity. It is precisely on account of our relation with God that we are valuable and ought to be loved by one another, and it is precisely in this divine-human communion that we achieve our end. For this reason the early church sought to know and love God together.[30]

Ambrose also is explicit, saying that following God establishes friendship. The final chapter of *Duties of the Clergy* presents the notion that genuine friendship depends on Christian faith and practice—a fitting extension for a bishop to make of Cicero's notion that friendship depends on virtue. In his own words, one "cannot be a friend to a man who has been unfaithful to God" (3.22.132). Faithfulness to God is a necessary condition for friendship. Again, "God Himself makes us friends instead of servants . . . He gave us a pattern of friendship to follow" (3.22.135). Following God establishes friendship. Finally, "he who does the will of God is His friend and is honoured with this name. He who is of one mind with Him, he too is His friend." Where Cicero left us wondering whether the community of friends depends on mutual possession of wisdom, Ambrose tells us plainly that community of friends depends on acquaintance with God.

In sum, on this account the love of God includes the love of man, for it is the activity of a community which loves God. Our proper good is to

29. Lactantius, *Anger of God*, chapter 14.

30. O'Keefe's and Reno's point that the early church read Scripture as a community is just as true of the early church's love of God. O'Keefe and Reno, *Sanctified Vision*, chapter 6.

be in a community that knows and loves God.[31] Within this community, there is no proper distinction between valuing a person instrumentally and valuing a person intrinsically; a person's "intrinsic" value is defined by his "instrumental" value, for his calling is to be a part of the community of them that love God. People are to be loved with a view towards their own good, and their own good is to be part of the holy community. Since our nature is communal and that community is a divine community, our good is precisely to be loved for God's sake. To treat humans as "ends in themselves," each solitarily maintaining himself as a *telos*, is to misuse the human being, to sever him from his proper good.[32] In the same spirit C. S. Lewis vividly portrays the danger of trying to love a human apart from God, spinning a tale of a mother who idolizes her son to the point that she prefers to lose God if she can have him to herself, in the process making life a misery for herself and her family.[33]

By way of contrast, consider Nygren, who very appropriately points out that there is no necessary conflict between loving God and loving creation, since God's creation is good.[34] However, he ends up saying that for Augustine love of creation is a mere instrument to the love of God.[35] Nygren overlooks two Augustinian themes: that loving something means treating it in the best way possible; and that the best way to treat creatures is to value them in and because of God.

More dangerously, Nussbaum thinks that when we desire only God the desires of the individual person are left behind; they no longer matter; we cannot desire God without ceasing to be human in any meaningful sense.[36] Nussbaum sees the human being as having value in himself, independently of God.[37] The finite world can flourish without God, and accordingly it and

31. Fortin, "Augustine and the Hermeneutics," 8–11.

32. As Burt observes, in loving human beings for God's sake, we achieve "our one true good;" *"Let Me Know You,"* 72.

33. Lewis, *The Great Divorce*, 90–98.

34. Nygren, 503–4.

35. Ibid., 510–22.

36. Nussbaum, *Upheavals*, 9. Nussbaum explores this aspect of Plato in Part II of *The Fragility of Goodness*; on Nussbaum's reading of *Symposium*, Plato is aware of the problem. *Therapy of Desire* (18–19) attributes the problem to the later Augustine.

37. Nussbaum remarks that our love for God does not differ in kind from our love for humans; the same love we direct to man should be directed to God. Of course she is right that our *dis*ordered love for a human should be redirected toward God. But from the perspective we are considering, that very redirecting allows for a different, more genuine love of man for the sake of God to take its place. See Nussbaum, *Upheavals*, 547. Nussbaum's criticism may have more success against ancient philosophers. See Pierre Hadot's remarks that ancient philosophy saw the happiest person as more than merely human; Hadot, *What Is Ancient Philosophy?* 211.

its inhabitants are on their own account lovable. But this fails to account for the central reason we humans are so often unhappy. Our desire is *not* finite; it always outruns the finite world, and thus it points to a higher world. A theistic framework can better address this problem of desire, meeting desire where it is and showing it what it may seek (and how it may seek it) to be satisfied. The finite world needs God to flourish. The only way to be truly human is to live as God created us, which is by loving God together and together desiring God above all. From this perspective Nussbaum's individual appears as an abstraction from a person's true significance; for a person's significance is grounded in his status as a creature of God, able to live in fellowship with God. Human nature and happiness are not subsumed, but realized, in the love of God.[38]

On this account it makes sense to love God above all and still love men, and church fathers have said as much. Is this Augustine's perspective? A number of scholars have argued that Augustine employs in *On Teaching Christianity* a perspective like the one I have outlined. Rist says "that one really does enjoy one's neighbor, but that the only way to do so without reducing his status to that of a material object is to enjoy him 'in the Lord' or 'in Christ.'"[39] No created thing has "a value in and of itself, independently of God"; to the contrary, "only if a man is loved 'in the Lord' can his value be recognized."[40] Baer's 1996 article develops these themes through close attention to *On Teaching Christianity*.[41] Hannam argues that the Augustinian ethic, "far from instrumentive, is meant to instruct . . . how one's neighbors can be most fully loved for who they truly are."[42] He points to Trinitarianism as the doctrine that secures the neighbor's own good even as the neighbor is loved for God.[43] A recent article by Stewart-Kroeker analyzes the Christological aspects of Augustine's theology of love, arguing that Christ who is both God and man, both destination and way, unites the love of neighbor with the love of God.[44] Matthew Levering's recent book clearly explains[45] why, on Augustinian ethics, to love but *not* for the sake of God is simply to

38. In a similar vein, Harding explains that Augustine, having critiqued pagan eudaimonism on its own terms, departs from it. Augustine recognizes the pagan goal of a happy life, but he understands that the satisfaction it requires cannot be afforded by anything in this world; Harding, *Augustine and Roman Virtue*.

39. Rist, *Augustine*, 165–66.

40. Ibid., 163, 166.

41. Baer, "The Fruit of Charity."

42. Hannam, "*Ad illud ubi permanendum est*," 170.

43. Ibid., 171.

44. Stewart-Kroeker, "Resisting Idolatry and Instrumentalisation."

45. Levering, *Theology of Augustine*, 3–6.

"fail to love each other or ourselves as we ought."[46] Also, in *The City of God* Augustine explains that the good of man is not *in* man, but *above* man (19.4, 25–26). Thus, the only way to love man is to *not* love him for his own sake. This is the sense of *On Christian Teaching* 1.35.39, and the sense in which we must understand 1.30.33's distinction between things we "use" (*uti*) and things we "enjoy" (*frui*). Human beings, when "used" and not "enjoyed," are not reduced to instruments of my own self-love, but are loved in the only way they can be properly loved—as creatures of God.[47] As *Confessions* says, "blessed is the man who loves you, and his friend in you, and his enemy for your sake" (4.9.14).

Let us look more closely at the distinction between love for man and love for God. To love God means to delight in God, to contemplate God with delight, and to take pleasure in God's sublime perfection. To love the neighbor means to want what is good for him, which is that *he* love and be delighted in God. Although we can also delight in man, love of man is unlike love for God in that it cannot stand on its own. For the love of man can be traced back to God in several ways. We love man because out of our love for God we obey God's command to love man. We love man as a creature of God, one in whom we see the image of God. That in our neighbor in which we delight is traceable back to God, from whom all good things derive. Thus, the neighbor is designed by his creator to be loved not as an independent being but as a being dependent on God, just as we are. In short, the love of man is of a different quality from the love of God; yet it treats the neighbor as he was meant to be treated and works for his good, so this is a genuine love for man, not a mere use or abuse of him.

We were created for fellowship with God and neighbor. It is right to love a person "as an end in himself" if that means loving him *for his own good*—for to love him for his own good is to love him as part of the divine community. But if to love someone "as an end in himself" means to regard him as having value independently of that community, then such love is a perversion, making the beloved into a sort of an idol and depriving him of his own proper good as a creature.

This perspective is key to understanding Augustine's ethics in the *Confessions* and is, moreover, the very rule given in *On Teaching Christianity* for the disambiguation of difficult passages in Scripture. Yet this very ethical notion, occupying the heart of Augustinian hermeneutics and theology, has

46. Ibid., 5.

47. Bourke says that "joy in the moral life depends on the Augustinian concept of *ordo*," and goes on to explain how order entails the direction of all things under "divine providence;" in other words, there simply is no satisfaction of desire if we love creatures apart from their Creator. See "Joy in Saint Augustine's Ethics," 43.

its roots in the Cassiciacum project of reordering desire. It is, in fact, the outgrowth of Cassiciacum's *Deum et animam scire cupio*—I yearn to know God and the soul. To these roots at Cassiciacum we now turn.

THE PERSPECTIVE AT CASSICIACUM

So much for Augustine's later writings; let us return to Cassiciacum to see how Augustine's emerging perspective allows us to respond to the problem of the love of God *and* man. The Cassiciacum dialogues display the rudiments of this creational perspective, and I suspect that a closer study would show that his thought as it matures develops this perspective.[48] Yet at Cassiciacum this perspective is, at best, undeveloped or in tension with the perspective according to which human beings are simply means to the end of loving God.[49] First, I shall show how at Cassiciacum Augustine is committed to the idea that we ascend to knowledge of God together. Then I shall show that there are hints of the notion that *knowing* God, the summit of the ascent to wisdom, is also a communal activity, and I shall also look at the limitations of this perspective at Cassiciacum. Then I shall address two aspects of Augustine's thought as it develops beyond Cassiciacum. Finally, by way of conclusion, I shall say a few words about desire and its conversion.

Coming to Know God Together at Cassiciacum

At Cassiciacum the ascent to God is thoroughly communal.[50] This marks it as a departure from Plotinus, who treats the ascent to God as the activity of a lone contemplative.[51] The pursuit of wisdom at Cassiciacum requires

48. Accordingly, even if Cary is right that it was not until much later that Augustine was able to fully integrate the love of God and neighbor (*Inner Grace*, 37), the rudiments of this integrated view had already been present at Cassiciacum. This is also evidence against the idea that Augustine's uniquely Christian view of friendship does not predate the *Confessions*. On this view see White, *Christian Friendship*, 196; and Lienhard, "Friendship, Friends," 372.

49. We should not be surprised if Augustine has not achieved a fully coherent philosophy, free of discrepancies and tensions, at Cassiciacum, as Rombs prudently remarks: "the reader must be careful to avoid the mistaken impression of a greater consistency of thought and systematic presentation in the young Augustine than is the case;" Rombs, xxiv.

50. On this theme Topping's comments are helpful; Topping, *Happiness and Wisdom*, 154–57. See also above, Chapter 3, under the subheading *Community as a Therapy for Desire*.

51. *Ennead* 1.2; also see above under the heading *Pagan Perspectives on the Communal Human Self*.

mutual dependence; Augustine and his friends rely on each other. Let us look at several passages and supporting evidence.

To begin, consider the language of the dialogues. The communal character of the philosophical quest is affirmed and reaffirmed when those on the quest are denoted in the plural. Augustine says "we are still seeking" (*b. Vita* 4.35), and Monica quotes Ambrose: "Cherish, O Trinity, those who pray" (*b. Vita* 4.35). Licentius sings psalms: "O God of hosts, convert us: and show Thy face, and we shall be saved" (*Ord.* 1.8.22).

The importance of communal prayer to the philosophical pursuit could hardly be overestimated. In *Contra Academicos* 2.7.18 Licentius prays for Augustine, and in the same scene all join in a touching display of care for Romanianus and for one another; in *De beata vita* 4.35 Monica prays.[52] In prayer they support each other on the quest for wisdom.

In *De ordine* the order of life takes priority over the order of education.[53] This order includes the social virtues of the ancients, but culminates in Christian charity. Augustine commends friendship and the golden rule to people who seek God, saying "let them have friends" and "Let them do to no one what they are unwilling to undergo" (2.8.25). The desire for God must be united with the love of man if we are to reach God.

In *Soliloquia* 1.1.1 Augustine decides to share the record of his contemplation of God with "a few of your fellow citizens." (In light of *Contra Academicos* 1.1.12 and *De beata vita* 1.6 he probably means fellow townsmen from Thagaste.) He wants those who are seeking God to join with him and help each other in the seeking (*Sol.* 1.12.20).

These passages show that the pursuit of God is a communal activity in Augustine.[54] An apt summary is in *De beata vita*: "I have decided not to disregard your minds when you are intent on God as I would certain oracles" (4.31). Community's place in ascent to God entails a new spiritual regimen. Fleeing the body's influences is not the central therapy prescribed for the soul. Rather, we should flee to Christ and to his church, immersing ourselves in the common life of the holy community. As part of this community we should practice the Christian virtues, loving one another in order to love God as we ought.

52. On prayer see above, especially chapter 2, under the subheading *Prayer as a Therapy for Desire*.

53. See above, chapter 4, under the subheading *Order of Life and Education*.

54. Kolbet: "The mature bishop believed that the healing process began by becoming incorporated into the Church: a remedial community not turned in upon itself, but turned toward Christ as the head of his broken body;" Kolbet, *Augustine and the Cure of Souls*, 132. This mature view of Augustine begins to take shape in his mind as early as Cassiciacum.

Of course, this aspect of community makes for a limited difference from the sort of pre-Christian notion of a solitary ascent typified in Plotinus; it does not by itself preclude that human beings are necessary for getting to God but *not* for knowing God once we have arrived. Perhaps community is a necessary part of our ascent to God simply because of our limitations in this life; perhaps it is an accident of our finite nature. Is there any more to community than that?

Knowing God Together at Cassiciacum

A human is created to be a communal being, a friend to God and other humans. Loving God and man rightly cannot be separated because community with each is our proper good. Numerous passages suggest this perspective.

Several examples may be found in *Contra Academicos*. In the prologue Augustine tells Romanianus that his friends at Cassiciacum have been praying that God "return you to yourself," and hastily adds: "for thus will He easily return you to us as well" (1.1.1). Augustine wants the best for Romanianus and his son, namely that they delight in God. In *Contra Academicos* 3.6.13 Augustine uses Cicero's definition of friendship, expressing his gratitude that Alypius agrees with him on divine and human matters and saying that such a friendship is a good "the value of which, I find, I cannot measure." A precious community is thus established by religious agreement. The conclusion to *Contra Academicos*, in its portrayal of Alypius's attitude to the finished dispute, alludes to the Cassiciacum community's participation in divine community. Alypius expresses his happiness that the Academics have been defeated and adds: "I do not reckon that this joy ought to be mine alone. Therefore, I will share it with you . . ." (3.20.44). Theological agreement grounds a theological friendship. This insight is consistent with ancient philosophy to the extent that ancient philosophers find in friendship a harmony of man's political and contemplative ends. But *Contra Academicos* 3.19.42 shows how, through the Incarnation, all people can love and share God together. Augustine alludes to the Platonic theme that political virtue pertains to this lower world, while knowledge of the highest is kept for the few. Thanks to Christ there is no need to keep knowledge secret. Ascent to God brings us together. Our loves are turned to one another by the conversion of desire to God.

Monica's "Cherish, O Trinity, those who pray" in *De beata vita* 4.35 is a touching, if all too brief, picture of community shared between the Trinity and a company of redeemed souls.

In *De ordine* 1.10.29 Augustine, lamenting the pride of Licentius and Trygetius,[55] says that "I wish nothing more for myself than I do for you . . . ." As Holt says,[56] this is apparently a reference to the biblical command to love one's neighbor. But the context of the passage suggests the church's rule of faith, the dual command to hold to the truth of the faith *and* to love God and neighbor.[57] A violation of orthodoxy upsets Augustine. Orthodoxy is closely tied to the practice of love; the truth about God issues in love among those who know that truth. After all, Christ commands, "Love your neighbor."[58] Thus we do not cease to live in community when we begin to know God; it is only when we begin to know God that we can begin to live in real community. In other words, if we are to love a person we must not do so for his own sake. Loving a person "for God's sake" does not mean construing him as having no value; it means that as a result of loving God I am enabled to love my fellow man.

De ordine 1.6.16 is another example of how movement toward God also brings us closer to one another. Observing Licentius's progress, Augustine says, "I was unable to contain myself for joy because I was seeing that my beloved friend's young man was also becoming my son: not only this, but that he was also now rising and growing into a true friend of mine . . . ."

An instance of the communal activity of a soul that loves God appears in *De ordine* 2.2.7 where Augustine discusses the importance of teaching the liberal arts.[59] Teaching others what it knows is the duty of a soul that knows God. Augustine implies that the wisest of us has responsibilities to the community. The incarnational undertone of the Cassiciacum dialogues reinforces this notion and implies that the wise man's duty to serve is an imitation of Christ. Nothing could compel lovers of God to love each other more than the imitation of Christ. The Truth himself gave himself in love to men; we, knowing the truth, should do the same. Moreover, unlike the philosopher in Plato's *Republic*, we should do so joyfully.

Examples also appear in *Soliloquia*. When he prays to the Holy Spirit in the opening prayer,[60] Augustine's language is redolent of a communal life organized by the Holy Spirit. He says, "O God, through whom we conquer the enemy . . . through whom we receive lest we perish altogether . . . by whom we are admonished to keep watch . . . through whom . . .

55. See above, Chapter 4, under the subheading *Pedagogy, Rhetoric, and Humility.*

56. "Wisdom's Teacher," 54 n. 28.

57. On the harmony of these rules, see O'Keefe and Reno, chapter 6.

58. Matt 22:39.

59. See above, Chapter 4, under the subheading *The Order of the Embodied Soul.*

60. See above, Chapter 5, under the subheading *Augustine's Prayer: The Trinitarian Quest for Reordered Desires.*

through whom . . ." (1.1.3). Lovers of God, then, are both brought to God in community and held by God in community. Acquaintance with God issues in the building up of a holy community organized and perfected by God. Only in the ascent to God is the formation of genuine community possible.

Finally, consider *Soliloquia* 1.2.7. Here Augustine, saying that "I love nothing but God and the soul," also says that he loves his friends for their souls. "They are men and I love them," he says, "because they are men, that is, because they have rational souls which I love . . . . And so the more my friends make good use of their rational soul—or at least insofar as they want to make good use of it—the more do I love them." This passage recalls Lactantius's use of Cicero. There is a community of rational souls. The love of the soul does not stop at one's own soul, but extends to all souls that do, or could, love God (even, as Augustine says, the souls of thieves). Indeed, the closer we get to God, the closer we get to each other. The love and knowledge of God establish a community of brotherly love among men. Our souls are meant for this loving community. In returning to God we return to our true nature and so are restored, like Romanianus to Augustine, to one another.

This is not the final word at Cassiciacum. A few chapters later (1.12.20) Augustine appears to shift to a different perspective. Reason asks, "why do you desire that the men whom you love either live or live with you?" He replies, "So that we may harmoniously inquire into our souls and God." Moments later he adds that he does "not desire their life or their presence for its own sake, but for the sake of finding wisdom." This suggests that a person has no value to me apart from his helpfulness in my own quest to get to God. Shortly afterwards, Augustine claims that "what is not loved for its own sake is not loved" (1.13.22), again suggesting that we should love our neighbor for the help he can offer in knowing God. However, an intriguing passage follows as Augustine claims that the fullness of wisdom will allow him to enjoy it together with his friends: "what limit can one have on the love of that beauty, in which not only do I not envy others, but I even seek many more who may desire with me, gawk with me, hold with me, and thoroughly enjoy with me; and the more we become friends, the more we will love her in common." Even as we are told that humans are not ends in themselves we are invited to join with them in love for God. While love for God is said to eschew love for man, it is accompanied by a wish for others to be happy in the same God. Whereas the Stoic sage's happiness is completely independent of the happiness of others, at Cassiciacum my happiness in God increases when others enjoy God with me.[61] Using the neighbor for God's sake, because it is what he is created for, is the right way

61. Brown comments on how different Cassiciacum's "shared love of beauty" is from the "strictly individual affair" that is the Plotinian ascent to the divine; Brown, *Eye of a Needle*, 166.

to treat people; it is also how we enjoy God, because it is how we are meant to enjoy God.

Reading 1.13.22 in light of 1.12.20, we would be forced to conclude that two perspectives are in play at Cassiciacum, in tension if not contradiction with one another. However, reading 1.12.20 in light of 1.13.22, it would seem that the language of the earlier passage is simply unclear and that Augustine at Cassiciacum consistently holds to the teleological perspective I have outlined in this chapter. This is the more charitable reading, and the more consistent of the two. Thus, here as well as in later works, Augustine believes that the love of God establishes a human community, and is indeed the only love able to establish true human community.[62] This is evidence that Augustine has moved beyond the ancient understanding of friendship. Not only is it possible to share wisdom with one's friends, but it even adds to our happiness. Our highest end is not merely to know God, but to know God together with others. Moreover, we are meant to know God together with as many as possible—with everyone whom Christ can reach (*c. Acad.* 3.19.42). Although the ancients never fully harmonized the political conception of the human self with the idea that we are meant to contemplate the divine, the Christian understanding of knowing God together unites our natural ends of living in community with one another and of knowing the highest.

Beyond Cassiciacum

Two aspects of Augustine's developing thought are not present at Cassiciacum in a mature form, yet have implications for the connection between the love of God and the love of man and constitute evidence that love for God and man are increasingly harmonized in Augustine's mind. First, Augustine's opposition to pride as the central sin and the root of disordered affections suggests that human happiness was never meant to be autonomous. Second, Augustine's understanding of the human self as a non-monadic entity reinforces the notion that human nature is meant to be communal.

As we have seen,[63] pride is the root of disordered desires, the cardinal sin. This truth is evident at Cassiciacum and only becomes more significant as Augustine continues to write. As Burns says, "Originally, however, and indeed fundamentally, he argued, a person turns . . . from the divine, the

62. I am grateful to John Spano for helping me see this aspect of 1.13.22.

63. See above: Chapter 2, under the subheading *Christ: Towards a Christian Theology of Desire*; Chapter 3, under the heading *The Port of Philosophy and the Land of the Happy Life*; and Chapter 4, under the subheading *Pedagogy, Rhetoric, and Humility.*

common good of all, and in pride prefers the self, created and private."[64] There is no room for community in self-centeredness. Happiness for us is never autonomous; pride, always claiming autonomy, defies community and the love of neighbor.[65] That self-centeredness is excluded from happiness ensures that the love of neighbor is included in happiness. Augustine's reference to neighbor-love in *De ordine* 1.10.29, juxtaposed with his students' pride, suggests as much;[66] the love of God leads to the love of one another. Pride may manifest itself in man's assertion of independence from God, but it also appears in an individual's assertion of independence from the community. Christianity eschews both manifestations of pride. Any attempt to know God as a solitary individual is a sinful act of pride, a vicious exaltation of my own intellect and virtue—and a marked contrast to the communal pursuit of God illustrated at Cassiciacum. Again, this suggests that life with, and accordingly love of, other human beings is essential to happiness.

Second, Augustine's notion of the soul is highly contextualized; it cannot subsist by itself in a solipsistic space, but exists in a multifaceted context, including the body, the human community, and the trinitarian God. The soul cannot be understood without reference to these things. The modern notion of the self is quite different. Consider the contrast between Augustine's treatment of "God and the soul" and Réne Descartes's treatment of the same. Descartes conceives of the soul as a monadic psychical entity.[67] Not only is it able to abstract itself from its history, from the body, and from other souls, but it profits by doing so. Not so the soul as Augustine understands it.[68] For Augustine the soul is bound to the body, is influenced by its history, is taught by others, and teaches others in turn. It prays for others and benefits from their prayers. It is an active entity, required by daily life to resist an Academic suspension of belief. That the soul is not independent of community undercuts the idea that it can or should know God all by itself. Its nature and its proper good are communal. It is not able, and should not attempt, to abstract itself from this context.[69] Above all, the soul is created for fellowship with a trinitarian God; it does not, cannot, and should not

64. Burns, "Ambrose Preaching," 380.

65. Ambrose also says that "friendship knows nothing of pride" (*Duties of the Clergy* 3.22.128), and that friendship should "be free from arrogance" (3.22.134).

66. See above under the subheading *Knowing God Together at Cassiciacum.*

67. Descartes, *Meditations on First Philosophy.*

68. Foley, "Cassiciacum and the So-Called Turn."

69. Gilson: "It is a remarkable feature of St. Augustine's doctrine that it always considers the moral life as something interwoven with social life. In his eyes, the individual is never separated from the city." See Gilson, *The Christian Philosophy*, 171.

try to be independent of its relation to God.[70] A soul abstracted from its communal nature would not be an incomplete soul—if it would even be a soul at all. The soul knows God in its proper context when it does so as part of its proper community. To know God apart from this context would not be best if it were even possible.

At bottom I suspect that no absolute distinction between egoism and altruism can be sustained by a worldview that recognizes the human person as a communal creature. Care for the self and care for others are distinguished as different aspects of the natural human community, but not separated. The pursuit of my own happiness in God thus cannot be separated from my care for others. Nor can an absolute distinction between love of man and love of God be maintained in a worldview that recognizes the community for which man is created as community with God.

It would be interesting to trace the Cartesian notion of the self and see what influence it has had on modern attempts to mediate egoism and altruism. To predict the outcome of such a study would be far too hasty, but it would not be amiss to suggest that the modern tendency to read Augustine as reducing the love of man to the love of God is rooted in modern presuppositions. Among them, perhaps, are the Cartesian notion of the monadic self and the belief in a divide between egoism and altruism.

To return to Augustine from the distraction that is modern thought: It is useful to note that Augustine scholars are not in agreement on the place of the Augustinian soul. The possibility of dispute arises because of the availability of an immaterialistic concept of place. Speaking rather broadly, an immaterialistic concept of place would allow us to plot the location of something by its distance from ultimate (immaterial) reality, or by the degree to which it is itself an immaterial rather than a physical thing—not by its coordinates on a spatial grid. Let us compare this notion in two readers of Augustine.

In the analysis of Cary,[71] Augustine's immaterialistic concept of place is an original development of Plotinus's concept of place. Plotinus's notion

70. On this theme Hanby's analysis is superb; see *Augustine and Modernity*, chapter 5. Hanby: "Augustine cannot be proto-Cartesian because the Augustinian self is only completed doxologically, by participation in the love and beauty of the Trinity through the mediation of Christ and his Body" (161). Hanby also supports Jean-Luc Marion in contrasting Augustine's recognition of his own thinking existence with Descartes's recognition; while the latter is, in and of itself, a substance capable of grounding a science, the former is wholly dependent on God and functions as a reminder to seek God (166–67).

71. Cary, *Augustine's Invention*. Passages in this book particularly relevant to an immaterialistic notion of place are found on pages 3–4, 27, 37, 39, 63–64, 67, 103–4, 108, 127–28, and 130–32.

was of a universalized immaterial region where the soul encounters the God that it, ontologically, *is*. One turns inward, and there finds God; but everyone else who turns inward finds God in the same place, for the inward turn is towards an immaterial region of reality that we all share, since we all are God. Augustine, to avoid making the soul ontologically one with God, treats the inward turn as only the first step towards finding God; an upward turn must follow it. One turns inward, and there begins to find God; but in *this* region of immaterial reality, the soul is alone; it does not in this space *share* knowledge of God with other souls.

Contrast this with Karl Vaught's trilogy on the *Confessions*.[72] Vaught summarizes the soul's journey to God as a journey taking place in *three* dimensions: the temporal, the spatial, and the eternal.[73] The temporal axis on which the soul is located is, of course, its literal location in time; but the soul also travels on this axis backward in time via memory and forward in time via anticipation. The spatial axis on which the soul is located traces its connection to the inner world of the soul and to the outer world of human community. The eternal axis on which the soul moves measures its distance from God. Vaught's analysis is quite different from Cary's, and is explicitly treated as *three*-dimensional: One can move closer to God (on the eternal dimension) no matter *where* one travels on the temporal and spatial axes. To move closer to God, for Vaught's Augustine, is not to move away from others.

The mere fact that Vaught was able to write his trilogy suggests that Cary's analysis, though interesting and insightful in various ways, is not the whole picture. The soul is communally located—at least that is how Augustine viewed the soul when he wrote the *Confessions*.

My own modest contribution in this chapter, if formulated in Vaught's language, would simply be to suggest that this Augustinian perspective is incipient at Cassiciacum.

Concluding Remarks

As *Confessions* 9.4.7 indicates, even at Cassiciacum "those healthful herbs which the Church provides" include the name of Christ and submission to his authority, a theme we have seen repeatedly in the dialogues. Yet some healthful herbs are not explored at Cassiciacum. Confident they can purify our lives, Augustine mentions divine mysteries he has yet to discover: "the sacred things into which we are being initiated, in which the life of the good

72. Vaught, *Journey toward God*, *Encounters with God*, and *Access to God*.

73. See, for example, *Journey toward God*, Introduction.

is most easily purified . . ." (*Ord.* 2.9.27). In the homily he heard on the occasion of his baptism and his first taking of the Eucharist in 387, Augustine would hear from Ambrose that these sacraments are effective for the healing of our souls.[74] As one who is unbaptized and not yet fully a member of the church, Augustine at Cassiciacum has not yet participated in the sacraments and knows little of them. Yet this remark in *De ordine* suggests that he may already have an inkling of what Ambrose will later tell him. He no doubt had already heard something about the spiritual healing of Scripture and Christian practices from Ambrose.[75] Prior to his baptism it is not possible for Augustine to analyze the spiritual healing of sacraments at Cassiciacum, and this is only one of the more obvious respects in which his understanding of desire's conversion and rehabilitation would be enriched over the years.

Even so, Cassiciacum tells us a great deal about the conversion of desire and the therapies which contribute to its renewal. We ought to love immaterial things over carnal things, above all desiring God and the soul. To save us from our evil desires God became a man, lived among us, and initiated a community in which our desires can be healed. The conversion of our desires requires help in the form of God's grace, and we must respond to grace by applying various therapies for our desires: submission to Christ's authority and imitation of him, joining the Christian community, and living humbly in imitation of Christ.

We must, finally, love God and our neighbor. The community of believers is founded and headed by the persons of the Trinity; this community unites the three divine Persons with those who love them. We are created for life in this community, and can be restored to it as a result of the Incarnation. In knowing and loving God as we should, we achieve a life in accordance with our created nature; thus we are fulfilled and happy. In this way the love of God includes the love and the right treatment of man.

Points of agreement with pagan philosophy are transformed in the light of Christ, church, and Scripture; the renewal of the ancient quest for the happy life is at the heart of Augustine's thought: "*Deus et animam scire cupio*" (*Sol.* 1.2.7). Though there are pagan notions of God and the soul, the *deus et anima* of Augustine are of a different kind. This soul cannot stand on its own, for it is created to love and depend on God. It dwells with other souls, whom it needs to know God, and with whom it is delighted to

74. This sermon is available as *On the Mysteries*, trans. H. de Romestin, E. de Romestin, and H. T. F. Duckworth. Kolbet has a useful discussion of Ambrose's teaching on the healing that comes through the Christian sacraments; see Kolbet, *Augustine and the Cure of Souls*, 106–7.

75. Kolbet, *Augustine and the Cure of Souls*, 77.

share God. This understanding of human nature makes it possible to love God above all yet still love man. At Cassiciacum we see some of the earliest inklings of the idea that only in loving the Creator above the creature is the creature itself fulfilled. As C. S. Lewis says in *Mere Christianity*, "Look for yourself, and you will find in the long run only hatred, loneliness, despair, rage, ruin, and decay. But look for Christ and you will find Him, and with Him everything else thrown in.[76]

76. Lewis, *Mere Christianity*, 227.

Bibliography

Adams, Robert M. "The Problem of Total Devotion." In *Friendship: A Philosophical Reader*, edited by Neer Kapur Badhwar, 108–32. Ithaca: Cornell University Press, 1993.

Alfaric, Prosper. *L'évolution intellectuelle de saint Augustin*. Paris: Émile Nourry, 1918.

Ambrose. *On the Duties of the Clergy*. Translated by H. de Romestin, E. de Romestin, and H. T. F. Duckworth. *Nicene and Post-Nicene Fathers, second series 7*. Edited by Philip Schaff and Henry Wace. Buffalo: Christian Literature, 1886.

———. *Exposition of the Holy Gospel According to Saint Luke, with Fragments on the Prophecy of Isaias*. Translated by Theodosia Tomkinson. Etna, CA: Center for Traditionalist Orthodox Studies, 1998.

———. *On the Mysteries*. Translated by H. de Romestin, E. de Romestin, and H. T. F. Duckworth. Nicene and Post-Nicene Fathers, second series 10, edited by Philip Schaf and Henry Wace. Buffalo: Christian Literature, 1896.

Anderson, James F. *St. Augustine and Being: A Metaphysical Essay*. The Hague: Martinus Nijhoff, 1965.

Anselm. *Proslogion: With the Replies of Gaunilo and Anselm*. Translated by Thomas Williams. Indianapolis: Hackett, 1995.

Aristotle. *Nichomachean Ethics*. Translated by W. D. Ross. In *The Basic Works of Aristotle*. Edited by Richard McKeon. New York: Random House, 1941.

———. *On the Soul*. Translated by J. A. Smith. In *The Basic Works of Aristotle*. Edited by Richard McKeon. New York: Random House, 1941.

———. *Physics*. Translated by R. P. Hardie and R. K. Gaye. In *The Basic Works of Aristotle*. Edited by Richard McKeon. New York: Random House, 1941.

Asiedu, F. "The Wise Man and the Limits of Virtue." *Augustiniana* 49 (1999) 215–34.

Athanasius. *The Life of Antony*. Translated by H. Ellershaw. In *Nicene and Post Nicene Fathers, second series 10*, edited by Philip Schaff and Henry Wace. Buffalo, NY: Christian Literature Publishing Co., 1892.

Augustine. *Against the Academics*. In *The Cassiciacum Dialogues of St. Augustine*. Translated by Michael P. Foley. Notre Dame, IN: University of Notre Dame Press, Forthcoming.

———. *Against the Academics*. Translated by Peter King. In *Against the Academics and The Teacher*. Translated by Peter King. Hackett: Indianapolis, 1995.

———. *The City of God*. Translated by Marcus Dods. In *Nicene and Post Nicene Fathers, first series 2*, edited by Philip Schaff. Buffalo, NY: Christian Literature Publishing Co., 1887.

———. *Confessions*. Translated by John K. Ryan. New York: Doubleday, 1960.
———. *On the Free Choice of the Will*. Translated by Anna Benjamin and L. H. Hackstaff. Upper Saddle River, NJ: Prentice Hall, 1964.
———. *On the Happy Life*. In *The Cassiciacum Dialogues of St. Augustine*. Translated by Michael P. Foley. Notre Dame, IN: University of Notre Dame Press, Forthcoming.
———. *Letters*. Translated by J. G. Cunningham. In *Nicene and Post Nicene Fathers, first series 1*, edited by Philip Schaff. Buffalo, NY: Christian Literature Publishing Co., 1887.
———. *The Nature of the Good Against the Manichees*. In *Augustine: Earlier Writings*, translated and edited by J. H. S. Burleigh. Philadelphia: Westminster, 1953.
———. *On Order*. In *The Cassiciacum Dialogues of St. Augustine*, translated by Michael P. Foley. Notre Dame, IN: University of Notre Dame Press, Forthcoming.
———. *Saint Augustine: The Retractions*. Translated by Sister Mary Inez Bogan. The Fathers of the Church 60. Washington, DC: Catholic University of America Press, 1968.
———. *Soliloquies*. In *The Cassiciacum Dialogues of St. Augustine*, translated by Michael P. Foley. Notre Dame, IN: University of Notre Dame Press, Forthcoming.
———. *St. Augustine: Against the Academics*. Translated by John O'Meara. New York: Paulist, 1978.
———. *On Teaching Christianity*. Translated by Edmund Hill. Hyde Park, NY: New City, 1996.
———. *Of True Religion*. In *Augustine: Earlier Writings*, translated and edited by J. H. S. Burleigh. Philadelphia: Westminster, 1953.
———. *The Usefulness of Belief*. In *Augustine: Earlier Writings*. Translated and edited by J. H. S. Burleigh. Philadelphia: Westminster, 1953.
Aurelius, Marcus. *The Meditations of Marcus Aurelius Antoninus*. Translated by A. S. L. Farquharson. Oxford: Oxford World's Classics, 1989.
Baer, Helmut David. "The Fruit of Charity: Using the Neighbor in *De Doctrina Christiana*." *Journal of Religious Ethics* 24.1 (Spring 1996) 47–64.
Beatrice, Pier Franco. "Quosdam Platonicorum Libros: The Platonic Readings of Augustine in Milan." *Vigiliae Christianae* 43 (1989) 248–81.
Berges, Sandrine. "Loneliness and Belonging: Is Stoic Cosmopolitanism Still Defensible?" *Res Publica: A Journal of Legal and Social Philosophy* 11.1 (2005) 3–25.
Bogan, Mary Inez. *The Vocabulary and Style of the Soliloquies and Dialogues of St. Augustine*. Washington, DC: Catholic University of America, 1935.
Bolyard, Charles. "Augustine, Epicurus, and External World Skepticism." *Journal of the History of Philosophy* 44.2 (2006) 157–68.
Boissier, Gaston. "La Conversion de Saint Augustin." *Revue des Deux Mondes* 85 (1888) 43–69.
Bolgiani, Franco. *La conversione di s. Agostino e l'VIIIo libro delle "Confessioni."* Torino: UniversitaÃ di Torino, 1956.
Boone, Mark J. "The Role of Platonism in Augustine's 386 Conversion to Christianity." *Religion Compass* 9.5 (2015) 151–61.
Bourke, Vernon J. "The Body-Soul Relation in the Early Augustine." In *Augustine: Second Founder of the Faith*, edited by J. Schnaubelt and Frederick Van Fleteren, 435–49, Collectanea Augustiniana 1. New York: Peter Lang, 1990.
———. "Joy in Augustine's Ethics." *The Saint Augustine Lecture Series* (1978) 9–57.

Boyer, Charles. *Christianisme et Néo-Platonisme dans la formation de saint Augustin*. 2nd ed. Rome: Catholic Book Agency, 1953.

Brickhouse, Thomas C. and Nicholas D. Smith. "Socrates' Gods and the *Daimonion*." In *Reason and Religion in Socratic Philosophy*, edited by Nicholas D. Smith and Paul B. Woodruff: 74–88. Oxford: Oxford University Press, 2000.

Brown, Peter. *Augustine of Hippo*. Berkeley: University of California Press, 2000.

———. *Through the Eye of a Needle: Wealth, the Fall of Rome, and the Making of Christianity in the West, 350–550 AD*. Princeton: Princeton University Press, 2012.

Burns, J. Patout. "Ambrose Preaching to Augustine: The Shaping of Faith." In *Augustine: Second Founder of the Faith*, edited by J. Schnaubelt and Frederick Van Fleteren, 373–86. Collectanea Augustiniana 1. New York: Peter Lang, 1990.

Burt, Donald X. *"Let me Know Myself . . ." Reflections on the Prayer of Augustine*. Collegeville, MN: Liturgical, 2002.

———. *"Let me Know You . . ." Reflections on the Prayer of Augustine*. Collegeville, MN: Liturgical, 2003.

Burton, Philip. "The Vocabulary of the Liberal Arts in Augustine's *Confessions*." In *Augustine and the Disciplines: from Cassiciacum to Confessions*, edited by Karla Pollman and Mark Vessey: 141–64. Oxford: Oxford University Press, 2007.

Byers, Sarah. "The Meaning of *Voluntas* in Augustine." *Augustinian Studies* 37.2 (2006) 171–89.

Cary, Phillip. *Augustine's Invention of the Inner Self: The Legacy of a Christian Platonist*. Oxford: Oxford University Press, 2000.

———. "God in the Soul: Or, the Residue of Augustine's Manichaean Optimism." *The University of Dayton Review* 22.3 (1994) 69–79.

———. *Inner Grace: Augustine in the Traditions of Plato and Paul*. Oxford: Oxford University Press, 2008.

———. *Outward Signs: The Powerlessness of External Things in Augustine's Thought*. Oxford: Oxford University Press, 2008.

———. "What Licentius Learned: A Narrative Reading of the Cassiciacum Dialogues." *Augustinian Studies* 29.1 (1998) 141–61.

Cessali, Laurent, and Nadja Germann. "Signification and Truth: Epistemology at the Crossroads of Semantics and Ontology in Augustine's Early Philosophical Writings." *Vivarium* 46.2 (2008) 123–54.

Chadwick, Henry. *Augustine of Hippo: A Life*. Oxford: Oxford University Press, 2009.

Cicero. *On Academic Skepticism*. Translated by Charles Brittain. Indianapolis: Hackett, 2006.

———. "Discussions at Tusculum." In *On the Good Life*, translated by Michael Grant. London: Penguin, 1971.

———. *On Duties*. Edited by M. T. Griffin and E. M. Atkins. Cambridge: Cambridge University Press, 1991.

———. *On Ends*. Translated by H. Rackham. Cambridge, MA: Harvard, 1914.

———. "Laelius: On Friendship." In *On the Good Life*, translated by Michael Grant. London: Penguin, 1971.

———. *The Nature of the Gods*. Translated by P. G. Walsh. Oxford: Oxford University Press, 1997.

———. *The Republic and The Laws*, translated by Niall Rudd. Oxford: Oxford University Press, 1998.

Clark, Mary T. Review of *St. Augustine's Early Theory of Man, A. D. 386–391 and St. Augustine's Confessions: The Odyssey of Soul*, by Robert J. O'Connell. *International Philosophical Quarterly* 11 (1971) 427–39.

Conybeare, Catherine. "The Duty of a Teacher: Liminality and *disciplina* in Augustine's *De Ordine*." In *Augustine and the Disciplines: From Cassiciacum to Confessions*, edited by Karla Pollman and Mark Vessey: 49–65. Oxford: Oxford University Press, 2007.

———. *The Irrational Augustine*. Oxford: Oxford University Press, 2006.

Cooper, Stephen A. "Scripture at Cassiciacum: I Corinthians 13:13 in the *Soliloquies*." *Augustinian Studies* 27.2 (1996) 21–46.

Courcelle, Pierre. *Les Confessions de Saint Augustin dans la tradition littéraire*. Paris: Études Augustiennes, 1963.

———. *Recherches sur les Confessions*. Paris: E. de Boccard, 1950.

Curley, Augustine J. *Augustine's Critique of Skepticism: A Study of* Contra Academicos. New York: Peter Lang, 1996.

Dennis, Phillip W. "The Three Augustines of *Contra Academicos*." Academia.edu, 1–26 (2007). https://www.academia.edu/22987961/The_Three_Augustines_of_Contra_Academicos.

Descartes, Réne. *Meditations on First Philosophy*. In *Discourse on Method and Meditations on First Philosophy*. Translated by Donald A. Cress, fourth edition. Indianapolis: Hackett, 1998.

Diggs, Bernard J. "St. Augustine Against the Academicians." *Traditio* 7 (1949–1951) 73–93.

Di Lorenzo, Raymond. "Ciceronianism and Augustine's Conception of Philosophy." *Augustinian Studies* 13 (1982) 171–76.

Djuth, Marianne. "Augustine, Monica, and the Love of Wisdom." *Augustinian Studies* 39.2 (2008) 237–52.

———. "Philosophy in a Time of Exile: Vera Philosophia and the Incarnation." *Augustinian Studies* 38.1 (2007) 281–300.

Dobell, Brian. *Augustine's Intellectual Conversion: The Journey from Platonism to Christianity*. Cambridge: Cambridge University Press, 2009.

Doucet D. "Le thème du médecin dans les premiers dialogues philosophique de saint Augustine." *Augustiniana* 39 (1989) 447–61.

Douglass, Laurie. "Voice Re-Cast: Augustine's Use of Conversation in De ordine and the Confessions." *Augustinian Studies* 27.1 (1996) 39–54.

du Roy, Olivier. *L'intelligence de la foi en le Trinité selon saint Augustin*. Paris: Études Augustiniennes, 1966.

Epicurus. *The Epicurus Reader: Selected Writings and Testimonia*. Translated and edited by Brad Inwood and L. P. Gerson. Indianapolis: Hackett, 1994.

Evans, G. R. *Augustine on Evil*. Cambridge: Cambridge University Press, 1982.

Felix, Minucius. *Octavius*. Translated by Robert Ernest Wallis. In *Ante Nicene Fathers 4*, edited by Alexander Roberts, et al. Buffalo, NY: Christian Literature Publishing Co., 1885.

Ferrari, Leo C. *The Conversions of Saint Augustine*. Villanova, PA: Villanova University Press, 1984.

———. "Truth and Augustine's Conversion Scene." In *Augustine: Second Founder of the Faith*, edited by J. Schnaubelt and Frederick Van Fleteren, 9–19. Collectanea Augustiniana 1. New York: Peter Lang, 1990.

Fleteren, Frederick E. Van. "Authority and Reason, Faith and Understanding in the Thought of St. Augustine." *Augustinian Studies* 4 (1973) 43.

Foley, Michael P. "Cassiciacum and the So-Called Turn to the Subject." Paper presented as part of the Oxford Patristics Conference. Oxford, August 10, 2007.

———. "Cicero, Augustine, and the Philosophical Roots of the Cassiciacum Dialogues." *Revue des Études Augustiennes* 45 (1999) 51–77.

———. "The Other Happy Life: The Political Dimensions to St. Augustine's Cassiciacum Dialogues." *The Review of Politics* 65.2 (2003) 165–83.

Fortin, Ernest L. "Augustine and the Hermeneutics of Love: Some Preliminary Considerations." In *The Birth of Philosophic Christianity: Studies in Early Christian and Medieval Thought*, edited by J. Brian Benestad, 1–19. Ernest Fortin: Collected Essays 1. Lanham: Rowman and Littlefield, 1996.

———. Foreword to *Augustine's Contra Academicos: A Study*, by Augustine J. Curley. New York: Peter Lang, 1996.

———. "The Nature of the Christian Message." In *Ever Ancient, Ever New: Ruminations on the City, the Soul, and the Church*, edited by Michael P. Foley, 31–45. Ernest Fortin: Collected Essays 4. Lanham: Rowman and Littlefield, 2007.

———. "The Patristic Sense of Community." In *The Birth of Philosophic Christianity: Studies in Early Christian and Medieval Thought*, edited by J. Brian Benestad: 61–77. In Ernest Fortin: Collected Essays 1. Lanham: Rowman and Littlefield, 1996.

———. "Reflections on the Proper Way to Read Augustine the Theologian." *The Birth of Philosophic Christianity: Studies in Early Christian and Medieval Thought*, edited by J. Brian Benestad, 95–114. Ernest Fortin: Collected Essays 1. Lanham: Rowman and Littlefield, 1996.

———. Review of *Saint Augustine's Early Theory of Man, A.D. 386–391*, by Robert J. O'Connell. In *The Birth of Philosophic Christianity: Studies in Early Christian and Medieval Thought*, edited by J. Brian Benestad, 309–11. Ernest Fortin: Collected Essays 1. Lanham: Rowman and Littlefield, 1996.

———. "The 'Rhetoric' of the Church Fathers." In *Ever Ancient, Ever New: Ruminations on the City, the Soul, and the Church*, edited by Michael P. Foley, 47–58. Ernest Fortin: Collected Essays 4. Lanham: Rowman and Littlefield, 2007.

Fredrekson, Paula. "Paul and Augustine: Conversion Narratives, Orthodox Tradition, and the Retrospective Self." *Journal of Theological Studies* 37.1 (1986) 3–34.

Hadot, Ilsetraut. *Artes libéraux et philosophie dans la pensée antique*. Paris: Études Augustiniennes, 1984.

Hadot, Pierre. *What Is Ancient Philosophy?* Translated by Michael Chase. Cambridge: Belknap, 2004.

Hallie, Philip P. "Classical Scepticism-A Polemical Introduction" In *Selections from the Major Writings on Scepticism, Man, and God*, translated by Sanford G. Etheridge and edited by Philip P. Hallie, 3-28. Indianapolis: Hackett, 1985.

Hanby, Michael. *Augustine and Modernity*. London: Routledge University Press, 2003.

Hannam, Walter A. "*Ad illud ubi permanendum est*: The Metaphysics of St Augustine's *usus-fruitio* Distinction in Relation to Love of Neighbor, *De doctrina Christiana*, I." In *Studia Patristica* 38, edited by M. F. Wiles and E. J. Yarnold. 169–73. Louvain, Belgium: Peeters, 2001.

Harding, Brian. *Augustine and Roman Virtue*. New York: Continuum Books, 2008.

———. "Epistemology and Eudaimonism in Augustine's *Contra Academicos*." *Augustinian Studies* 37.2 (2006) 247–71.

———. "Skepticism, Illumination, and Christianity in Augustine's *Contra Academicos*." *Augustinian Studies* 34.2 (2003) 197–212.

Harnack, Adolph von. *Augustins Konfessionen*. Geissen: J. Ricker, 1888.

Harrison, Carol. *Augustine: Christian Truth and Fractured Humanity*. Oxford: Oxford University Press, 2000.

———. *Rethinking Augustine's Early Theology: An Argument for Continuity*. Oxford: Oxford University Press, 2008.

Heβbrüggen-Walter, Stefan. "Augustine's Critique of Dialectic: Between Ambrose and the Arians." *Augustine and the Disciplines: from Cassiciacum to Confessions*, edited by Karla Pollman and Mark Vessey: 184–205. Oxford: Oxford University Press, 2007.

Heil, John. "Augustine's Attack on Skepticism: The Contra Academicos." *The Harvard Theological Review* 65.1 (1972) 99–116.

Henry, Paul. *Plotin et l'Occident*. Louvain: WC Brown, 1934.

Holt, Laura. "Wisdom's Teacher: Augustine at Cassiciacum." *Augustinian Studies* 29.2 (1998) 47–60.

Holte, Ragnar. *Béatitude et Sagesse*. Paris: Études Augustiniennes, 1962.

———. "Monica, 'the Philosopher.'" *Augustinus* (1994) 293–316. http://www.invado.se/holte/monica.pdf.

Howard-Snyder, Frances, et al. *The Power of Logic*. 4th ed. New York: McGraw-Hill, 2009.

Howland, Jacob. "Re-Reading Plato: The Problem of Platonic Chronology." *Phoenix* 45.3 (1991) 189–214.

Gilson, Etienne. *The Christian Philosophy of Saint Augustine*. Translated by L. E. M. Lynch. New York: Random House, 1960.

———. Review of "L'évolution intellectuelle de saint Augustin." *Revue Philosophique* (1919) 497-505.

Jackson, M. G. St. A. "Augustine All at Sea: An Interpretation of the Opening Paragraphs of *De beata vita*." In *Studia Patristica* 18.4, edited by Elizabeth A. Livingston, 71–77. Louvain, Belgium: Peeters, 1990.

James, William. "The Will to Believe." In *The Will to Believe and Other Essays in Popular Philosophy: And Human Immortality*, 1–31. New York: Dover, 1956.

Kevane, Eugene. *Augustine the Educator: A Study in the Fundamentals of Christian Formation*. Westminster, MD: Newman, 1954.

———. "Christian Philosophy: The Intellectual Side of Augustine's Conversion." *Augustinian Studies* 17 (1986) 47–83.

Kirwan, Christopher. "Augustine Against the Skeptics." In *The Skeptical Tradition*, edited by Myles Burnyeat, 205–23. Berkeley: University of California, 1983.

Kleingeld, Pauline, and Eric Brown. "Cosmopolitanism." In *Stanford Encyclopedia of Philosophy*, edited by Edward N. Zalta. 2006. http://plato.stanford.edu/entries/cosmopolitanism/.

Klingshirn, William E. "Divination and the Disciplines of Knowledge according to Augustine." In *Augustine and the Disciplines: From Cassiciacum to Confessions*, edited by Karla Pollman and Mark Vessey, 113–40. Oxford: Oxford University Press, 2007.

Kolbet, Paul R. *Augustine and the Cure of Souls: Revising a Classical Ideal*. Notre Dame, IN: University of Notre Dame Press, 2010.

Lactantius. *On the Anger of God*, translated by William Fletcher. Ante-Nicene Fathers 7, edited by Alexander Roberts, et al. Buffalo: Christian Literature, 1886.

Lear, Gabriel Richardson. *Happy Lives and the Highest Good: An Essay on Aristotle's "Nichomachean Ethics."* Princeton: Princeton University Press, 2004.

Levering, Matthew. *The Theology of Augustine: an Introductory Guide to His Most Important Works*. Grand Rapids: Baker, 2013.

Lewis, C. S. *The Great Divorce*. New York: Macmillan, 1946.

———. *Mere Christianity*. San Francisco: HarperCollins, 2001.

Lienhard, Joseph T. "Friendship, Friends." In *Augustine Through the Ages*, edited by Allan D. Fitzgerald, et al., 372–73. Grand Rapids: Eerdmans, 1999.

Madec, Goulven. "Connaissance de Dieu et action de graces. Essai sur les citations de l'Epître aux Romains, 1, 18–25." *Revue des Études Augustiniennes* 2 (1962) 273–309.

———. *Introduction aux 'Révisions' et à la lecture des Œuvres de saint Augustin*. Paris: Études Augustiniennes, 1996.

———. "The Notion of Philosophical Augustinianism: An Attempt at Clarification." *Mediaevalia* 4 (1978)125–46.

———. *Saint Augustin et la philosophie*. Paris: Études Augustiniennes, 1996.

Marrou, H. I. *Saint Augustin et la fin de la culture antique*. 2nd ed. Paris: De Boccard 1949.

Mallard, William. "The Incarnation in Augustine's Conversion." *Recherches Augustiniennes* 15 (1989) 80–98.

McLynn, Neil. "Ambrose of Milan." In *Augustine Through the Ages*, edited by Allan D. Fitzgerald, et al., 17–19. Grand Rapids: Eerdmans, 1999.

———. "Disciplines of Discipleship in Late Antique Education: Augustine and Gregory Nazianzen." In *Augustine and the Disciplines: from Cassiciacum to Confessions*, edited by Karla Pollman and Mark Vessey, 25–48. Oxford: Oxford University Press, 2007.

McWilliam, Joanne. "The Cassiciacum Autobiography." *Studia Patristica* 18.4, edited by Elizabeth A. Livingston, 14–43. Louvain, Belgium: Peeters, 1990.

———. "Cassiciacum Dialogues." In *Augustine Through the Ages*, edited by Allan D. Fitzgerald, et al., 135–43. Grand Rapids: Eerdmans, 1999.

Milliken, John. "In a Fitter Direction: Moving Beyond the Direction of Fit Picture of Belief and Desire." *Ethical Theory and Moral Practice* 11.5 (2008) 563–71.

Miner, Robert. "Augustinian Recollection." *Augustinian Studies* 38.2 (2007) 435–50.

Mosher, David L. "The Argument of St. Augustine's Contra Academicos." *Augustinian Studies* 12 (1981) 89–113.

Mourant, John A. "Augustine and the Academics." *Recherches Augustiniennes* 4 (1966) 67–96.

———. "The Emergence of a Christian Philosophy in the Dialogues of Augustine." *Augustinian Studies* 1.0 (1970) 70–88.

Nash, R. H. "Some Philosophic Sources of Augustine's Illumination Theory." *Augustinian Studies* 2 (1971) 47–67.

Naugle, David K. *Reordered Loves, Reordered Lives: Discovering the Deep Meaning of Happiness*. Grand Rapids: Eerdmans, 2008.

Neiman, Alven Michael. "The Arguments of Augustine's 'Contra Academicos.'" *Modern Schoolman* 59 (1982) 255–80.

———. "Augustine's Philosophizing Person: The View at Cassiciacum." *New Scholasticism* 58.2 (1984) 236–55.

Norris, Richard A. "Immortality." In *Augustine Through the Ages*, edited by Allan D. Fitzgerald, et al., 444–45. Grand Rapids: Eerdmans, 1999.

Nussbaum, Martha. *The Fragility of Goodness: Luck and Ethics in Greek Tragedy and Philosophy*. Cambridge: Cambridge University Press, 1986.

———. *The Therapy of Desire*. Princeton: Princeton University Press, 1994.

———. *Upheavals of Thought: The Intelligence of Emotions*. Cambridge: Cambridge University Press, 2001.

———. "The Worth of Human Dignity: Two Tensions in Stoic Cosmopolitanism." In *Philosophy and Power in the Graeco-Roman World: Essays in Honor of Miriam Griffin*, edited by G. Clark and T. Rajak, 31–49. Oxford: Clarendon, 2002.

Nygren, Anders. *Agape and Eros*. Translated by Philip S. Watson. Chicago: University of Chicago Press, 1982.

O'Connell, Robert J. "Alypius' Apollinarianism at Milan (Conf. 7.25)." *Revue des Études Augustiniennes* 13 (1967) 209–10.

———. "On Augustine's 'First Conversion': Factus Erectior (*De Beata Vita* 4)." *Augustinian Studies* 17 (1986) 15–29.

———. "Enneads VI, 4–5, in The Works of St. Augustine." *Revue des Études Augustiniennes* 9 (1963) 1–39.

———. "The Enneads and St. Augustine's Image of Happiness." *Vigiliae Christianae* 17.3 (1994) 129–64.

———. *Saint Augustine's Early Theory of Man, A.D. 386–391*. Cambridge, MA: Harvard University Press, 1968.

———. *Saint Augustine's Platonism: The Saint Augustine Lecture, 1981*. Villanova: Villanova University Press, 1984.

———. "The Visage of Philosophy at Cassiciacum." *Augustinian Studies* 25 (1994) 65–76.

O'Donnell, James J. *Confessions, Vol. 3: Commentary on Books 8–13*. Oxford: Oxford University Press, 1992.

———. *The Confessions of Augustine: An Electronic Edition*. Online Edition by Anne Mahoney for The Stoa Consortium (1992). http://www.stoa.org/hippo/.

O'Daly, Gerard. *Augustine's Philosophy of Mind*. Berkeley: University of California Press, 1987.

———. "Did St. Augustine Ever Believe in the Soul's Pre-existence?" *Augustinian Studies* 5 (1974) 227–35.

———. "Memory in Plotinus and Two Early Texts of St. Augustine." In *Platonism Pagan and Christian: Studies in Plotinus and Augustine*, 462–69. Aldershot, Great Britain: Ashgate, 2001.

———. "The Response to Skepticism and the Mechanisms of Cognition" in *The Cambridge Companion to Augustine*, edited by Elenore Stump and Norman Kretzman, 159–70. Cambridge University Press, 2006.

O'Donovan, Oliver. "*Usus* and *Fruitio* in Augustine, *De Doctrina*, I." *Journal of Theological Studies* 33.2 (1982) 361–97.

O'Ferrall, Margaret More. "Monica: A Reconsideration." *Recherches Augustiennes* 10 (1974) 23–43.

O'Keefe, John J., and R. R. Reno. *Sanctified Vision: An Introduction to Early Christian Interpretation of the Bible*. Baltimore: Johns Hopkins University Press, 2005.

O'Meara, John J. Introduction to *St. Augustine: Against the Academics*, translated by John J. O'Meara, 3–33. New York: Paulist, 1978.

———. "Plotinus and Augustine: Exegesis of 'Contra Academicos II Point 5." *Revue Internationale de Philosophie* 24 (1970) 321–37.

———. *Prolegomena to the Contra Academicos of St. Augustine*. Thesis, University of Oxford, 1944.

———. *Studies in Augustine and Eriguena*. Edited by Thomas Halton. Washington, DC: Catholic University of America Press, 1992.

———. *The Young Augustine: The Growth of St. Augustine's Mind up to His Conversion*. Staten Island: St. Paul Publications, 1965.

Pettit, Philip. "Desire." In *Routledge Encyclopedia of Philosophy*, edited by E. Craig. London: Routledge, 1998. http://www.rep.routledge.com/article/V009.

Plato. *Phaedo*. Translated by G. M. A. Grube. In *Plato: Complete Works*, edited by John M. Cooper. Indianapolis: Hackett, 1997.

———. *Protagoras*. Translated by Stanley Lombardo and Karen Bell. In *Plato: Complete Works*, edited by John M. Cooper. Indianapolis: Hackett, 1997.

———. *Republic*. Translated by G. M. A. Grube. In *Plato: Complete Works*, edited by John M. Cooper. Indianapolis: Hackett, 1997.

———. *Symposium*. Translated by Alexander Nehamas and Paul Woodruff. In *Plato: Complete Works*, edited by John M. Cooper. Indianapolis: Hackett, 1997.

Plotinus. *The Enneads*. Translated by Stephen MacKenna. London: Penguin, 1991.

———. *The Essential Plotinus: Representative Treatises from The Enneads*. Translated by Elmer O'Brien. Indianapolis: Hackett, 1964.

Plutarch. *How a Young Man Should Study Poems*. Translated by Simon D. Ford. Boston: Little, Brown, & Co., 1878. http://bostonleadershipbuilders.com/plutarch/moralia/study_poems.htm.

Pollman, Karla. "Augustine's Hermeneutics as a Universal Discipline!?" In *Augustine and the Disciplines: from Cassiciacum to Confessions*, edited by Karla Pollman and Mark Vessey: 206–31. Oxford: Oxford University Press, 2007.

Porphyry. *On the Life of Plotinus and the Arrangement of His Work*. In *Plotinus: the Enneads*, translated by Stephen MacKenna. Abridged by John Dillon. London: Penguin, 1991.

Pucci, Joseph. *Augustine's Virgilian Retreat: Reading the Auctores at Cassiciacum*. Toronto: Pontifical Institute of Mediaeval Studies, 2014.

Roberts, David E. "Augustine's Earliest Writings." *The Journal of Religion* 33 (July 1953) 161–81.

Roberts, Robert C. *Emotions: An Essay in Aid of Moral Psychology*. Cambridge: Cambridge University Press, 2003.

Rist, John M. *Augustine: Ancient Thought Baptized*. Cambridge: Cambridge University Press, 1994.

———. "Plotinus and Christian Philosophy." *Cambridge Companion to Plotinus*, edited by Lloyd P. Gerson: 386–413. Cambridge: Cambridge University Press, 1996.

Rombs, Ronnie. *Saint Augustine and the Fall of the Soul: Beyond O'Connell and His Critics*. Washington, DC: Catholic University of America, 2006.

Russell, Robert P. "Cicero's Hortensius and the Problem of Riches in Saint Augustine." *Augustinian Studies* 7 (1976) 59–69.

Teske, Roland J. *To Know God and the Soul: Essays on the Thought of Saint Augustine*. Washington DC, Catholic University of America Press, 2008.

Schroeder, Tim. "Desire." *Philosophy Compass* 1.6 (2006) 631–39.

Seneca. *On Anger*. Translated by John W. Basore. London: Heinemann, 1928.

———. *On the Happy Life*. In *Seneca: Dialogues and Essays*, translated by John Davie, 85-111. Oxford World's Classics. Oxford: Oxford University Press , 2007.

———. *On Providence*. In *Seneca: Dialogues and Essays*, translated by John Davie, 3-17. Oxford World's Classics. Oxford: Oxford University Press , 2007.

———. *On the Tranquility of the Mind*. In *Seneca: Dialogues and Essays*, translated by John Davie, 112-39. Oxford World's Classics. Oxford: Oxford University Press , 2007.

Sextus Empiricus. *Outlines of Pyrrhonism*. In *Selections from the Major Writings on Scepticism, Man, and God*, translated by Sanford G. Etheridge and edited by Philip P. Hallie, 29-128. Indianapolis: Hackett, 1985.

Shanzer, Danuta R. "Augustine's Disciplines: *Silent diutius Musae Varronis*." In *Augustine and the Disciplines: from Cassiciacum to Confessions*, edited by Karla Pollman and Mark Vessey, 69–112. Oxford: Oxford University Press, 2007.

Silk, Edmund T. "Boethius' Consolatio Philosophiae as a Sequel to Augustine's Dialogues and Soliloquia." *Harvard Theological Review* 32.1 (1939) 19–39.

Smith, James K. A. *Desiring the Kingdom: Worship, Worldview, and Cultural Formation*. Grand Rapids: Baker, 2009.

Stewart-Kroeker, Sarah. "Resisting Idolatry and Instrumentalisation in Loving the Neighbour: The Significance of the Pilgrimage Motif for Augustine's *Usus–Fruitio* Distinction." *Studies in Christian Ethics* 27 (2014) 202–21.

Stock, Brian. *Augustine the Reader: Meditation, Self-knowledge, and the Ethics of Interpretation*. Cambridge: Harvard University Press, 1996.

Theiler, Willy. *Porphyrios und Augustin*. Halle: M. Niemeyer, 1933.

TeSelle, Eugene. *Augustine the Theologian*. London: Burns and Oates, 1970.

Testard, Maurice. *Saint Augustin et Cicéron*. Paris: Études Augustiennes, 1958.

Topping, Ryan N. S. *Happiness and Wisdom: Augustine's Early Theology of Education*. Washington, DC: Catholic University of America Press, 2012.

Trout, Dennis E. "Augustine at Cassiciacum: *Otium Honestum* and the Social Dimensions of Conversion." *Vigiliae Christianae* 42 (1988) 132–46.

Van Fleteren, Frederick E. "Authority and Reason, Faith and Understanding in the Thought of St. Augustine." *Augustinian Studies* 4 (1973) 33–71.

———. "The Cassiciacum Dialogues and Augustine's Ascents at Milan." *Mediaevalia* 4 (1978) 159–82.

Vaught, Carl J. *Access to God in Augustine's Confessions: Books X–XIII*. Albany: State University of New York Press, 2005.

———. *Encounters with God in Augustine's Confessions: Books X–XIII*. Albany: State University of New York Press, 2003.

———. *The Journey toward God in Augustine's Confessions: Books X–XIII*. Albany: State University of New York Press, 2003.

Vessey, Mark. Introduction to *Augustine and the Disciplines: from Cassiciacum to Confessions*, edited by Karla Pollman and Mark Vessey: 1–21. Oxford: Oxford University Press, 2007.

Vlastos, Gregory. "Socratic Piety." *Proceedings of the Boston Area Colloquium in Ancient Philosophy* 5 (1989) 213–38.

Wetzel, James. *Augustine and the Limits of Virtue*. Cambridge: Cambridge University Press, 1992.

White, Carroline. *Christian Friendship in the Fourth Century*. Cambridge: Cambridge University Press, 1992.

White, Nicholas. "The Classification of Goods in Plato's *Republic*." *Journal of the History of Philosophy* 22 (1984) 393–421.

Wilken, Robert Louis. *The Christians as the Romans Saw Them*. New Haven: Yale University Press, 1984.

———. *The Spirit of Early Christian Thought: Seeking the Face of God*. New Haven: Yale University Press, 2003.

Winkler, Klaus. "La Théorie Augustinienne de la Mémoire à Son Point de Depart." In *Augustinus Magister* 1, 511-19. Paris: Études augustiniennes, 1954.

* 9 7 8 0 2 2 7 1 7 6 6 6 5 *
ND - #0068 - 030626 - C0 - 229/152/11 - PB - 9780227176665 - Gloss Lamination